P9-DEL-525

THE MYTH OF THE MILITARY-NATION

THE MYTH OF THE MILITARY-NATION

MILITARISM, GENDER, AND EDUCATION IN TURKEY

AYSE GUL ALTINAY

palgrave
macmillan

THE MYTH OF THE MILITARY-NATION
© Ayse Gül Altinay
All rights reserved. No part of this book may be used or reproduced in any manner whatsoever without written permission except in the case of brief quotations embodied in critical articles or reviews.

First published in 2004 by
PALGRAVE MACMILLAN™
175 Fifth Avenue, New York, N.Y. 10010 and
Houndmills, Basingstoke, Hampshire, England RG21 6XS
Companies and representatives throughout the world

PALGRAVE MACMILLAN is the global academic imprint of the Palgrave Macmillan division of St. Martin's Press, LLC and of Palgrave Macmillan Ltd. Macmillan® is a registered trademark in the United States, United Kingdom and other countries. Palgrave is a registered trademark in the European Union and other countries.

ISBN 1–4039–6281–2 hardback

Library of Congress Cataloging-in-Publication Data

Altinay, Ayse Gül, 1971–
    The myth of the military nation : militarism, gender, and education in Turkey / Ayse Gül Altinay.
        p. cm.
    Includes bibliographical references and index.
    ISBN 1–4039–6281–2 hardback
        1. Civil-military relations—Turkey. 2. Militarism—Turkey.
        3. Education—Turkey. I. Title.
JF195.A48 2004
355.02′13′09561—dc22   2004044798

A catalogue record for this book is available from the British Library.

Design by Newgen Imaging Systems (P) Ltd., Chennai, India.

First edition: December 2004

10 9 8 7 6 5 4 3 2 1

Printed in the United States of America.

To Nusret, Erdal, and Hakan

CONTENTS

ACKNOWLEDGMENTS

When I began this project in 1997 as a graduate student, I could not have imagined that so many people and institutions would become a part of it. As I traveled between Durham, Istanbul, and New York, I knew that I had the best of many worlds. I am grateful to everyone who shared these travels, and the many troubles in between, and gave me support and inspiration.

This book has been possible with generous support from a number of institutions. I thank them all. The Social Science Research Council-MacArthur Foundation, International Peace and Security Fellowship provided me with two years of research funding and valuable contacts. I have also received financial assistance from Duke University Graduate School, Department of Cultural Anthropology, Ford Seminar in Integrative International Studies, John Hope Franklin Center, and the Center for International Studies. The Political Science and International Relations Department at Boğaziçi University hosted me for three semesters, providing me valuable access to their library and other privileges. I spent the fall semester in 1998 at Columbia University and received kind support from the Institute for War and Peace Studies, and the Middle East Institute. I would particularly like to thank Karen Barkey for her hospitality and friendship during that semester. The Research Fund of Sabancı University enabled me to do further archival and ethnographic research in the past three years, and to hire research assistants whose help was crucial in this process.

Over the past four years, different parts of this book have been presented at conferences in Azerbaijan, Britain, Canada, Israel/Palestine, Lebanon, the Netherlands, Sweden, Turkey, and the United States. I am grateful to all these transnational encounters filled with criticism, helpful suggestions, and stimulating debate. They have greatly contributed to my thinking and, I hope, writing.

Many people have graciously shared my journey toward this book in the past six years. At Duke, I had the privilege of working with an outstanding group of academics, who assisted in my growth as a scholar and a person. My advisor Orin Starn has shaped my thinking about anthropology, academia, and the world in fundamental ways. It is thanks to his guidance, critical interventions, insight, and continuous support that I was able to carry out this project. I cannot thank him enough. Anne Allison's teaching and thinking on gender and feminist anthropology have been crucial in shaping my work. She has also greatly inspired me as a person. Charlie Piot, besides being an invaluable teacher, has always been there when I needed help and advice. I have benefited greatly from working with Katherine Ewing in Durham and in Istanbul. I owe her special thanks for continual encouragement. I have had many stimulating conversations with Arif Dirlik and learned a lot from his critical interventions. His close reading of the earlier version of this book was also most helpful. From Catherine Lutz, I have learned a great deal about militarization, as well as responsible social science. I am grateful to you all! I hope that I have managed to integrate at least some of your advice and warnings into this book.

During my "home/fieldwork" in Turkey, I benefited tremendously from the valuable insights, encouragement, and support of Yeşim Arat and Taha Parla. I could not have gone through the ups and downs of research in a very difficult field without their guidance and wisdom. My colleagues at Sabancı University have been wonderful in the past three years of teaching, research, and painful writing ordeals. I would particularly like to thank Ayşe Öncü, Annedith Schneider, Leyla Neyzi, and Tara Hopkins for friendship and much needed solidarity. Hülya Adak has been a special friend and colleague. I feel very fortunate that we happened to land on this campus together. My gratitude to Ahmet Evin, Ahmet Alkan, and Halil Berktay for valuable assistance and encouragement. Sabancı University has been an ideal academic home since I came back to Turkey. I could not have imagined a more stimulating group of students and an academic setting that takes academic freedom and research as seriously. I greatly appreciate the wisdom and commitment of Tosun Terzioğlu in making this possible.

Cynthia Enloe's work has been a major source of influence and inspiration in this project. I have also had the pleasure of getting to know and learn from her personally. I am deeply appreciative of the tremendous encouragement and feedback she has given me. I am also grateful to Betty Reardon, Rela Mazali, and Haggith Gor Ziv for pushing me to think more critically about the militarization of education, for all their advice and input, and for giving me hope about the future of feminist critique and solidarity.

Numerous people have helped me at different stages of research and writing. Nilgün Bayraktar and Yunus Doğan Telliel deserve special thanks for their meticulous and enthusiastic research support over the course of almost three years. Arzu Yüksel, Ezgi Dikici, and Seda Müftügil have also been wonderful research assistants. In the final stages of this book, Amy Spangler's meticulous and caring editorial interventions made a tremendous difference. It has been a pleasure to work with her and to have her as a friend. Ferah and Zelal made crucial parts of my interviews possible. I am very much indebted to both of them. Ferda Ülker's valuable help, hospitality, and friendship have turned research into feminist fun. I have learned a great deal from my conversations with Inci Ağlagül, Yavuz Atan, Mehmet Bal, Oğuz Sönmez, Mehmet Tarhan, Osman Murat Ülke, Coşkun Üsterci, and Uğur Yorulmaz. I thank them deeply for sharing their lives and ideas with me. Many others who have been a part of this research will have to remain anonymous. I am indebted to them all. At Palgrave Macmillan, I have had the pleasure of working with David Pervin. I am grateful for all his helpful advice, responsiveness, and patience.

Many friends have been there for me all along—sharing life, and giving me hope and strength. Marro Inoue, Ya-Chung Chuang, Yektan Türkyılmaz, and Şenay Özden were special friends as I was writing this manuscript. Deniz Altınay gave me crucial support during archival research and was always a good friend. I am also grateful to Nadire Mater, Tansel Güney, Müge Sökmen, Ayşe Erzan, Ayşe Buğra, and Nebahat Akkoç for their insights, inspiration, and friendship.

Gültekin Altınay, Yılmaz Altınay, Deniz Altınay, Cem Sorguç, Cenk Karayazgan, Barış Karayazgan, Nilhan Karayazgan, and Suade Taşlıca have been more than family. Their support and encouragement has been invaluable. It gives me great pain that Yılmaz Altınay is not with us anymore, and that he could not live to see "the book" that has kept me away from so many family occasions.

Finally, I would like to thank my parents, Nusret and Erdal Karayazgan, and my soul mate, Hakan, for all that they have been and have done for me. Hakan has shared every moment of this long journey and read every single line that I wrote. I dedicate my work to them with great love, gratitude, and admiration.

INTRODUCTION

The state is not the reality which stands behind the mask of political practice. It is itself the mask which prevents our seeing political practice as it is. There *is* a state-system: a palpable nexus of practice and institutional structure centered in government and more or less extensive, unified and dominant in any given society. There *is*, too, a state-idea, projected, purveyed and variously believed in in different societies at different times. We are only making difficulties for ourselves in supposing that we have also to study the state—an entity, agent, function or relation over and above the state-system and the state-idea.

Philip Abrams

[Since the 1980s] anthropological thoughts turned on how to write less imperial ethnographies, but not ethnographies of imperialism. Our practice of anthropology has not prevented many of the hundreds of thousands of college graduates who have taken our courses from being shocked by the violent opening of the 21st century.

Catherine Lutz

In August 1999, Turkey's Minister of Culture Istemihan Talay called a press conference. His purpose was to introduce a new book titled *Türk Ordusu* (The Turkish Military).[1] "Turks have been known as a military-nation throughout history," the minister proclaimed. "The Turkish military is synonymous with Turkish national identity. Our military has won great victories, glory and honor for our nation" (*Hürriyet*, 11 August 1999).[2] The use of the term "military-nation" by a state official in 1999 was hardly out of the ordinary, and, indeed, Talay was not the first Minister of Culture to invoke the idea of the military as a key and sacred institution in Turkish society and the idea that every (male) Turk is born a soldier.[3] The book he was introducing with such fanfare was built on the same idea; a state-published work full of statements by Mustafa Kemal Atatürk (a speech that he made in 1938 was reprinted), the current president, prime minister, and other luminaries all centered on the "historical" and "heroic" character of Turkish armed forces. The first section of the book was titled: "*Türk Askerlik Kültürü*" (Turkish Military Culture).

What brings together "the military" and "culture" in Turkey's social and political life? Why would the Ministry of Culture, and not the Ministry of Defense or the General Staff, see it as its task to publish a 500-page book on the Turkish military? Suat Ilhan, the director of *The Atatürk High Council for Culture, Language and History*, offers one answer: "Characteristics related to the military are bound to make a great contribution to the shaping of the culture of a society so unified with its military as ours. The fact that the military has all the cultural characteristics of the society, that it manifests these characteristics, and that it serves as a center of education for most of these cultural values is an inevitable, in fact, necessary, consequence" (Ilhan 1989, 361). Ilhan ominously warns: "If we think of military culture, with its historical achievements as well as its contemporary impact, as separate from the cultural whole, then our national culture will lose its unity and identity" (363).

This book offers a different view. I show that "military culture" and "military-nation" are products of history, artifacts of a century of practices and discourses. My goal is to chart the intricate links between the ideas about the nation, the military, the state, and culture, and make intelligible the specific forms of militarism prevalent in Turkey at the turn of the twenty-first century. I hope to begin to look at "the mask" that "the state" and "the military" have been in the Turkish context.

Silencing the Present

Militarism and militarization, as political and analytical concepts, are not new. Historian Volker R. Berghahn (1982) points out that the concept of "militarism" was first popularized by Pierre Proudhon in the 1860s. Berghahn lists several defining features of its uses since then: the introduction of compulsory conscription as a modern practice in the nineteenth century, the impact of the two world wars, the debates on Japanese and German militarisms, the differentiation between liberal and Marxist critiques of militarism, the civil–military relations debates in the Third World, and the "military-industrial complex" in the West. Definitions since Berghahn's account in 1982 have become even more diverse.

The analysis in this book follows the lead of recent scholarship, which has differentiated between (1) military as a social institution, (2) militarism as an ideology, and (3) militarization as a social process (see Cock 1991; Enloe 1993; Chenoy 1998; Feinman 2000). I understand militarism to be a set of ideas and structures that glorify "practices and norms associated with militaries" (Chenoy 1998, 101). In this sense, militarization is "a step-by-step process by which a person or a thing gradually comes to be controlled by the military or comes to depend for its well-being, on militaristic ideas" (Enloe 2000, 3). Militarization is successful when it achieves a discourse of "normalcy" in public discussions surrounding the power of the military in civilian life, politics, economics, and people's self-understandings. In Turkey, this normalization has been achieved through a variety of discourses and reinforced by a lack of academic curiosity and scrutiny. With the exception of works by political theorist Taha Parla (see Parla 1991c, 1998), the terms "militarism" or "militarization" have been absent in the vocabulary of Turkish social science and cultural criticism until recently.[4]

The one widely used term that connotes a negative display of military power is "darbe" (literally "blow"). This is an expression of direct intervention by the military in the political system. There are several instances of such use in Turkish history: 27 May 1960, 12 March 1971, 12 September 1980, and 28 February 1997.[5] There are many more instances of daily monitoring of the political process by the military high command through the National Security Council and other mechanisms since the early 1960s. This role of the military in Turkish politics has been analyzed by both Turkish and non-Turkish scholars and observers.[6] As theorist Michel Foucault has argued, however, modern power works as much through "productive" mechanisms as through "negative" ones. The military is as much a site of (masculine) national desire and production, as it is a force of coercion. Militarism as an ideology that has become intertwined with nationalism, as well as militarization as a process that *shapes* culture, politics, and identities in Turkey, are in need of further analysis with a broader understanding of modern power.

Anthropologist Michel-Rolph Trouillot suggests, "history is the fruit of power, but power itself is never so transparent that its analysis becomes superfluous. The ultimate mark of power may be its invisibility; the ultimate challenge, the exposition of its roots" (Trouillot 1995, xix). In my attempt to expose the dynamics of militarism and militarization in Turkey, the ultimate challenge has *not* been the *invisibility* of the military and its power, but the discrepancy between its strong presence and visibility, and the lack of critical analyses of this strong presence. I kept returning to a single central question: How is it possible that the military as an institution and "military-nationhood" as an idea have been so omnipresent, yet a discussion of militarism and militarization so absent? I believe that this question holds one of the keys to understanding the workings of militarism in Turkey. Silences, after all, form "an integral part of the strategies that underlie and permeate discourses" (Foucault 1990, 27).

Building upon archival research, participant observation, and extensive interviews with individuals, this historical ethnography aims to highlight both the silences and visible transformations through which military needs and militaristic presumptions in Turkey have become normalized in the past century. Looking at a variety of sites including the myth of the "military-nation," gender ideologies, compulsory conscription, conscientious objection, and education, I seek to render militarism and militarization visible in their various forms. To follow up on Abrams's conceptualization, this is not a study of the military-system, or the military as an institution,[7] but a study of militarism and militarization, that is, the ways in which the "military-idea" has been produced and maintained as a gendered discourse by Turkish nationalism, and the practices of military service and education. As anthropologist Arturo Escobar suggests: "cultures ... are characterized not only by rules and values but also by ways of knowing" (1995, 13). In exploring the links between nationalism, militarism, and gender in Turkey, my project fits within a broader trend in anthropology where different "ways of knowing" are being discussed in relation to the state-system and the state-idea in contemporary societies.

Anthropology of the State and the Military

Recently there has been a renewed interest by anthropologists in the state as a research site.[8] This move has come after several decades of self-critique in the discipline whereby the neglect of power and history in analyses of cultures came under attack from a number of vantage points. In the 1960s and 1970s, Marxist anthropologists stressed the impact of colonialism and capitalism on cultures around the world, drawing attention to the connectedness between cultures as well as the power dynamics that produce unequal exchanges between them (see Mintz 1960; Asad 1973; Wolf 1982). At around the same time, feminist anthropologists began writing about the power dynamics *within* societies around the world that produced unequal gender relations (Rosaldo and Lamphere 1974; Reiter 1975). This growing attention to power and history was reinforced by what has been called the post-modern turn in anthropology in the early 1980s, when the "politics and poetics" of writing and representation (see Clifford and Marcus 1986) became central in debates about the discipline. Since then anthropological approach to cultures as coherent, timeless and discrete has been criticized from all angles (Abu-Lughod 1991, 147).

There is widespread agreement today that culture is "not an object to be described, neither is it a unified corpus of symbols and meanings that can be definitively interpreted. Culture is contested, temporal, and emergent. Representations and explanation—both by insiders and outsiders—is implicated in this emergence" (Clifford 1986, 19). As an extension of this approach, anthropological explanations and representations themselves are seen as being "in, not above, historical and linguistic processes" (Clifford 1986, 2).

A retrospective look at anthropological works produced prior to the 1980s reveals anthropology's embeddedness in both progressive and oppressive political processes. Developing anti-racist approaches or drawing attention to the uniqueness and value of *all* cultures would be examples of the former. Yet anthropology has also contributed to historical discourses that have homogenized and marginalized non-Western peoples of the world. For instance, Orin Starn has shown how anthropological research on the "Andean cultures" of Latin America prior to the 1980s had produced its own discourse of Orientalism, in the form of "Andeanism," where Andean peasants were represented as being "outside the flow of history," overlooking "the climate of sharp unrest across the impoverished countryside" and ignoring "the intensifying linkages of Peru's countryside and cities, villages, and shantytowns" (Starn 1991, 64). Ethnographies of the Andes produced in the 1960s and 1970s provided "detailed pictures of ceremonial exchanges, Saint's Day rituals, weddings, baptisms, and work parties" and not the "terrible infant mortality, minuscule incomes, low life expectancy, inadequate diets, and abysmal health care" (1991, 79). Having downplayed poverty's effects and the sharp unrest in Peru's countryside, anthropologists were taken by total surprise when Shining Path with its Maoist revolutionary political discourse became a popular force in the Andes in the early 1980s. Anthropologists, that is, the "experts" of Andean culture, had "missed the revolution."

Since the 1980s, the critique of "culture" and its representations in anthropology has led to a growing interest in the workings of power and history in the making of people's everyday lives in different parts of the globe, as well as their connections with one another. Yet the anthropological bias of working "from below" has largely prevented anthropologists from directly engaging power structures such as corporations, the military, the World Bank, the UN, the growing NGO sector, or the state.[9] Omission of the state is a particularly critical one in studies of twentieth century societies, as this century has, above all, witnessed the consolidation of an international system of nation-states in all parts of the world. Anticolonial struggles have brought into being some 140 new nation-states in the latter half of the century and forces of nationalism and state-formation have shaped the lives of all populations and individuals, almost without exception. In the words of anthropologist Aiwa Ong, "because we have tended to focus on the political dynamics of culture from below, we have paid very little attention to the ethnography of the state as an institution of government producing society" (Ong 1999, 50).

Conversely, it can be argued that those disciplines that had states at the center of their analysis have paid very little attention to "the political dynamics of culture from below." A large body of work in political science, international relations, military history, and even political sociology written prior to the 1980s approached the state and its institutions as unified entities that are represented by their decision-makers. In the late 1970s, Philip Abrams was criticizing political sociology for seeking to give a social account of the state as a "thing" whose reality was taken for granted. In strong opposition to this perspective, Abrams argued that the state is an essentially imaginative construction and an ideological project.

Building upon Abrams's work, sociologists Philip Corrigan and Derek Sayer published their book *The Great Arch* in 1985, in which they analyzed English state formation as a cultural revolution, as "moral regulation (rendering natural, taken for granted, obvious, what are in fact ontological and epistemological premises of a particular and historical form of social order)" (Corrigan and Sayer 1985, 2). In other words, Corrigan and Sayer looked at "state forms culturally and cultural forms as state-regulated" (1985, 3).

In the early 1980s, a similar emphasis on "culture" also became prevalent in analyses of nationalism and nation-states. Benedict Anderson, for instance, in his much influential work, *Imagined Communities,* suggested that we approach nationality, nation-ness, and nationalism as "cultural artifacts of a particular kind" (1991, 6). What we can call the new generation of nationalism studies is built upon the recognition of the cultural complexities of nations and nation-states.

This turn to "the cultural" in studies of the state and the nation took other forms in political science and international relations. Security studies, a Cold War sub-discipline, had become an established academic field by mid-1980s dominated by the neorealist paradigm, where the existence and legitimacy claims of nation-states were (in fact, to a certain extent, still *are*) taken for granted. However, this disciplinary picture has been changing at least since 1989, when many security studies scholars, almost overnight, lost the political basis of their work: with the disintegration of the Soviet bloc, issues like armament or military balance between the superpower blocs lost their significance (Weldes et al. 1999, 5). Just as the anthropologists of the Peruvian Andes had missed the coming of the Shining Path revolution, security studies scholars of the Cold War had missed the coming of the "velvet revolution."

As a result, the post–Cold War era has witnessed a proliferation of critical work on what constitutes security—as well as insecurity (Buzan 1991; Buzan et al. 1998; Campbell 1992; Shapiro and Alker 1996; Weldes et al. 1999). Questioning the legitimacy claims of states as the agencies of security with military concerns at the center, these works shift their emphasis to the society, ordinary citizens, the environment, economic and social inequalities, and so on; look at identities in the plural; and argue that "*all* social *insecurities* are culturally produced" (Weldes et al. 1999, 1).

In other words, what we have today is a growing interdisciplinary field where the intricate relations between culture, nationalism, the state, and its citizens are explored by scholars from a large spectrum of disciplines. Yet, what is still missing in this growing literature, are analyses of militarism and militarization. One area of scholarly inquiry, feminist studies, has been crucial in addressing this lack and introducing new questions through which we can better understand the state-idea and the military-idea. Recent feminist scholarship on the military include analyses of soldiers' experiences in the military; cultural and political significance of military service in contemporary societies; women's varied roles in the military-system as wives, girlfriends, prostitutes, and soldiers; soldiering and violence against women; the impact of militaries and war preparations in particular locales; as well as the relationship between soldiering, gender, and citizenship in the nation-state system.[10] Gender, feminist scholars argue, is not yet another category to add to our checklist. Rather, a scholarly lens that takes questions about men/masculinity and women/femininity seriously promises to reshape our vision altogether.

I see my work as coming out of this interdisciplinary field. I approach state-making as a gendered cultural revolution; a revolution whose discursive power is derived from nationalism and is enabled by modern apparatuses of power. This revolution has involved a number of militarizing processes. The institution of a "citizen-army" usually based on universal male conscription has defined the nation at birth as a "military-nation." What I hope to show in this book is that military service provides one of the most important sites where the nation-idea is married to the state-idea, naturalizing the connection between the two. A state protected by a "national army" (or "citizen-soldiers") can be the tip of the iceberg concealing state-idea being protected by the nation-idea. None of these linkages are automatic. Their establishment has required a vast range of political and cultural maneuvers.[11] For instance, discourses on masculinity have contributed greatly to the marriage of these two ideas by *naturalizing* male participation in the military as "protectors" of their families and of the nation. By defining national pride through masculine pride in the practice of military service, nation-state builders have simultaneously *culturalized, masculinized,* and *militarized* an emerging political process (see Enloe 1989).

Through a combined historical and ethnographic lens, this book seeks to unravel some of these maneuvers in the context of Turkey, where the military-idea has remained particularly strong since the early days of state-making.

The Book

The research for this historical ethnography has spread over six years and can be characterized as, what anthropologist George Marcus (1995) calls, multi-sited ethnography. Rather than focusing on a single, bounded site (geographic, spatial, institutional, or topic-wise), I examine the ways in which different threads that have to do with the state, nationalism, military, and gender are interwoven together in a large cultural, historical space. This interweaving does not suggest a seamless formation. While I analyze attempts at making it seamless, I also look for the contradictions and silences embedded in each thread.

The six chapters in the book are organized as follows: chapter one looks into the discourses on the "military-nation" focusing on the formative years of the Turkish Republic, that is the 1920s and the 1930s. I argue that the myth that "the Turkish nation is a military-nation" became state ideology in this period, supported by the

Turkish History Thesis, an official account of Turkish history that defined state-building and military service as cultural/national/racial characteristics (using the three terms almost interchangeably). I further suggest that this discursive move has established military service in Turkey as a cultural practice, rather than a state practice or a citizenship obligation. I discuss the implications of this *culturalization of military service* throughout the book.

Chapter two addresses women's relationship to the myth of the military-nation, focusing on the life story of Sabiha Gökçen, Mustafa Kemal Atatürk's adopted daughter, Turkey's first military pilot, and the world's first woman combat pilot. In her memoirs, Gökçen depicts Turkish women as the "military daughters of a military-nation" and finds much pride in her participation in the Dersim military operation in 1937. Drawing upon Gökçen's memoirs, writings about her in national and international media, the Grand National Assembly discussions on compulsory military service and women, as well as recent debates in feminist and nationalist historiographies, this chapter examines the connections established between conceptions of citizenship and the military, as well as between male and female citizenship, starting with the early years of the Turkish Republic. I show that the practice of compulsory military service has created a major gender difference administered by the state, and that the decision-makers were well aware of the gender implications of this practice from the very beginning. This awareness further highlights the gendered nature of the nationalist project and the need to interrogate the intimate relationship between masculinities, femininities, national imagining, and the state.

Chapter three focuses on the practice of compulsory conscription drawing from historical material and official discourse, as well as interviews with men who have been through it. Corrigan and Sayer, in their analysis of state-formation as a cultural revolution, suggest that state-making involves both a totalizing and an individualizing process. It totalizes by representing people as part of a community and individualizes them within the state community as "citizens, voters, taxpayers, ratepayers, jurors, parents, consumers, homeowners—individuals" (1985, 5). What is missing in this list is the category of the "citizen-soldier," in other words, the individual (male) members of states who, since the French Revolution, have become obliged to kill and die in the name of "the nation." As sociologist Sara Helman suggests "conscription frameworks" should be viewed as "an integral part of the totalizing and individuating technologies of the state" (1997, 309). Invented during the French Revolution, perfected by Prussia in the nineteenth century, and effectively used both in wartime *and* in peacetime by many nation-states since then, military service has historically defined first-class citizenship and has shaped the lives of men and women throughout the world.

Yet, despite these crucial links between military service, nationalism, citizenship, and gender, until recently neither social historians nor theorists of nationalism have paid much attention to this nation-state practice. Benedict Anderson, for instance, talks about the formation of standing, conscript armies in the nineteenth century in a footnote (1991, 87). As a result, military service, or different conscription practices, have remained in the domain of military historians, and have been analyzed mainly from the perspective of military strategy, that is as a "manpower" issue. Yet as historian Victor Gordon Kiernan suggests "...to see [conscription] solely as a method of conducting wars is to see very little of it" (Kiernan 1973, 141). In an effort to see more of conscription, I look at it historically and ethnographically as a disciplinary (in Foucault's sense), nationalizing and masculinizing citizenship practice. At the same time, I discuss the contradictions and ambivalences of this experience from the perspective of the men who have been through it.

The first citizens of Turkey, the last nation-state emerging out of the Ottoman Empire, had suffered from more than ten years of constant warfare. For them, military service meant war and death (see Zürcher 1996). Therefore, establishing universal male conscription was no easy task. The myth of the military-nation was a crucial component of the move from military service as a citizenship obligation to military service as cultural essence. As the publication of the book *Turkish Military*, by the Ministry of Culture suggests, after eighty years of nationalist myth-making and practice, the "military-nation" as a cultural given has become common sense. More recently, the fifteen-year war (1984–1999) in Turkey's Southeast between Kurdish nationalists, organized under the Kurdistan Workers' Party (PKK), and the Turkish Armed Forces has re-associated military service with war and death, without necessarily disassociating it from "culture."

A highly influential book by journalist Nadire Mater (1999) on the testimonies of soldiers who have done their military service fighting in the Southeast, *Mehmedin Kitabı: Güneydoğu'da Savaşmış Askerler Anlatıyor* (Mehmet's Book: Soldiers Who Have Fought in the Southeast Speak Out), points to the ambivalent feelings of most soldiers about military service, as well as to their trauma having faced war and death. Despite the high numbers of young men who "evaded" conscription during the 1980s and 1990s by continuing their education or simply by not registering, the only public and political resistance to military service has been articulated by a small group of conscientious objectors, which is the topic of chapter four. Based on interviews with conscientious objectors and their supporters, I tell the story of this marginal movement and discuss the consequences of their "taboo-breaking" actions. In the absence of a conscientious objection clause in Turkish laws, the objectors I have interviewed risk spending a life-time in jail in the vicious cycle of forced "surrender" to the assigned military unit, trial and imprisonment for "insubordination," transfer to the military unit upon the completion of the sentence, and further imprisonment for "persistent insubordination." This chapter addresses the impasse created by the sons of the "military-nation" refusing to be soldiers.

Chapters five and six take us into the realm of education through a compulsory high school military course unique to Turkey: a course that was called *Preparation for Military Service* when it was introduced in 1926 and is now called *National Security Knowledge*. In chapter five, I analyze the militarizing role given to schools and the educating role given to the military in the early years of the Turkish Republic. In the words of an official of the Ministry of Culture in 1938, "Just as the army is a school, so is the school an army." I suggest that the close relationship established between the military and national education (seen as the "two fronts" of the new nation) has contributed significantly to the development of a militaristic understanding of Turkish citizenship, as one based on duties and responsibilities to a military-nation. Moreover, I discuss the implications of the *normalization* of a course on the military taught by military officers as part of the core curriculum since 1926.

The recent changes in the course, which I discuss both in chapters five and six, throw further light on the militarization of politics and identities in Turkey and point to the need to take this course seriously. Drawing upon interviews and focus-group discussions with young people from different parts of Turkey, chapter six addresses the strong feelings of "insecurity" based on the religious and ethnic identities created by the hegemonic security discourse and reinforced by the military course in high schools. This final chapter seeks to understand the militarization of lives in the 1990s in light of Turkish cultural history, and also to highlight the demands for and challenges of demilitarization as Turkey enters the twenty-first century as a plural, but not a pluralist, society.

(De)Militarizing the Social Sciences

> From its inception, social science itself has been part and parcel of this work of construction of the representation of the state which makes up part of the reality of the state itself.
>
> *Bourdieu 1999, 55*

The consequences of militarization in the realm of academic discussions were brought home to me in two different occasions in the past year. The first was in the context of a conference where I was presenting a paper on the militarized aspects of textbooks and pointing to the need to demilitarize education. All presenters, including myself, were analyzing contemporary textbooks in terms of human rights criteria. In the middle of my talk, I saw someone raising their hand to ask a question from the back rows. He was requested by the organizers to wait till the end of the presentation. As soon as I finished, this enthusiastic participant identified himself as "an officer in the War Academy," and shared his comment:

> In your talk, you criticized the treatment of military service as a "sacred practice" in the textbooks. I disagree with this approach. Military service is sacred because the human being is sacred. Death is sacred because the human being is sacred. I mean, the sacredness of military service and death stems from the sacredness of the human being.

He continued to tell me about the "modern" and "democratic" nature of military education and urged me to go to the military schools and see it with my own eyes. In response to this comment, I said:

> Your approach is a valid approach. If we were to name it, we would have to define it as a "militarist" approach because it sanctifies death and the military. We have another approach, that of human rights, which also "sanctifies" the human being, but then departs in a different direction to sanctify life, and not death. The question we have at hand is whether we should continue to organize *civilian* education around these militaristic values, or re-write our textbooks based on the international human rights criteria. This is what we need to decide upon.

In his rebuttal, the officer again emphasized the democratic nature of the military education system and elaborated on the need to guard Atatürk's principles with care.

Receiving such a response from the audience, particularly from an officer, was not surprising. What was frustrating was that this comment was the *only* comment my talk received from an audience of more than one hundred people in the following forty-five minutes of discussion. The presence of a military officer in the room and his objection to my presentation had silenced a room full of people. All remaining comments and questions were addressed to the other presenter on the panel. After the panel, several people came to me to ask their questions privately and to tell me how relieved they were that the discussion had not become more "heated."

About six months later, I was a facilitator on a panel on education, where an officer-teacher from the Naval High School presented his pedagogical techniques for democratizing the classroom and engaging the students in the course. It was indeed a very thought-provoking and well-prepared presentation. I, for one, had a lot of questions to ask, but as the facilitator, I had to turn to the audience first. Among the audience, there were high school teachers, faculty members from schools of education, as well as academics from other fields. No one had a question or a comment. I went ahead and asked a question, and, after hearing the answer, I turned to the audience one more time. Again, no response. I said, "Well, I will keep asking my questions then. You talked about addressing the various prejudices that students have. Could you please share with us your methods for dealing with gender prejudices in an all-male classroom?" This time adopting a more defensive tone, the officer-teacher explained that they had a woman officer who instructed the students in human rights, and that no student would graduate from the Navy High School or from any other military school with gender prejudices.

It was only after this second question and answer between the officer-teacher and myself that the audience joined in the discussion. I would have interpreted this as a common need for "warming up" if it weren't for several members of the audience who came to me afterwards to thank me for breaking the wall between themselves and the officer who was presenting. "If you had not asked those questions in such a calm and confident manner, no one would have talked. You know, there is that invisible wall that prevents us from engaging with an officer," said a woman high school teacher.

Both of these incidences bear witness to the uncanny nature of public silence on issues related to the military in Turkey. I agree with Timothy Mitchell's suggestion that "we must take seriously the elusiveness of the boundary between state and society, not as a problem of conceptual precision but as a clue to the nature of the phenomenon" (Mitchell 1999, 77). This book aims to read into such silences and silencings, with the hope of normalizing the discussion around them. It is only with such discussion, I believe, that we will begin to understand the "military-idea" so prevalent in our everyday lives, as well as in our intellectual practices.

PART 1
THE MILITARY-NATION

CHAPTER ONE

THE MYTH OF THE MILITARY-NATION

Sabiha Gökçen, one of Atatürk's adopted daughters, participated in the Dersim Operation in 1937 and became the first woman combat pilot in the world. In her memoirs, she writes about Atatürk's response to her success in the operation upon her return to Ankara: "I am proud of you, Gökçen! And not just me, the whole Turkish nation that has been following this incident very closely is proud of you. . . . We are a military-nation. From ages seven to seventy, women and men alike, we have been created as soldiers." (Gökçen 1996, 125–126)

Halil Inalcık, a highly-respected historian of the Ottoman Empire and Turkey, wrote an article in 1964, titled "Osmanlı Devrinde Türk Ordusu" (The Turkish Military in the Ottoman Period) where he argued that "the Turkish nation has conserved its military-nation characteristic from the beginning of history till today" and that Turks are used to living as *hakim* (dominant) and *efendi* (master). *Inalcık 1964, 56.* This article appeared in the journal Türk Kültürü (Turkish Culture) and was re-printed in the same journal in 1972 and in 1994.

In 1937, Hasan-Ali Yücel, a parliamentarian and educator who later served as the Minister of Education for eight years (1938–1946) collected some of his writings in a volume where he recited the following story: When a general of the Turkish Army told him, partly joking, that he would not let anyone who is not a soldier kiss his hand, Yücel felt offended: "Is there a Turk who is not a soldier? I am a soldier, too, my dear Pasha." (Yücel 1998, 39)

As the utterances of Turkey's legendary leader, most famous historian, and the most celebrated (and remembered) Minister of Education make clear, the idea that the Turkish nation is a military-nation (*ordu-millet* or *asker-ulus*)[1] is one of the foundational myths of Turkish nationalism. The popular saying, "*Her Türk asker doğar*" (every Turk is born a soldier) is repeated in daily conversations, school textbooks, the speeches of public officials and intellectuals, and is used as a drill slogan during military service. Its legitimacy goes without saying. In this chapter, my aim is to attempt a genealogy of the term *military-nation* and discuss the making of the myth that "the Turkish nation is a military-nation."

The Military-Nation: Beginnings

The first reference to the term "military-nation" I have been able to identify in the English language is an 1803 book published in Britain: *The French Considered as a Military Nation Since the Commencement of Their Revolution*. It is a "negative" reference in the sense that the author(s) are alarmed at the formation of the French conscript army and its possible consequences for Britain, as well as its consequences for the future of warfare in general. According to historian Orhan Koloğlu, the term "military-nation" appeared in the Ottoman language in the 1860s. On 21 January 1864, the newspaper *Tasvir-i Efkar* published an essay introducing a new publication called *Ceride-yi Askeriye* (Military Journal) and referred to "the Ottoman nation" as a "combatant nation"[2] (Koloğlu 1999, 344). In 1884, a year after its original publication in German, Baron von der Goltz's influential work *Das Volk in Waffen* (The Nation in Arms) was translated into Ottoman as *Millet-i Müsellaha* (literally, the nation in arms or armed nation). In 1888, the second edition of the translation came out. It is remarkable that Ottoman was one of the first languages this book was translated into (three years before the first English translation) and that a second edition came out in four years.

First appropriated into the discourses of Ottoman nationalism, Goltz's ideas continued their influence into the discourses of Turkish nationalism as they turned into official ideology in the early 1930s. This continuity was hardly surprising. As historian Hasan Ünder (1999a, 48) notes, "Atatürk and most of the other founders of the Turkish Republic were soldiers and had received their education in military schools whose curricula had been designed by German military experts. Most of their teachers were German or, if they were Ottoman, they had been trained in Germany."[3]

Goltz's book was a major source for the new textbooks written by Mustafa Kemal (Atatürk)[4] and his adopted daughter Afet (Inan) in the early 1930s. Afet, who was a high school teacher in the 1920s and later became a historian and anthropologist, is best known for her contributions to the *Turkish History Thesis* (see below) and to the series of textbooks compiled under the volume *Vatandaş İçin Medeni Bilgiler* (Civilized Knowledge for the Citizen). Although Afet appeared as the sole author of *Vatandaş İçin Medeni Bilgiler* when it came out in 1931, it was known that Mustafa Kemal had assumed an active part in the writing process, guiding her and, at times, directly dictating passages. In 1964 (and later in 1988), *Vatandaş İçin Medeni Bilgiler* was reprinted with Mustafa Kemal's handwritten notes and an introduction by Afet Inan, revealing that the collection was indeed co-authored by Mustafa Kemal and herself: "I see it as my responsibility to set the historical record straight. Although these books have come out under my name, they have been written based on Atatürk's ideas and criticisms and the narrative style belongs solely to him" (Inan 1988, 7).

As Hein and Selden suggest (1998, 3), "textbooks provide one of the most important ways in which nation, citizenship, the idealized past, and the promised future are articulated and disseminated in contemporary societies." *Vatandaş İçin Medeni Bilgiler*, used as a textbook at several levels of secondary and high school education in the 1930s, can be read as an official treatise on the structures and discourses of government in the formative years of Republican Turkey. Its different sections discuss ideas about the state, the republic, the nation, military service, laws, citizenship, and the economy. It is a valuable resource for analyzing the ways in which the new state was constructing itself and how Ankara wanted to educate its students. Moreover, Mustafa Kemal's own participation in the writing and commissioning of the new textbooks as the president of the country reveals the importance attached to these texts by the ruling elite.

One of the textbooks that became a part of the *Vatandaş İçin Medeni Bilgiler* collection was *Askerlik Vazifesi* (Military Service or Military Duty). It was first published in 1930 by the Ministry of Education, with Afet (Inan) as the author, for use in the military course in secondary and high schools. The concise, but well-written narrative of the book is based heavily on Goltz's analysis in *Das Volk in Waffen*, with certain sections being direct translations (see Ünder 1999a). Without any reference to Goltz or the concept of "nation-in-arms" he had made popular, the book outlines the characteristics of contemporary (*asri*), national (*milli*) armies and emphasizes the need for every citizen to participate in the country's defense through military service.

As in *Das Volk in Waffen*, the main approach in the textbook *Askerlik Vazifesi* towards history is universalistic and evolutionary.[5] Human (tribal) communities in ancient times are presented as having been based on self-defense and the arming of all members of the community (Afet 1930, 22). As people settle down in towns, a new class, that is, a military class, comes into existence: "In this age the army was constituted only during war time and by a part of the nation" (Afet 1930, 23). The third stage is that of standing armies: "After gunpowder was discovered, arms were perfected, and modes of warfare became complicated, it became necessary to work everyday to be prepared for war" (Afet 1930, 23). The rest of the text lays out some of the characteristics of this "contemporary army" (*asri ordu*) and further clarifies the army in question as being a "pure national army" (*halis milli ordu*) as opposed to an army of paid soldiers and volunteers (Afet 1930, 35).

Although *Askerlik Vazifesi* is based on Goltz's account of military and human history in *Das Volk in Waffen*, the future is conceived differently in the two texts. For Goltz, it is imaginable that "the day will come when the present aspect of war will disappear, when forms, customs, and opinions will again be altered" (Goltz 1887, x). But that day, according to Goltz, is "a long way off" (xi). In the textbook written by Afet Inan and Mustafa Kemal Atatürk, there is a latent assumption that national armies mark the end of the universal (evolutionary) history. The only change that might occur is the disappearance of armies, but that, according to them, will remain a dream: "It is often suggested that armies should disappear altogether. You will always hear this suggestion, which is a humanistic (*insaniyetperverane*) idea. It is indeed desirable to see the implementation of this idea, but that is not possible. It will always remain a brilliant Ideal" (Afet 1930, 36–37).

As discussed in chapter five, *Askerlik Vazifesi* is remarkably different in its style and line of argument about militaries and military history from textbooks used in the same course after the mid-1930s. It is also different from what was soon to become official ideology on the military characteristics of the Turkish nation. This difference, I argue, results from two related developments in this period: (1) the writing of a national history based on Central Asian origins through the *Türk Tarih Tezi*

(Turkish History Thesis) and a turn to a racial understanding of Turkishness in the 1930s, and (2) the subsequent re-interpretation of military service as *cultural/national/racial* characteristic, rather than as a "necessity of our times" and a duty for the nation-state. Both of these developments have helped shape the myth of the military-nation as an essential component of Turkish nationalist discourse.

The next four sections are devoted to a critical analysis of these developments. I first trace Turkish nationalism from the Ottoman nineteenth century through the early years of the Turkish Republic. Then I concentrate on the institutionalization of state nationalism in the 1930s, and particularly on the writing of the Turkish History Thesis. The third section that follows discusses the discursive and institutional maneuvers in the realm of military service that enabled the construction of the myth that "the Turkish nation is a military-nation." And finally, I suggest that this myth has assumed the status of what Bakhtin calls an "authoritative discourse" in Turkey.

From Ottoman Nationalism to Turkish Nationalism

Turkish nationalism was one of the last ethnic nationalisms to develop within the borders of the Ottoman Empire. It was only around the turn of the century that Turkish nationalism became an articulate ideology. By the end of the 1910s, a decade of much loss and suffering as a result of the Balkan Wars and the World War I, accompanied by an intense intellectual debate on "how to save the Ottoman State,"[6] it had turned into a prominent force. Starting with the French Revolution, nationalist ideas had permeated the minds and actions of both the elite and the diverse groups of people living on Ottoman lands. The Ottoman state, through reforms in its legal system, the military and political structure, was taking measures towards becoming a "nation-state" with a centralized administrative structure, a modern education system, a new conception of rights and duties for its subjects, and a citizen-army.[7] Initially, this was seen as a transformation of the Ottoman state and polity. The reorganization of the state was aimed at creating "citizens" and an "Ottoman nation" out of the subjects of the Empire. However, especially with the increase in the number of ethnic nationalisms (Bulgarian, Greek, Serbian, Albanian, Arab, etc.) in the Empire and the loss of territories, the feasibility of keeping the Empire together as a multiethnic, multireligious "national" community became a burning issue.

One of the first people to articulate the tensions between empire and nation-state was Yusuf Akçura (1878–1935). A historian and one of the first ideologues of Turkish nationalism, Akçura wrote an influential essay in 1904, which was published in Cairo in the journal *Türk*. In this essay, titled *Üç Tarz-ı Siyaset* (Three Kinds of Politics), Akçura argued that, for the Ottoman state, there existed three main visions of the future: Ottomanism, Islamism, and Turkism. According to Akçura, the first two had already influenced the Ottoman state, whereas the third was a new idea.

Ottomanism was the effort to create a new nation called the "Ottoman nation" within the existing borders of the Empire along the lines of the United States of America (Akçura 1976 [1904], 19). This involved the sharing of the same rights and duties by Muslim and non-Muslim communities in the Empire, equality among all groups, and freedom of expression and religious belief. Akçura suggested that "the policy of creating an Ottoman nation" had begun with Sultan Mahmud II (r. 1808–1838), when ideas of nationalism were still under the influence of the French Revolution and were, thus, based on "will" (*vicdani istek*) rather than "descent and race" (*soy ve ırk*) (20). According to Akçura, Sultan Mahmud II and his followers were "deceived" by the French notion of nationalism by believing in the possibility of keeping the different racial and religious communities in the Empire together under one nation based on notions of equality and freedom (20). However, in Akçura's terms, the "recent interpretation of the laws of nationality by the Germans as being based on race" and "the victory of this interpretation in Europe" not only meant the toppling of Napoleon's French Empire, but it also had an impact on the Ottoman Empire. The Ottomanist policies of the Empire based on the notion of will had lost their legitimacy (20). It was not "will" but common "race" that formed nations.

In Akçura's periodization, *Islamism* came next to dominate the agenda of Ottoman intellectuals and the Palace, following the failure of the Ottomanist policy (21–23). According to Akçura, the advocates of Ottomanism turned to Islamism as they realized, mainly through their studies in Europe, that the principles of religion and race were gaining political significance in the West and that the French model of nationalism was inapplicable to "the Orient" (21). They found their new direction in a call for the unity of all Muslims under the Ottoman state and the caliph (who had been the Ottoman sultan since the early sixteenth century), which came to be labeled as Pan-Islamism by Europeans (21). Akçura sees this policy as having been one of the causes of the growing tensions, hatred, and rebellion among the diverse religious communities of the Empire and of the increasingly negative feelings against the Turks in Europe (23).

Akçura's introduction of "a political Turkish nationalism based on race" (23) follows this narrative of double-failure. For Akçura, Ottomanism was bound to fail and Islamism is difficult, whereas taking the direction towards a racially based Turkish nationalism appears to be inevitable. He acknowledges *Turkism* as a "brand new" policy not having any basis in the history of the Ottoman state or in any other Turkish state in history (23) and suggests that it is still not very popular (24). To him, this policy would involve the Turkification of other Muslim elements in the Empire (33). Its dangers included the exclusion of certain ethnic groups (*kavim*) that would resist Turkification, and growing antagonism between Russia, which had Turkic populations under its rule, and the Ottoman state. According to Akçura, the limitations of Islamism and Turkism were similar in degree, making a straightforward answer to the question of "which political direction will be more useful and feasible for the Ottoman State" a difficult one (36). Although it is clear that he was fascinated with the "brand new" idea of Turkism, Akçura ended his essay with the reiteration of this question, the answer to which was either Islamism or Turkism.

Despite this open-ended conclusion, *Üç Tarz-ı Siyaset* has been received as one of the earliest articulations of (Pan)Turkish nationalism and is often referred to as the "Communist Manifesto of Turkism" (Zürcher 1994, 134). As Erik Jan Zürcher suggests, by the end of the Balkan Wars (1912–1913), Ottomanism was "a dead letter" (1994, 134) and Turkish nationalism was gaining prominence and turning into a program, mainly through the organization *Türk Ocakları* (Turkish Hearths) and its journal *Türk Yurdu* (Turkish Homeland). However, competing visions of Turkish nationalism were also being voiced at this time. For instance, Ahmed Ferid (Tek), a leading public intellectual, published a rebuttal in the same journal, arguing that Ottomanism, despite its shortcomings, was the best option for maintaining unity in the Ottoman Empire. Historian Şükrü Hanioğlu argues that until 1913, Ahmed Ferid's position was much more popular among the Ottoman intelligencia than Yusuf Akçura's (Hanioğlu 1985a).[8]

Another key intellectual of this period was Ziya Gökalp (1875–1924), a passionate and prolific contributor to the journal *Türk Yurdu*, who also theorized about the relationship between nationhood, culture, race, and ethnicity.[9] He criticized his contemporaries for confusing these concepts with each other and devoted his energy to developing a "sociological" approach to the burning questions at hand:

> What...is a nation? What kind of unifying force is there that is superior to, and dominant over, racial, ethnic, geographic, political, and volitional forces? Sociology teaches us that this unifying force lies in education and culture; in other words, in the community of sentiments.
>
> Nation is not a racial, ethnic, geographical, political, or voluntary group or association. Nation is a group composed of men and women who have gone through the same education, who have received the same acquisitions in language, religion, morality, and aesthetics. The Turkish folk express the same idea by simply saying; "The one whose language is my language, and whose faith is my faith, is of me". Men [*sic*] want to live together, not with those who carry the same blood in their veins, but with those who share the same language and the same faith. Our human personality is not our physical body but our mind and soul. (Gökalp 1959, 136–137)

As the emphasis on "the same language and the same faith" reveals, Gökalp was known for his efforts to create a synthesis between Islam and Turkish nationalism, while at the same time emphasizing the need to "modernize." His volumes on Turkish nationalism, partly inspired by Durkheimian sociology, became foundational sources for the nationalism of first the ruling Union and Progress Party (*Ittihat ve Terakki Partisi*) between 1908–1920 and later of Mustafa Kemal and the People's Party (*Halk Fırkası*). According to Taha Parla, Gökalp's corporatist thinking has helped to define "mainstream political discourse and action" in Turkey to this day (1985, 7).[10] Yet the Republican era also witnessed major divergences from Gökalp's formulations of Turkish nationalism (see Parla 1985). With the development of the Turkish History Thesis in the early 1930s, Turkish nationalism became "racialized" and the synthesis that Gökalp was trying to achieve between Islam and westernization was dropped in favor of a radical interpretation of "laicism."[11]

First, however, came a defining period: the War of Independence (1919–1923).

Turkification of the War of Independence

The War of Independence was not fought in the name of "the Turkish nation" as later historiography would have us believe. It was fought in the name of "the

Anatolian and Rumeli Muslim people" (see Zürcher 1994; Rustow 1959). The Congresses of Erzurum and Sivas in 1919 were essential in the initiation of a joint struggle by the many (armed and unarmed) organizations that had formed around the country under the name *Müdafaa-i Hukuk Cemiyetleri* (Societies for the Defence of Rights).[12] When the Grand National Assembly (*Büyük Millet Meclisi*) was formed in April 1920 in Ankara, as an alternative to the Istanbul government, Mustafa Kemal gave an opening speech, presenting a detailed account of the national struggle that was taking place. While reciting the results and minutes of the Erzurum Congress, he outlined the "*hududu milli*" (national borders) that had been set by the participants in the Congress and explained:

> These borders have not been drawn only with military considerations, they are national borders. They have been set as national borders. But it should not be assumed that there is only one kind of nation within the Islamic element inside these borders. Within these borders, there are Turks; there are the Çerkes; as well as other Muslim elements. These borders are national borders for *kardeş* [sibling] nations that live in a mixed way and that have totally unified their goals. [In the article concerning borders], the privileges of each of the Muslim elements within these borders, which stem from their distinct milieu (*muhit*), customs (*adat*) or race (*ırk*), have been accepted and certified with sincerity and in a mutual fashion.[13]

In a subsequent speech, Atatürk revisited the question of who made up the "nation":

> Gentlemen . . . What we mean here, and the people whom this Assembly represents, are not only Turks, are not only Çerkes, are not only Kurds, are not only Laz. But it is an intimate collective of all these Muslim elements. . . . The nation that we are here to preserve and defend is, of course, not only comprised of one element. It is composed of various Muslim elements. . . . We have repeated and confirmed, and altogether accepted with sincerity, that [each and every element that has created this collective] are citizens who respect each other and each other's racial, social, geographic rights. Therefore, we share the same interests. The unity that we seek to achieve is not only of Turks or of Çerkes, but of Muslim elements that include all of these.[14]

As these speeches, along with the minutes of the initial congresses that unified the struggle of armed groups around Anatolia and Rumeli into a national struggle, make clear, the War of Independence was hardly a "Turkish" War of Independence, but has become one through official historiography, which was set to work soon after the Republic was founded in October 1923. By the early 1930s, not only had the war been re-conceived as a *Turkish* War of Independence, but the existence of all other "Muslim elements" (the Kurds, the Çerkes, the Laz) as distinct ethnic groups, let alone "*sibling* [*kardeş*] *nations*," had become silenced. Articulate theories of total denial of their distinct identities would soon follow (Parla 1992; Yeğen 1999; Yıldız 2001).[15]

The efforts to define Turkishness and Turkish nationalism began in mid-1920s and became intensified after a series of radical reforms by the new state, which abolished the sultanate and the caliphate[16] (1924). A new law was passed to centralize education (*Tevhid-i Tedrisat Kanunu*—Unification of Education Law, 1924);

the European calendar was adopted (1926); the alphabet was changed from Arabic to Latin (1928); and new civil and penal codes (based on Swiss and Italian codes respectively) were put in place (1926). As Zürcher suggests, these reforms were made possible by (and accompanied) the establishment of an authoritarian regime: "From the promulgation of the Law of Maintenance of Order in March 1925, Turkey's government was an authoritarian one-party regime, and, not to put too fine a point on it, a dictatorship" (Zürcher 1994, 187).

The Law of Maintenance of Order (*Takrir-i Sükun Kanunu*) was passed to "empower the government for two years to ban by administrative measure any organization or publication which it considered to cause disturbance to law and order" (Zürcher 1994, 179) after an attempted rebellion in Eastern Turkey by a Kurdish *Nakşibendi*[17] leader, Sheik Sait. This law remained in effect until 1929 and was used not only against the Kurdish rebels in the East, but also to silence opposition to government policies in other parts of Turkey as well. Major national and provincial newspapers were closed down and almost all remaining press was placed under government control in this period of rapid and radical reform. Turkification of the state began in the same period and was enhanced through efforts to "write Turkish history" in the 1930s. By the late 1930s, the new Turkey had been constructed as a "Turkish" state. The production of the *Turkish History Thesis* marks an important stage in the making of a hegemonic Turkish nationalism based on ideas of race and ethnicity.

The Turkish History Thesis and the Racialization of Culture

Using Charles Tilly's (1992) differentiation between *state-led* nationalisms and *state-seeking* nationalisms, one can argue that the history of nationalisms from the Ottoman Empire to the Turkish Republic followed a tortuous path. It started with a state-led Ottoman nationalism based on new notions of citizenship and rights for all ethnic and religious groups in the Empire, soon to be accompanied by competing views of oppositional but state-inspired Islamic and Turkish nationalisms; along with numerous state-seeking nationalisms (Greek, Bulgarian, Serbian, Armenian, Arabic, etc.). The War of Independence (1919–1923) can be viewed as a state-seeking, place-based (Anatolia and Rumeli) Muslim nationalism. Starting with the early years of the new nation-state (Turkey), this nationalism turns into a state-led ethnic/racial Turkish nationalism which aims to suppress differences within the national borders and Turkify all other ethnicities whose names were clearly articulated (Çerkes, Kurd, Laz, etc.) during the War of Independence.

The ideological basis for Turkification was developed through a rewriting of Turkish and Ottoman history in the 1930s. At first a history commission was established under the organization *Türk Ocakları* (Turkish Hearths).[18] A new textbook titled *Türk Tarihinin Ana Hatları* (The Main Tenets of Turkish History) was produced in the same year (1930), but it was found to be "unsatisfactory" by both Mustafa Kemal and other historians (see Uzunçarşılı 1939). In 1931, *Türk Ocakları*, remnants of the Ottoman-Turkish nationalist movement, were closed and a new organization under the name *Türk Tarih Tetkik Cemiyeti* (The Society for the Study of Turkish History; later to be named *Türk Tarih Kurumu*—Turkish

Historical Society) was formed to further historical research and writing. In 1932, *Türk Dil Kurumu* (Turkish Linguistic Society) joined these efforts concentrating on the linguistic aspects of history writing. These two societies, both formed by Atatürk, were the central bodies for the intellectual production of Turkish nation and nationalism in the 1930s. Turkish History Thesis and its linguistic counterpart the Sun-Language Thesis (*Güneş-Dil Teorisi*) were researched by these societies, under the directives and close scrutiny of Mustafa Kemal. According to historian Etienne Copeaux, their establishment marked a crucial step in the centralization and "absolute control of all intellectual life in Turkey" (Copeaux 1998, 40), as well as in the *"etatization"* and *"ideologization"* of history (Copeaux 1998, 35).

Only three months after its formation, the Turkish Historical Society published a four-volume history textbook titled *Tarih* (History), ready for use in the 1931–1932 academic year. This was the first articulation of the Turkish History Thesis. These four volumes were reprinted in large quantities (20,000–30,000) throughout the 1930s. In 1939, Prof. Ismail Hakkı Uzunçarşılı, a parliamentarian and a member of the Turkish Historical Society, explained how this book was written in an article titled "As Turkish History Was Being Written":

> Each person [participating in the writing of this book] had produced a certain section of the book, based on their area of expertise. They then read out their theses and accepted criticisms. Atatürk, as the benefactor of the Historical Society, was present during these first readings. For approximately a month, the theses were read out loud, discussed and criticized from four o'clock till midnight in the libraries of Çankaya [the Presidential House]. (Uzunçarşılı 1939, 350)

In 1932, a year after the publication of this official treatise written under Mustafa Kemal's supervision, the first history congress was gathered in Ankara. This congress was more an attempt at *introducing* the Turkish History Thesis and *enlightening* school teachers who had used the new textbook in the previous academic year, than an occasion for an academic discussion on Turkish history (Ersanlı-Behar 1992, 119; Copeaux 1998, 46). In fact, what was most striking about this process was that the discursive turn to "science" as the basis of history (particularly anthropology) was going hand in hand with increasing intolerance towards any theory or suggestion that would contradict the official thesis. Curiosity and skepticism toward the material presented by "official" historians, such as Mustafa Kemal's adopted daughter Afet (Inan), were regarded as anti-patriotic and dangerous.[19]

This resulted in self-censorship and an increasingly singular conception of what Turkish nationalism should be about and who the Turks were. According to political scientist Büşra Ersanlı-Behar, the writing of an official history under the directives and close supervision of Mustafa Kemal "not only created the pressures of an ethnic hegemony [on history writing], but more importantly, it provided the legitimacy for an understanding of history limited to the political powers. Together with the Republic, historians were seen as nation-state makers, and their political mission was seen as being more important than their scientific inquiry" (Ersanlı-Behar 1992, 13). The "mission" was clear: To look for "proof" for the original thesis through historical and anthropological inquiry. By the Second History Congress, which met in 1937, the Turkish History Thesis had already established itself, together with Atatürk's single-party rule. In the words of Şemsettin Günaltay (1938), the Second History Congress had witnessed the "absolute victory" of the thesis.

Atatürk's adopted daughter Afet (Inan) deserves special attention here. Although she was only in her twenties, and initially a fresh high school teacher, she headed the first history commission in the writing of *Türk Tarihinin Ana Hatları* (1930) and was one of the writers (and the only woman writer) of the four volumes of *Tarih* (1931). Later, she would be a prominent voice in the Turkish Historical Society. Hers was a "mission" to prove the history and language theses proposed by Mustafa Kemal Atatürk and his followers. In the words of Ersanlı-Behar, she was the "designated historian" (1992, 126). After Atatürk's death, this is how she wrote about the origins of her interest in history and anthropology:

> In 1928, in French geography books, there was a statement about Turks belonging to the yellow race and, thus, having a secondary status in European thinking in terms of their genotype. I showed it to him [Mustafa Kemal] and asked: "Is this true?" He said: "No, this cannot be true. We need to work on this. You should study this." I began studying this issue as part of my duty to teach history in 1929. Atatürk had the most recent history books brought to Turkey. He established a library with these books. He gathered the historians in the country around him. We listened to what they had to say. All of his parliamentarian or minister colleagues would leave Atatürk's room with a book in their hands. (Afet 1939, 244)

Afet Inan complemented her work as a historian with an anthropology Ph.D. thesis in 1939 titled *Türkiye Halkının Antropolojik Karakterleri ve Türkiye Tarihi* (On the Anthropological Character of the Turkish People and Turkish History)[20] that was written at the University of Geneva in Switzerland under the supervision of anthropologist Eugène Pittard.[21] The thesis was based on anthropometrical research on the "skulls" of 65 thousand "Turks," the main argument being that the Turks were a *brachycephalic* (broad-headed) race, a characteristic that defined the "white" race (Inan 1947). Her turn to anthropology for further study was to be expected since race was the organizing category in the Turkish History Thesis regarding the "origins" and history of "the Turks."[22] The argument that the Turks were a *brachycephalic* race had first been made in the first volume of *Tarih* (1931) and further elaborated in the First History Congress in 1932 by Afet (Inan) herself.

The Turkish History Thesis and its crucial linguistic counterpart, the Sun-Language Thesis (*Güneş-Dil Teorisi*) which was introduced in 1936, were based on a racialized conception of the history of all civilization at the center of which lay the Turkish race, culture and language. The main arguments of both theses can be outlined as follows (see Günaltay and Tankut 1938; Günaltay 1938):

- The original homeland of the Turks is not Mongolia, but Turkistan.
- Turks are not members of the Mongoloid "yellow race," but of the *brachycephalic* white race.
- Neolithic civilization was first created in Central Asia by the Turks.
- Due to climactic changes (mainly drought) Turks of Central Asia migrated to different parts of the world and introduced Neolithic civilization to Asia, Europe, and America.

- The Turks developed the early civilizations in Mesopotamia and Egypt.
- Early civilizations in Anatolia (Asia Minor) such as those of the Hittites were also of Turkish origin.
- Turkish language is the oldest language of high culture and is the origin of Sumerian and Hittite languages.
- The Turks have formed many states in history.

Three main issues stand out in these theses, which have formed the basis of the new textbooks and the population policies of the Turkish Republic from the 1930s onward: (1) development of an ethnic/racial understanding of "culture," (2) glorification of the Turkish "race" as the basis of civilization and high culture in world history, and (3) formation of a "dual geographic framework" (Copeaux 1998, 32) whereby Central Asia is the "main" homeland, while simultaneously the current location of Turkey (Anatolia) is claimed to have Turkish origins long before the Ottoman Empire. According to Copeaux (1998, 32), the emphasis on Central Asian origins was aimed at the marginalization of Ottoman and Islamic influences in Turkish history, and the arguments over Anatolia served to subside the Armenian and Greek land claims over Turkey. "We, the Turks, were here long before the Greeks and Armenians" was the main subtext of these arguments. They were also used to develop arguments for the Turkic origins of all other Muslim populations in modern Turkey. The Kurds, the Laz, and the Çerkes were no longer "sibling nations" but Turks who had "forgotten" their Turkishness or were in "denial" of their Turkish origins.

Where did Ziya Gökalp, arguably the most influential ideologue of Turkish nationalism, stand in this "(re)turn to race" in theories of the Turkish nation? Gökalp's premature death (in 1924) prevented him from being an active agent in this process. Yet, before he died, he clearly stated his position in relation to the concepts of race and culture. In 1923 he wrote: "Nations have nothing to do with race, organic heredity or organic degeneration. A nation is a group that has its own culture" (Gökalp 1977, 11). Racial difference, for Gökalp, was socially constructed:

> Every race can reach the highest levels of civilization. Progress and civilization are not unique to the European race. While certain ethnicities that belong to the European race are today backward civilization-wise, certain races that are not of the European race and are considered to be of second-class by foreign scholars have reached the civilization levels of Europe ... Real and objective science has shown us that in democracies the first truth is that "races are equal". (Gökalp 1977, 8)

Other "truths" that should be the bases of democracy for Gökalp were: Equality of the nations, equality between men and women, and equality among castes and classes. The reasons for inequality were social and historical: "The difference in the capabilities of races and nations, as well as men and women, are not due to biological reasons, but social ones" (Gökalp 1977, 15). Culture, which was the basis of nationhood, too, had an historical character: "People living in a country might belong to different ethnic groups. As long as they share a common way of life and do not mix up with people from other countries, after a long time, they turn into a single nation with a shared culture" (Gökalp 1977, 10). He added that culture could not be transmitted through heredity, but could only be taught through education (Gökalp 1977, 9).

What we see in the 1930s is a synthesis of Gökalp's theories on national culture, including his emphasis on a Turkey-based nationalism, and Yusuf Akçura's ongoing contributions toward a racialized history.[23] Construction of an idealized racial past with an alternative geographic standpoint (centered in prehistoric Central Asia) was used for rewriting human history, but not for drawing the borders of the existing Turkish state. Rather, it was used as the background for a Turkey-based nationalism. Why such a background and not another? It would be difficult to answer such a counterfactual question. But we can talk about the intended effects of this particular nationalist construction, which include, among others, to instill pride in Turkishness, to pursue claims over the existing geography against the Greeks and the Armenians, to enforce policies of Turkification over all Muslim groups in Anatolia (by reminding them of their "real" origins), to legitimize secularist policies through the invention of pre-Islamic "traditions," and to sever ties with the Ottoman Empire by marginalizing its importance in Turkish history (H. Berktay 1990; Copeaux 1998).

As historian Halil Berktay argues, one of the crucial arguments that combine nationalist history and contemporary politics in Turkey is that Turks have formed numerous "states" in history.

> [According to the Turkish History Thesis] Turks never went through a "barbaric" phase; in 209 B.C. (when Mo-tun/Mete became the leader of the Huns), Turks appeared in history as a "nation" with their "military" and "state"; and since then, they have established sixteen states (according to some, more than a hundred states, dozens of big states, and a few super empires!). (H. Berktay 1990, 64)

Conceptualization of Turkish history as a history of state-making not only contributes to the overall theme of high civilization among the Turks, but also provides "an organic unity" (H. Berktay 1990, 63) between history and contemporary politics. State-making, in these narratives, appears as a character of the Turkish race, which provides a powerful standpoint for the modern Turkish state against its own minorities (e.g., the Kurds who have never had a state of their own), as well as its neighbors (particularly Armenia[24]). Moreover, the Ottoman Empire becomes only *one* of the many states established by the Turks, adding to its marginalized status in Turkish historiography.

Before the advancement of the Turkish History Thesis, Ottoman and European history books described Turks as "tribal" people. Afet Inan recites Atatürk's opposition to this argument: "Turks could not have formed an empire in Anatolia as a tribal people. There should be a different explanation. History should reveal this [alternative explanation]" (quoted in Inan 1939, 244). Embedded in Atatürk's statement is evolutionary thinking that was characteristic of his times: Tribal societies are primitive and civilization is defined in close proximity to "statehood." The alternative explanation, which would soon be "revealed" by official historians, was based on a leveling of all Turkish history as "civilized." According to the Turkish History Thesis, Turks had formed their own "states" from time immemorial and had carried their skills as "state-makers," along with civilization, wherever they went.

Tarih, the four-volume history book written by the Turkish Historical Society in 1931, defined Turks as "members of a great race that has brought into being different states, civilizations, and societies in the historical period and in pre-historic times" (*Tarih I*, 20). These included the ancient Egyptian civilization and state, the Hittite Empire in Anatolia, Sumerian civilization in Mesopotamia, as well as the Great Hun Empire in Central Asia, the Seljuks, Timur's Empire, the Mogul Empire in India, the Turkish-Ottoman Empire and finally, the Turkish Republic. It was added in italic letters that the Turkish Republic was the best state established by the Turks so far. This list has changed over time[25] and some of the claims (such as the Turkishness of Egyptian civilization) made in earlier historiography have been dropped. Yet the claim that no other nation has established more states in history than the Turks has remained a constant and formed the background to the myth of the military-nation. It was thanks to Turks being a military-nation that they could establish so many states in history. This narrative of the Turkish nation and state-making naturalized military service (in fact the military itself) as a *cultural institution*, rather than a modern state institution. It is in this interlocking of state, nation, culture, and race throughout history that the idea of military-nationhood assumes the position of a foundational myth.

Roland Barthes (1972, 143), in his discussion of myth, argues that "in passing from history to nature, myth acts economically: it abolishes the complexity of human acts, it gives them the simplicity of essences, it does away with all dialectis, with any going back beyond what is immediately visible, it organizes a world which is without contradictions because it is without depth, a world wide open and wallowing in the evident, it establishes a blissful clarity: things appear to mean something by themselves." As Anne Allison (1994, 81) suggests, the concept of *naturalization* in Barthes refers to the conceptionalization of something as "cultural" in order to make it seem as "natural." In this sense, the turn to a *cultural* interpretation of military service in 1930s Turkey can be read as an effort to *naturalize* military service in the eyes of the population that had identified it with war and death.

Military Service in the Age of Nationalism

As Lucassen and Zürcher (1999, 1) argue, the phenomenon of universal conscription which, in the nineteenth and twentieth centuries, was the "predominant system of military recruitment . . . has received surprisingly little attention from social historians." Zürcher's (1999) edited volume *Arming the State: Military Conscription in the Middle East and Central Asia 1775–1925* is a timely attempt at exploring the links between nationalism, state-making, and military service in Ottoman history. Lack of historical attention to military service has contributed to its naturalization as an ahistorical, cultural practice. In the previous section, I tried to outline the maneuvers in nationalist historiography that prepared the context for this naturalization. I now concentrate on the maneuvers in the realm of the military. The term "military-nation" marks the connectedness of these maneuvers and necessitates a discussion of both in relation to each other. In what follows, I summarize the changes in the Ottoman military structure in eighteenth and nineteenth centuries and discuss the introduction of compulsory military-service as a modern state practice.

The Ottoman military had a unique structure that proved successful from the fourteenth century, when the first standing army of Janissaries was formed, till the eighteenth century, when military reform came to dominate the agenda of the palace. As it had developed throughout the centuries of expansion, the Ottoman army consisted of various groups of soldiers. The two main classes were the Janissaries (a salaried standing army established in 1363, long before its counterparts in Europe) and the fief holding semifeudal soldiers. The Janissaries were first recruited from among the slaves and later from among the non-Muslim (mainly Christian) population. They were directly tied to the palace, receiving their salaries from the treasury and undergoing a special education program, which enabled some of them to achieve positions of power among the ruling elite, including the post of the grand-vizier.[26] The fief holders, on the other hand, were distributed throughout the Empire and were called in to join wars as needed with their own forces. There were also a small group of soldiers recruited directly by the palace for specific tasks in the army.

Sultan Selim III (r. 1789–1807), in the early 1790s, launched a series of reforms under a program called New Order (*Nizam-i Cedit*) that included the formation of a new army to be trained with modern techniques to balance the power of the Janissaries. Although this new army could not maintain itself, and Sultan Selim III was killed during a rebellion against it, these reforms started a process which resulted in the elimination of Janissary troops by Sultan Selim's successor, Mahmud II, in a bloody campaign of annihilation in 1826, and was followed by the formation of yet another army, *Asakir-i Mansure-i Muhammediye* (Trained Victorious Soldiers of Muhammad). From this period till the end of the Ottoman Empire, military reforms were at the center of modernization policies (Kayalı 1985).

It was first during the Tanzimat reforms in 1839 that each region in the Empire was asked to provide a certain number of soldiers on a regular basis (Kayalı 1985, 1253). The law regulating the time of this onetime service to five years was passed in 1843 and was based on the Prussian Conscription Law of 1814 (Çoker 1985, 1260). In 1856, the population eligible for military service was expanded to include the non-Muslim minority (Kayalı 1985, 1254), although until the 1910s the majority of the non-Muslims avoided military service by paying the applicable tax.[27] A new law in 1870 declared that all (male) Ottoman subjects, except for certain groups (including judges, teachers, imams, sheiks, doctors, and the disabled), were obliged to register their names and to participate in the lottery for military service (Çoker 1985, 1264). In 1909, the exceptions were lifted and all Ottoman male subjects, except the family of the Sultan, were made eligible for military service.

These reforms in the military structure were not taking place in a vacuum. The nineteenth century was characterized by change in all aspects of society and the ruling elite in the Ottoman Empire as it was in other parts of Europe. The most radical change came with the proclamation of the Gülhane charter in 1839 that marked the beginning of *Tanzimat*, a new era of reforms that led to the adoption of the first constitution in 1876. This charter announced new laws that regulated the government, administrative and fiscal policies, the military, the judiciary, and the rights of all members of the Ottoman polity. According to Bülent Tanör (1985, 14), the Tanzimat reforms marked an attempt to "reinstate political unity and stability by redefining state activities through a framework of legal trust" as opposed to the military-theocratic framework that was beginning to lose its legitimacy. Similarly, historian Ilber Ortaylı (1985, 1546) defines the Tanzimat as an important step in the "civilianization of state administration."

Despite the fact that the Tanzimat reforms were initiated and carried out by civilian administrators and that civilianization of the Ottoman state was one of the most significant end-results, modernization in the Ottoman nineteenth century is often characterized by, or rather defined vis-à-vis the military reforms of the period (Ahmad 1993; Kayalı 1985; Berkes 1978). Yet one aspect of these reforms rarely receives adequate interrogation: the changing relationship between Ottoman subjects and the palace with the development of a conscription system as the basis of the new modern army. The introduction of conscription, which never became effectively universal under Ottoman rule, not only signaled the modernization of the Ottoman military, as it is often argued, but it also meant that the ordinary population would, for the first time, come into direct contact with the Ottoman center and that their services would be mobilized *directly by the state* (Berkes 1978, 89). Moreover, it changed soldiering from a lifetime occupation to a temporary service to the state demanded from a larger part of the population with each reform package.

This reform period, starting in late eighteenth century and continuing into the last days of the Ottoman Empire, marked a paradigmatic shift in the relations between the Ottoman state and its subjects. Being the subject of the Ottoman Empire no longer meant simply the payment of taxes, but involved a new conception of rights and duties towards the state, parallel to developments in the rest of Europe. "As direct rule expanded throughout Europe" sociologist Charles Tilly writes, "the welfare, culture, and daily routines of ordinary Europeans came to depend as never before on which state they happened to reside in. Internally, states undertook to impose national languages, national educational systems, national military service, and much more" (Tilly 1992, 115–116). In implementing these reforms, the Ottoman state was responding to the formation of an international state system based on a different conception of rule and power than before. In turn, these reforms were to start an irreversible process whereby subjects of an empire turned into citizens of nation-states, with the Turkish Republic being one of the states to be born out of the disintegrating Ottoman Empire. The next section deals with what became of military service and its discourses during the war years of 1912–1922 and during the Republican era (1923 onward).

From "A Necessity of The Times" to (Invented) "Tradition"

The first conscription law in the Republican period was in 1927, the year of the first census. That should not be a coincidence. As Lucassen and Zürcher (1999, 10) suggest, a reliable census is one of the "prerequisites for the successful introduction of a conscript army." Until 1927, the army of the Republic had been based on the system inherited from the Ottoman army, including recruitment practices. Although we do not have adequate historical material to comment on the functioning of the new recruitment system set in 1927, the increase in the number of soldiers in this period is quite revealing: "It has been estimated that as late as 1932 the size of the Turkish army was little greater than that existing in 1922 (78,000 men). It was not until 1939 and 1940 that the Turks mobilized a substantially greater force, possibly something in the neighborhood of 800,000" (Lerner and Robinson 1960, 27). What is suggested here is that there was a 900 percent increase in the number of conscripted soldiers between 1932 and 1939—which indicates that conscription evasion and desertion in the pre-1939 period may have been considerably high.[28] The increase in recruitment reveals the extent to which the bureaucratic apparatuses of government were in need of development throughout Mustafa Kemal Atatürk's rule and explains the attention paid to the discussion of the necessity of armies and significance of military service in the textbook written by Atatürk and Afet Inan in the 1930s. There *was* a real need to persuade young men throughout the country to serve in the military.[29]

When the Republic was founded, the population that inhabited its territories had already experienced constant warfare since 1912. The Balkan Wars had resulted in the death of large numbers of men serving in the military, as well as in the influx of more than one million refugees. The World War I had been even more disastrous, with certain parts of Anatolia turning into battlefields. During the Dardanelles campaign alone, 90,000 soldiers had lost their lives, with 165,000 wounded (Zürcher 1996, 233).[30]

The number of army deserters was also extremely high. According to Zürcher (1996, 233), one-fourth of all recruits called up for service during the war did not turn up in the first place. Furthermore, many would escape on the way to the battlefields. This was not very difficult because "it was socially acceptable to the villagers" (Lucassen and Zürcher 1999, 13), which meant that the deserters could receive assistance on their escape routes. The poor conditions in the army (lack of proper clothing, food, and means of transportation), combined with war conditions brought the rate of desertion to "unmanageable proportions" (Zürcher 1996, 234). By 1918, there were about half a million deserters in the Ottoman army (Lucassen and Zürcher 1999, 14). In other words, the army that was to undertake the Independence War was one with a very high rate of evasion and desertion.

This history of loss and suffering highlights the links between warfare and military service that marked the experiences of recruits and their families alike in the ten years of war between 1912 and 1922. Zürcher reviews the songs of World War I that reveal the sense of loss: "the prevailing sentiment in the lyrics of the songs is ... nearly always that those who went on campaign had no chance of returning and that they would die in some far off desert" (Zürcher 1996, 236), "there is no heroism here, and no patriotism.... More than anything they express a feeling of hopelessness and doom, of being sacrificed. In the eyes of the people who sang these songs, being called to the colors was a death sentence. In many cases, of course, they were right" (Zürcher 1996, 237). World War I was followed by the War of Independence, which lasted until 1922. Therefore, when the new conscription law of the Turkish Republic was passed in 1927, military service was still closely linked to war and a sense of loss. The discourses that were produced in the 1930s would slowly divorce military service from the recent wars and the Ottoman past, and relocate it in the terrain of culture/nation/race.

One of the earliest writings of Mustafa Kemal on the military is a review piece he wrote as a letter to the author of the book *Zabit ile Kumandan* (The Officer and

The Commander) in 1914. Here Mustafa Kemal outlines his views on contemporary armies:

> Contemporary armies are not comprised solely of those who join the military on their own will, but all members of the nation are obliged to perform military service. Those who do not want to join, along with those who do, are, and should be, obliged to perform their duty to their homeland (*hizmeti vataniye*). (*Atatürk'ün Askerliğe Dair Eserleri* [1959], 20)

This depiction of universal conscription as the unique characteristic of contemporary armies was in line with the evolutionary historiography Mustafa Kemal and Afet (Inan) were to recapitulate in *Askerlik Vazifesi* (Military Service) in 1930 (borrowing from Goltz). The recognition of the existence of "those who do not wish to join" the military was also an underlying subtext in *Askerlik Vazifesi*: The longest section in this textbook was the section titled *Orduların Lüzumu* (The Necessity of Armies).

Yet, with the development of Turkish nationalism as discussed above, discourses on military service were to take on a different character. The evolutionary, universalistic history that had explained its emergence in "the theatres of war" (Goltz 1887, ix) was eventually replaced with a nationalist history based on a mythical construction of "Turkish culture starting in Central Asia" (*sic*). Contemporary uses of the term "military-nation" are based on this move of turning a characteristic of contemporary armies into a cultural/national/racial characteristic.

The final (fourth) volume of the official history textbook, *Tarih* (1931, 1934), which was the first articulation of the Turkish History Thesis, ends with a short but poignant section titled "Turkish Military and National Defense" (*Tarih* [1931], 344–348). The section starts out with a discussion of "Turkishness and Military Service" (344) where it is argued that Turks are the best soldiers because they carry the cultural elements that make good soldiers. It is added that Turks "love military service"[31] and never despair, even when faced with the most powerful of enemies (344). According to the writers, there is a fundamental distinction between "military training" and "military spirit":

> Military training can be given in a matter of years, whereas military spirit is an ore that is born from the hammering of the abilities and capabilities of humankind throughout the centuries on the anvils of experience, and transformation into steel in the fire of life that has been fanned with raging storms. That is why the Turkish nation is the nation with the most developed military spirit. . . . A nation with high military spirit is a nation with a history of civilization; one that embodies deep and far-reaching knowledge [*derin ve engin irfan*]. It is natural that the *Turkish race*, which has been the ancestor [*ata*] of all major civilizations since the first days of humanity, perfected this spirit. (*Tarih* [1931], 344–345, original emphasis)

As in other parts of the Turkish History Thesis, in this narrative, too, culture, nation, and race are used interchangeably. What is most striking here is that a discussion of the Turkish military and national defense in official historiography starts with a narrative that locates military service in culture. Before the writers embark on a discussion of the military as an *institution* in late Ottoman period (345–346), during the Independence War (346) and in the Turkish Republic (346–348), they give primacy to the *idea* of military-nationhood, which is constructed as a cultural/national/racial characteristic. Moreover, it is also noteworthy that this narrative defines "civilization" through military power, revealing a deeply militarized sense of national history and national self.

In short, the Turkish History Thesis and the myth of the military-nation established the citizen-army of the Turkish Republic no longer as "the necessity of the times" and the present stage in a universal, evolutionary history of warfare (as Goltz's book and the official textbook *Askerlik Vazifesi* had argued), but as the basis of Turkish cultural/national/racial character throughout history. Military service, an obligation set by the nation-state for its male citizens was turned into an "invented tradition" (Hobsbawm and Ranger 1983) that combines the realms of culture and politics in the body of the "military-nation."

What are the implications of this discursive shift? First, the marriage of military service with an ahistorical sense of culture/nation/race has accompanied a distancing (if not a divorce) of military service from wars, fighting, and possible death, connections that the ten years of warfare had firmly established. Second, it has placed military service outside the realm of history, making it immune to historical change (or the imagination of such change in the future). Third, this shift places military service outside the realm of political debate as well. If the nation is "by its very nature" a military-nation, then challenging compulsory military service would not be about discussing the nature of the relationship between the state and its citizens; it would necessitate a challenge to the essential characteristics of the Turkish culture/nation/race. Fourth, this formulation leaves little room for an independent, nonmilitary, civilian sphere in national politics and cultural practice. If every Turk is born a soldier, then all Turkish life goes on (or should go on) in khaki. Imagining "the outside" would be equivalent to being a non-Turk, if not a traitor.

Conclusion: Military-Nationhood as an Authoritative Discourse

> Mythic and symbolic discourses can thus be employed to assert legitimacy and strengthen authority. They mobilize emotions and enthusiasm. They are a primary means by which people make sense of the political process, which is understood in a symbolic form. (Schöpflin 1997, 27)

The myth that the "Turkish nation is a military-nation" has achieved the status of what Bakhtin identifies as the "authoritative word." It has been the basis of Turkish (nationalist) historiography according to which Turks have formed many states and created many civilizations throughout history all owing to their military spirit. In the words of historian Halil Inalcık:

> The Turkish nation has preserved its military-nation character from the beginnings of history till today. . . . If the Turk is . . . marching on the forefronts of world history, that is because of his unshakable national characteristics, military character, his grand military virtues and his ability to engage in total war for his rights and freedom. The Turk has inherited this character from his history that goes back thousands of years. (Inalcık 1964, 56)

As Bakhtin argues, "the authoritative word is located in a distanced zone, organically connected with a past that is felt to be hierarchically higher. It is, so to speak, the word of the fathers. Its authority was already *acknowledged* in the past. It is a *prior* discourse" (Bakhtin 1994, 342). Questioning this history and the status of this foundational myth would, then, be "akin to taboo" (Bakhtin 1994, 342).

This authoritative discourse is intricately linked to an authoritative practice: military service. Universally compulsory for all men since 1927, military service has been the embodiment of military-nationhood. For at least three generations now, all men have gone through the military for one to two years of their lives (in some cases longer) and, as I try to show in the following chapters, the barracks have been a major site for the "imagining of the nation" (Anderson 1991) and of masculine national identity.

Around the same time as the writers of the Turkish History Thesis, including Atatürk himself, were acknowledging the "victory" of their theses, Alfred Vagts, a military historian, was finishing his lengthy treatise on militarism that was to become the most renowned and comprehensive work in this field: *A History of Militarism: Civilian and Military* (1937). Vagts argued that militarism, a modern phenomenon, was closely linked to the emergence of mass armies (which were based on the conscription system) starting with the French Revolution. "The standing army in peacetime," Vagts suggested, "is the greatest of all militaristic institutions" (Vagts 1959 [1937], 41). According to Vagts, "militarism flourished more in peacetime than in war" (1959, 15) and there were two kinds of militarism: Militarism of the military and civilian militarism. He defined civilian militarism as:

The unquestioning embrace of military values, ethos, principles, attitudes; as ranking military institutions and considerations above all others in the state; as finding the heroic predominantly in military service and action, including war—to the preparation of which the nation's main interest and resources must be dedicated, with the inevitability and goodness of war always presumed. (1959, 453)

Alfred Vagts was not alone in his concern about the militarizing role of conscript mass armies. The introduction of military service to the "theatres of war" (Goltz 1887) had both fascinated and alarmed the politicians, intellectuals, and the ordinary people of the nineteenth century and early twentieth centuries. In 1905—before, in Gramsci's terms, the idea of military service became "common sense"—Tolstoy likened military service to slavery: "Continental powers without a murmur submitted to the introduction of a universal military service, that is, to the slavery, which for the degree of degradation and loss of will cannot be compared with any of the ancient conditions of slavery" (Tolstoy 1990 [1905], 41).

Recent studies have revealed the agonizing histories of resistance whereby eligible men in great proportions went as far as dismembering themselves to evade military service in a variety of settings from Napoleon's France (Weber 1976; Woloch 1994) to Mehmed Ali Pasha's Egypt (Fahmy 1997) to the Ottoman territories (Zürcher 1999). The establishment of military service as a compulsory and universal modern state practice was nowhere an easy task; nor was it a smooth process. As Cynthia Enloe suggests, "there is a reason that so many states in the world have implemented military conscription laws for young men: most of those men would not join the state's military if it were left up to them to choose" (2000, 245).

The history of conscription in Turkey is still in need of research and analysis. For instance, how did the Turkish state manage to increase its number of military recruits 900 percent in less than a decade (i.e., in the 1930s)? We do not know. What we do know is that, eighty years after the establishment of the Turkish Republic, military service has become a "sacred" institution central to the "national order of things" (Malkki 1995) and that military-nationhood is an authoritative discourse. And together, they contribute to a unique form of "civilian militarism" in Turkey.

Starting in the early nineteenth century, the Ottoman military, since the 1920s, and the Turkish military have modeled themselves after the armies of Europe (mainly France and Germany). Those armies have since then changed their conscription practices as well as their internal structures (Horeman and Stolwijk 1998). Such changes in Turkey are more difficult because military service is much more than a citizenship rite (Feinman 2000). Through the myth that the Turkish nation is a military-nation, military service has been constructed as an essential characteristic of the Turkish nation, an authoritative "tradition" as opposed to a historical necessity: "Every Turk is born a soldier!" This move has "sanctified" the practice of military service in the name of nationhood, placing it outside of history and outside of political debate.

There is more to the myth of the military-nation as an "authoritative discourse": It is a highly gendered discourse that has important implications for gendered citizenship and gendered self-identification. Just as "Turkish culture" is defined through the military, Turkish masculinity is defined through military-service. In state discourse, as well as in the perception of many Turkish citizens, men become "men" only after serving in the military. This discourse on masculinity has contributed to the *culturalization* (and thus, *naturalization*) of military service. Part II will explore the links established between military service, masculinity, and nationhood, as well as the stories of those who have challenged them.

Yet, before I move on to a discussion of masculinity and military service, I would like to ask the question "where are the women?" (Enloe 1989) in the making of the myth of the military-nation. Since women do not serve in the military, is the "military-nation" a male nation? Are women automatically excluded? What role(s) have they been allowed or invited to play in this myth? The following chapter addresses these questions focusing on the striking life story of one woman, Sabiha Gökçen. The story of Gökçen (and how she chooses to tell it) reveals more than the gender tensions of the nationalist project as it was being crafted; it illustrates the extent to which militarism has shaped Turkish history and self-understanding alike.

CHAPTER TWO

WOMEN AND THE MYTH: THE WORLD'S FIRST WOMAN COMBAT PILOT

But the educated man's sister—what does "patriotism" mean to her?

Virginia Woolf

The current conscription law in Turkey dates back to 1927. The law was passed without much debate in the Grand National Assembly, except for a short but very significant discussion at the very beginning. The first article of the law suggested that "every man who is a citizen of the Turkish Republic, is hereby, given the obligation to perform military service." When this article was read in the Assembly, one member, Hakkı Tarık Bey, had a question:

> Sir, we see that here and there women are engaged in suffrage activities, asking for the right to vote and be elected for office. I personally believe that women should get this right. It is only a matter of time.... If voting and becoming a candidate is a national issue, participating in the country's defense is also a similar right, a similar duty. I realize that the first article of the compulsory military service law has only included men. I would like to ask whether you have taken women's services into consideration, or to what extent. (*TBMM Zabıt Ceridesi* [1927], 385)

He received two responses to his inquiry, neither claiming that women were incapable of fighting or doing military service or anything of that sort; rather both respondents acknowledged the participation of women in the Independence War and suggested that they were confident that women would do the same in the future, if that were needed. They did not need conscription for that! But apparently men did ...

In the words of Sylvia Walby (1996, 243), "nationalist projects are simultaneously gender projects." The debate in the Turkish Grand National Assembly reveals the extent to which the compulsory military service law passed in 1927 was as much a part of the state's gender project as it was of its nationalist project. At the same time, this debate reinforces the need to see military service not only as a practice that is about national defense, but also as one that defines the relationship between male and female citizens, and their state. When it is only men who become soldiers, military service inevitably defines male citizenship and masculinity in an opposition to female citizenship and femininity. Through continuous, compulsory and universal peacetime military service, masculinity, first class citizenship, the state, and the military are interwoven together as parts of an intricate whole. Masculinity becomes directly tied to the state (Enloe 2000; Nagel 1998).

Of course, none of this is specific to Turkey, but in Turkey, too, by bringing male citizens together in the barracks and separating them from female citizens, lawmakers created a major source of gender difference that *was defined and administered by the state*. Given equal suffrage rights, there is no other citizenship practice that differentiates as radically between men and women as compulsory male conscription. What is striking about the Assembly discussion in 1927 is that lawmakers were well aware of this fact. As Hakkı Tarık Bey suggests, just as voting and becoming a candidate are practices that shape the "rights and duties" of citizens in their relationship to their state, so is compulsory military service. This is another major characteristic of military service, which is made invisible by the myth of the military-nation. By defining men's compulsory participation in the military as a *cultural/national/racial characteristic of Turkishness*, this myth naturalizes military service, while at the same time naturalizing a state-sponsored *political* differentiation between male and female citizens as *cultural* differentiation.

What are the implications of this culturalized gender differentiation for women? Where do women stand in the myth of the military-nation? Through the life story of Sabiha Gökçen, Turkey's (and the world's) first woman combat pilot, I seek to show that in the early phases of the Turkish nationalist project, women were first and foremost designated the position of motherhood, and in exceptional cases, the position of the "warrior heroine." At the same time as I trace the making of the woman warrior in the story of Gökçen, I also inquire into the history of women's participation in the Turkish military and the nationalist project, Gökçen's contributions to official-history writing, and the feminist critiques of this historiography. I conclude the chapter by juxtaposing the gender tensions of the nationalist project and the ethnic tensions of second wave feminism.

Tracing Sabiha Gökçen

Sabiha Gökçen came of age in the early 1930s as the adopted daughter of the president of a new republic and chose a career untypical for a woman in any part of the world in those years. She first became a pilot, later joined the Turkish Air Force in its early years of formation, learned how to fly combat planes, and participated in an internal war effort in 1937, at the age of 24. She is not only Turkey's first woman *military* pilot, but she is also known as the world's first woman *combat* pilot.

In the words of Yeşim Arat, "the image of Sabiha Gökçen in her air force uniform, with respectful male onlookers, including her proud father, is ingrained in the collective consciousness of at least the educated urbanites in Turkey" (1997, 98–99). Being an educated urbanite in Turkey, this was also the case for me when Sabiha Gökçen literally "flew" into my life on 29 October 1998. I was spending a semester at Columbia University in New York, after more than a year of research in Turkey, when a friend visited me. She had flown Turkish Airlines from Istanbul and had received a complimentary book on this flight. The book was a long interview done with Sabiha Gökçen back in 1956. It was translated into English, published as a book in both languages for the seventy-fifth anniversary of the Turkish Republic, and distributed to everyone who flew Turkish Airlines on 29 October, the day the Republic was founded back in 1923. The book mentioned Gökçen's title as the world's first woman combat pilot and her desire to join the war effort in North Korea in 1950 to "do her part there for the free world" (Kıvanç 1998, 80). Her request was found "reasonable" by the president of the time, but there was a major obstacle: the United Nations did not allow women soldiers to engage in combat. As Sabiha Gökçen would not accept serving behind the lines, she did not go to Korea. Her desire to fight for the second time remained "unfulfilled" (Kıvanç 1998). The first time had been in 1937 during a large-scale military operation in Dersim, a Kurdish-Alevi dominated province in Turkey's Southeast. Upon learning about this military operation, Gökçen had gotten special permission from Atatürk and had assumed combat duty together with her peers from the Air Force. She had been awarded a special national medal for her success in this operation and had become "the first woman combat pilot in the world."

Most of this information was new to me. The images of Sabiha Gökçen, ingrained in my consciousness, started gaining a different meaning—or rather, meanings. In January 2001, only months before Sabiha Gökçen died at age 88,[1] Istanbul's second airport was opened and named after her:

> Development of Anatolia shall begin from the Anatolian Coast of Istanbul. Sabiha Gökçen Airport is getting ready to open new horizons for Turkey, just like the woman combat pilot of Turkey that it is named after.[2]

Since 2001, as I take the Sabiha Gökçen Airport exit everyday on my way to the Sabancı University campus, I am reminded of Gökçen's legacy as a pioneer woman and national heroine. In what follows, I aim to unravel some of the new and old images of Sabiha Gökçen ingrained in the consciousness of many Turkish citizens like me. My main source will be Gökçen's own memoirs published in 1982, in commemoration of Mustafa Kemal Atatürk's hundredth birthday.

Young Woman Pilot of the Young Republic

Sabiha (Gökçen) was born in 1913 in Bursa, the first capital of the Ottoman Empire, a green city on the foothills of Uludağ (The Great Mountain). Having lost both her parents at a young age, Sabiha was living with her elder brother and sister when Mustafa Kemal visited Bursa for the first time as the president of the new Turkish Republic in 1924 and for the second time in 1925. Sabiha Gökçen's memoirs start with a chapter titled "On the Threshold of Sacred Days," which describes the war-torn condition of Bursa at the dawn of Atatürk's visit to the city in 1924, in Gökçen's words, a "sacred incident" (Gökçen 1996, 13).

We learn from the memoirs that, although Sabiha had a great desire to see Mustafa Kemal during this first visit, she was not able to even get close to him. When he visited Bursa again a year later, however, he stayed in the mansion right next to Sabiha's home. Moreover, her brother was given service duty in the mansion. Watching Mustafa Kemal for a couple of days from the windows and balcony of her house, twelve-year-old Sabiha finally decided to jump over the fence and meet him in person. And she did: "I shouldn't have done that. Even when I was young, I was a brave girl" (Gökçen 1996, 20). While being interrogated by the guards upon her entry to the mansion's backyard, she shouted that she wanted to see Gazi Pasha and kiss his hand.[3] Finally, Mustafa Kemal called her to approach, let her kiss his hand, and rubbed her hair, "as if he were [her] father" (21). Sabiha Gökçen describes this moment as having "reached the unreachable" (21).[4]

During her conversation with Mustafa Kemal, Sabiha told him that she had lost both her parents, and that she wanted to go to a boarding school both for further education and in order not to be a burden on her siblings any longer. At the end of their conversation, Mustafa Kemal asked Sabiha if she would be interested in being his adopted daughter and moving to Ankara with him. For the young Gökçen, this proposal was a "miracle" (24). After consulting with her family, she accepted the offer and left with Mustafa Kemal for Ankara, the nation's new capital. From that day on, she was "Atatürk's daughter Sabiha" (25).

Sabiha started a new life in Ankara. She received education in the Presidential House from a private tutor, together with Zehra and Rukiye, Mustafa Kemal's other adopted daughters.[5] After she finished her studies at the primary school level, she continued her education in two schools in Istanbul, both American colleges for girls. However, she developed a sickness and moved to the sanatorium in one of the islands off the Istanbul Coast, Heybeliada. Because her medical condition remained unstable, Mustafa Kemal decided to send her to Vienna, to the same healthcare facility where he had received treatment. She got better in Vienna and came back home. With the reoccurrence of her sickness, Mustafa Kemal sent her to Paris this time. As soon as her treatment in Paris was over, Sabiha Gökçen returned to Ankara, finding it difficult to "be away from [her] country, from Pasha, and from [her] people" and not showing much interest in Paris, a city "that everyone else loved and admired" (Gökçen 1996, 55). She had improved her French during this stay, but was still not clear as to what she should do with her life. Later, she would describe the years between 1930 and 1935, including her stay in Paris, as "dull, empty years" (Kıvanç 1998, 28).[6]

In the meantime, the "Surname Law" (Soyadı Kanunu) was passed in 1934, requiring everyone to adopt a surname. It was at this time that Mustafa Kemal was given the surname, Atatürk, meaning "father of all Turks." It was Mustafa Kemal himself who gave the surname Gökçen to Sabiha, meaning "related to the sky." Sabiha Gökçen corrects a misconception that people have about her surname in her memoirs: "A lot of people think that I was given my last name after I started aviation. However, it was about a year after Atatürk gave me this name that I met up with the skies and started flying" (Gökçen 1996, 81). Gökçen had no interest in aviation until she attended the opening ceremony of the newly founded aviation society, Turkish Bird, in May 1935. When she watched the performances of the Russian aviators with their planes during this ceremony, she told Atatürk that she would also like to experience flying. Atatürk's reply was affirmative: "I like your courage . . . aviation would in fact be a good match with your last name Gökçen" (Gökçen 1996, 81). Sabiha Gökçen started with parachuting and continued with flying. From that point on, her "future [was] in the skies" (81); "Atatürk's daughter [was] to become the daughter of the skies" (96).

Gökçen completed her training in the *Turkish Bird* in a couple of months and was sent to Russia for further training to become an aviation teacher together with seven other (male) students from Turkey (Gökçen 1996, 98). After receiving her teaching certificate in Odessa, she returned to Ankara and continued her training at the Air Academy (*Askeri Tayyare Okulu*) in Eskişehir, a small town midway between Istanbul and Ankara. According to Gökçen's memoirs, after her first solo flight, Atatürk approached her and revealed his plans for the future of his pilot daughter: "Thank you Gökçen ... You have made me very happy. Now, I can tell you what I have planned for you.... You may become the world's first woman military pilot. Can you imagine how proud it would make us feel to have a Turkish girl become the world's first woman military pilot? I will act now and make arrangements for you to receive special training at the Eskişehir Air Academy" (Gökçen 1996, 109).

Gökçen joined the Air Academy in early 1936, at the age of twenty-three. Her training was special indeed. First of all, she was the only woman at the Air Academy. She was also shorter than the average male students, for which they readjusted one of the planes so that her feet were able to reach the pedals (112). While other students were trained in groups of three or four, Gökçen received personal training on the airplane that was adjusted to her height. As a result, she finished the initial training under the supervision of an aviation teacher earlier than her peers and started flying solo. Unlike the students and the officers in the Academy, Gökçen lived in a rented apartment in the city, together with her primary school teacher, Nüveyre Uyguç, who was asked by Atatürk himself to accompany and assist Gökçen, and Hatice Bacı, presumably a woman who helped with house chores (112).

Gökçen spent two years in the Academy, getting training both as a pilot and as a soldier/officer (111). During this time, she participated in two military activities. The first one was the 1936 Thracian Maneuvers. Gökçen does not mention these maneuvers in her own memoirs. There is a hint in the interview she gave to Halit Kıvanç in 1956 as to why she does not like talking about this first time when she put her military training into practice:

> The 1936 Thracian maneuvers were the first time Sabiha Gökçen applied her military training. Until then it had all been theory, with very little practice, but now the Turkish flightgirl would have a chance to gain some valuable experience. She was very excited, as she would be sent on a reconnaissance mission with Atatürk among the spectators viewing from below. During the reconnaissance she had seen a formation on the ground, but what was it? A regiment? A battalion? She couldn't be sure, and was mortified upon landing. General Baransel put the question to her:
> "What sort of force was the formation you sighted? What was it?"
> "Well, Sir ... I mean ..."
> "Try and remember the units you've seen here. Which one did it resemble?"
> Teasingly, the people gathered round called out: "Say it was a division!" The young girl was so humiliated, especially before Atatürk, that she couldn't speak. But right at that moment he showed his greatness and wisdom by coming to her aid. "Don't worry", he said, "these missions require a great deal of experience. Learning always takes time and experience." (Kıvanç 1998, 44)

A year after these maneuvers, in 1937, Gökçen had a second chance to prove that she had learned her lessons well—this time, in a combat situation involving real people and live ammunition. In early 1937, the government initiated a military operation in Dersim, a province in Turkey's Kurdish dominated Southeast, which was not made public until months after the operations had started. In her memoirs, Gökçen refers to this incident as the "Dersim Operation" and makes it clear that she does not intend to discuss it in detail: "Here, I will not go into the reasons and the consequences of the Dersim operation. What I, together with my friends, tried to do in this operation was to carry out a duty given to me by my country" (Gökçen 1996, 125).

Yet, being a woman military pilot, she was not given this duty automatically, the way her "friends" were. Making his daughter a military pilot may have been a planned course of action on Atatürk's part, but letting his daughter, a "young girl," fight in a real war situation was a different matter. The next section is about Gökçen negotiating her gender identity to be able to "serve her country" in this operation on the road to becoming the world's first woman combat pilot.

"She is no Longer a Young Girl, but a Young Soldier"

On a spring day in 1937, Sabiha Gökçen observed a "joyous excitement" (Gökçen 1996, 115) among her peers at the Academy. She tried to learn what was happening, but was given unsatisfactory answers. Finally, she was told that they were not authorized to talk about the operation that they would be leaving for the next day. She immediately found her commander and asked about the operation, volunteering to take part in it. Her commander said that he could not make the decision for her to go into real combat and that Atatürk, as Gökçen's father and as the president of the country, needed to be consulted. Gökçen asked the commander if she could borrow one of the planes to fly to Ankara and talk to Atatürk face to face. Upon receiving this permission, she indeed flew to Ankara and convinced Atatürk, who was at first hesitant, to let her take part in the operation. Later that day, this is how Atatürk explained his decision to colleagues and friends at the dinner table:

> Here is another duty that has called upon the Turkish girl. Gökçen will join the Dersim operation tomorrow morning with her plane. *She is no longer a young girl, but a young soldier.* Just as I am confident that she will perform as well as her colleagues and fulfill her duty, you, too, should be confident . . . She is aware of how dangerous this mission is. I know that if she is made to stay behind, such discrimination may result in her withdrawal from aviation, an occupation she loves. She was trained to take part in such situations. So? So she will leave early in the morning for Dersim. (Gökçen 1996, 118, emphasis added)

Sabiha Gökçen did leave for Dersim the next morning, flew combat planes, and dropped bombs throughout the month-long air operation. But there is more to the story that highlights the gender tensions of her taking part in this operation. While her participation in actual combat was to become a hallmark for what Turkish women could accomplish in any profession, including a military profession, being a woman also gave her another duty: In order to save her honor (and her nation's) she was given the duty to kill herself if she were to get caught by the enemy. This is the conversation she had with Atatürk on the issue (again from her memoirs):

> *Atatürk:* I will let you go . . . if your desire to go is this strong. But this is a military operation and you can only join if the Commander in Chief, Marshall Çakmak, gives the appropriate permission. But you should not forget this: You are a girl. And the mission at hand is a very difficult one. You will be faced with a band of deceived men. They too have some weapons. In case of an accident, you might have to do emergency landing and surrender to them. You will not know what this means until it happens to you. Have you thought about what you would do in such a situation?
> *Gökçen:* You are right. The plane might always have a technical problem and force me to land, or it might crash. If something this unfortunate happens, don't you worry; I will never surrender to them alive. (Gökçen 1996, 117)

This was apparently the answer Atatürk was expecting to hear from his daughter. Gökçen remembers him being very touched by her response. He said:

> Gökçen, then, I will give you my own pistol. . . . I hope that you will not face any risk. But if anything that will put your honor to risk should happen, do not hesitate to use this pistol against others or to kill yourself. (Gökçen 1996, 117)

Taking the pistol from her father, Gökçen first kissed Atatürk's hand and then the pistol, and said: "I will not forget your words for as long as I live and will always keep this promise!" (118). Thus, Sabiha Gökçen left that late April morning for Dersim, well equipped to protect her country *and* her honor as a "young girl." She might have become a young soldier, but she was also a young woman whose sexuality needed to be protected and negotiated as she was given permission to go into war. In Atatürk's view, the threat to her honor (through rape, an unspoken, unnamed act in this narrative) was the ultimate danger, not death. Her permission to go was based on her readiness to kill herself in order to protect her honor, and her nation's. The chapter in Gökçen's memoirs that talks about this operation is titled: "*The Dersim Operation and the Pistol That Would Protect My Honor!*" (Gökçen 1996, 111).

After Dersim: "Daughter of Turks, Daughter of the Skies, Daughter of Atatürk . . ."

Sabiha Gökçen spent more than a month in Dersim, flying almost everyday, "one day as an observer, one day as a pilot" (Gökçen 1996, 122), dropped numerous bombs and successfully handled several risky situations as she flew over the mountainous Dersim province. One day, when she got lost in bad weather and was about to run out of fuel, she remembered her promise to Atatürk: Even if she could use a parachute to jump before the plane crashed, she might have to kill herself with Atatürk's own pistol. Fortunately, she and the co-pilot managed to make it back to the base before they had to make this hard decision. When the air operation came to an end, Gökçen returned to Ankara.

After the Dersim Operation, Sabiha Gökçen was a national heroine. Prime Minister Ismet Inönü was one of the first people to congratulate her: "Like Atatürk, we are watching your work, success, and courage very closely...You are like the Turkish women who carried ammunition to us throughout the [Independence] war. They were doing their service on the ground, you are—and will be—doing yours in the sky" (Gökçen 1996, 131). For Atatürk, too, Gökçen's achievements meant a lot:

> I am proud of you, Gökçen! And not just me, the whole Turkish nation that has been following this incident very closely is proud of you...You should be proud of yourself for showing to the whole world, once again, what our young girls can do... *We are a military-nation. From ages seven to seventy, women and men alike, we have been created as soldiers.* (Gökçen 1996, 125–126, emphasis added)

In other words, by participating in this internal war effort, Gökçen had achieved three things simultaneously: First, she had taken her place beside the women who had fought for the country's independence, and had thus proven herself to her military-nation. Second, she had proven her nation, as a nation-in-arms that can also make use of its young women, to the whole world. Moreover, she had flown combat planes, fought with the enemy, and had come back alive to have her father experience "one of the happiest days of [his] life" (Gökçen 1996, 127).

There was much glory for Gökçen in the aftermath of the operation. A special ceremony was held in Ankara on 28 May 1937 to honor Sabiha Gökçen's achievements, where over three hundred guests were invited, among them the prime minister, chief of staff, other ministers, journalists, and military officers (Gökçen 1996, 143). She was given the Special Medal of the Turkish Aviation Society, presented to her by Prime Minister Ismet Inönü. The journal *Havacılık ve Spor* (Aviation and Sports), a popular biweekly of the times, dedicated a whole issue, in June 1937, to Sabiha Gökçen and provided detailed information about the commemorating ceremony and the media attention that she had received afterwards. In his article titled "Daughter of Turks, Daughter of the Skies, Daughter of Atatürk...," Behçet Kemal Çağlar, a leading writer and poet, wrote that Gökçen had given him a chance to—once again—feel proud to be a Turk and likened her to a heroine of pre-Islamic Turkish (or Turkic) history, who had gained popularity with the advent of the officially manufactured Turkish History Thesis in the early 1930s (see chapter one). Another writer described her as "one of the granddaughters of the 'anonymous woman' who fought silently, but with great sacrifice, in the Anatolian struggle for independence" (*Havacılık ve Spor* [1937], 3, 122). Yunus Nadi, the owner and editor in chief of one of the leading newspapers of the time, *Cumhuriyet* (Republic), showed her as an example not just to "the patriotic woman youth, that is, Turkish citizens of her own kind," but to the "whole Turkish youth" (*Havacılık ve Spor* [1937], 3, 125). What all these writings had in common was an effort to congratulate Sabiha Gökçen and to place her either in a version of nationalist history, or a nationalist future.

Sabiha Gökçen was a national heroine. Yet there was a striking silence about how she had become one. The Dersim Operation had not been in the news at all, leaving the general public ignorant of this internal war effort. There was no mention of the operation during either the commemoration ceremony or the articles written about Gökçen in the newspapers and journals of the period. According to the *Havacılık ve Spor* journal, she had earned this medal because of her "success during her courses and field practice at the Air Academy and her heroic service during a recent maneuver with live ammunition" (*Havacılık ve Spor* [1937], 3, 117). A similar approach was assumed by the speakers at the ceremony, including Fuat Bulca, the President of the Turkish Aviation Society, in his opening speech:

> The medallion regulation of the Turkish Aviation Society suggests that medals be awarded to "pilots who have shown sacrifice to the point of risking their lives." It is for this reason that the Turkish Aviation Society has decided to award brave Gökçen, who has shown success in air force units and has gained the appreciation of the Chief of Staff, Marshall [Çakmak]. (*Havacılık ve Spor* [1937], 3118)

But what was it that Gökçen had done to show "sacrifice to the point of risking [her] life"? Even if it was known to everyone, no one expressed it publicly. The name of Dersim does not appear in Gökçen's speech either. There is only a subtle comment about the operation in the way she thanks Marshall Çakmak: "I am deeply grateful to Sir Marshall, Chief of Staff, for giving me the opportunity to gain valuable experience by allowing me to take part as a volunteer soldier in conducting certain military services in recent days" (*Havacılık ve Spor* [1937], 3118).

It was not until 15 June 1937, about three weeks after the air operation over Dersim had ended, that national and international media started writing about what was going on in this region. The tone in the national newspapers and journals was triumphant and self-congratulatory. Ismet İnönü's speech at the Grand National Assembly on 14 June 1937 was quoted as the main source of information on the operation, yet there were hints that the operation had been known to the journalists long before this speech but was censored or self-censored. One daily newspaper published a special column on Sabiha Gökçen explaining the earlier silence on her military activities:

> Several days ago, when it was said that our first woman pilot Sabiha Gökçen was awarded a special medal, there was mention of her services during some air maneuvers. The nature of these services was not made explicit. The reason was that the measures that were being taken to eliminate the last remnants of Feudalism were of historical significance. It was left to Ismet İnönü's speech to inform the nation and the world in detail of these measures. As this speech has made public the whole truth, we can now talk explicitly about Sabiha Gökçen's services. (*Tan*, 15 June 1937, published in Kalman 1995, 271)

The column went on to explain her bravery and accomplishments, including her dropping "the final bomb that would eradicate Feudalism" during the operation. Years later, when the chief of staff published a detailed account of the Dersim operation in 1972, a 50-kg bomb that Sabiha Gökçen had dropped on the "fleeing rebels," which had resulted in "severe losses," was also mentioned (*Türkiye Cumhuriyetinde Ayaklanmalar (1924–1938)* [1972], 388). Yet it was hardly the "final bomb," since it had taken more than a year after that bomb for the military forces to gain control over the Dersim province.

From Dersim to Tunceli

Dersim had been a troubled, and troubling, province for both the Ottoman state and the new Turkish Republic for almost a century. It was a mountainous region, barely accessible in the absence of roads, and its population was almost predominantly Kurdish[7] and Alevi.[8] They had rebelled against the centralizing policies of first the Ottoman state and later its successor, the Turkish government in Ankara. It was almost an autonomous region, with the help of its tough geography, where the growing apparatuses of the modernizing Turkish state had not been able to establish themselves: There were no military posts, police stations, schools, or even roads. Young men of the region resisted military service, and no taxes were paid. Determined to maintain this status, people of Dersim remained armed and resistant to any form of governing.

On 25 December 1935, a special law, called "Law Regarding the Administration of the Tunceli Province," was passed in the Grand National Assembly that would change the administrative structure of the Tunceli province. With this law, the governor of Dersim would be the military commander of the province with powers equivalent to that of ministers in the cabinet. The thirty-eight articles of the law cited the extraordinary powers of the Governor/Commander, as well as the limitations to the judicial process. According to the law, the Governor/Commander could relocate people within the same city or, if necessary, ask people not to leave the city, and could take power away from (elected) mayors and give it to (appointed) state administrators. He could also appoint military officers to these administrative posts and postpone the investigation of charges against any individual for as long as he saw fit. Furthermore, suspected felons would not be able to see the indictment until the court hearings and did not have the right to appeal to a higher court. The verdicts were final. All death sentences, unless the governor/commander ordered for their deferral, were to be carried out immediately (Beşikçi 1992). As Beşikçi points out (1992, 40), when this law was passed, there was no province under the name of Tunceli. It was two weeks later, on 4 January 1936, that another law would establish the Tunceli Province, in place of the Dersim Province.

By April 1937, when full-fledged military operations—including the air raids that Sabiha Gökçen participated in—began, Dersim had already been renamed as Tunceli and was being governed by semi-military rule. In his speech at the Grand National Assembly on 14 June 1937, Prime Minister Ismet Inönü referred to the operation as being part of a special reform program that they had designed for the Tunceli Province. This reform program included, besides the military operations, construction of "roads, schools and military/police outposts" (Kalman 1995, 269).

Following Inönü's speech, numerous articles and news pieces appeared in the national media on Dersim and the military campaign. In one of the early commentaries, Dersim was called "a century long sickness" and the reform program of the government was praised. According to this writer, "the saddest part of it all" had to do with the ethnic identification of the people of Dersim:

> The people of Dersim, who are essentially Turks and who used to speak Turkish, have fallen foreign to Turkish ways as a result of the sunni vs. kızılbaş[9] issue on the one hand and a constant fear of attack on the other. They have partially forgotten their

language, learned Kurdish, and started to think they are Kurds... Kurdishness was forcibly inculcated among many Turks who, only a generation ago, did not speak anything but Turkish. (Yalman 1937)

There were two major discourses surrounding Kurdishness expressed in the coverage of the events in Dersim. One was to accept, as the above quote suggests, that Kurds and Kurdishness exist, but not among these people or in this particular province. The second discourse was one of total denial: "What is called Kurdish language is a degenerated form of Turkish that has mingled with Persian!" (*Kurun*, 20 June 1937). This approach of denial was soon to become official state policy. Sociologist Mesut Yeğen suggests that the main characteristic of the Turkish state discourse has been its "deep 'silence' on the *Kurdishness* of the Kurdish issue" (Yeğen 1999, 555). Starting with the early days of state-formation, the Kurdish issue has been defined as "either political reaction, tribal resistance or regional backwardness, but never as an ethno-political question" (Yeğen 1999, 555). Until the 1990s, the Turkish nationalist discourse and the state maintained that Kurds were mountain Turks, with toughened identities and language (Kirişçi and Winrow 1997, 108). In fact, the origin of the term "Kurd" was attributed to the sound that came out of walking in the snow on the mountains: "kart, kurt, kart, kurt."

The official figure on the number of Kurds from Dersim killed in the military campaign was five thousand. Kurdish sources estimate much greater figures (see Kalman 1995; Kaya 1999). Yet, the change from Dersim to Tunceli was not over even after the operations and would require at least another year of intense military operations and years of militarized "reform," where many were killed, large populations were displaced and relocated, roads, schools, and military posts were built, and the name Dersim erased from all records. The change from the Kurdish name Dersim to the state-manufactured Turkish name Tunceli in this province is emblematic of the deep "silencing" of "the *Kurdishness* of the Kurdish issue" (Yeğen 1999) and the articulation of military force as the main mechanism to deal with this issue.

I remember reading Sabiha Gökçen's chapter on Dersim (with the name Dersim in the title) and being very surprised to see her use the name. In her memoirs, she breaks a sacred silence by remaining faithful to the original name of the province she has bombed.[10] Yet there is a much deeper silence in her account. Gökçen refers to Dersim as the operation that made her the world's first woman combat pilot; she talks about the bravery of her peers and of herself during the operation; she pays special attention to her negotiation over her sexuality and to getting Atatürk's pistol to protect her honor. Yet, there is little mention of the people of Dersim and of the thousands of men, women, and children who were killed by the bombs, some of which she had dropped. There is only one remark that signals her ambivalence about war and violence, in her 1956 interview: "Believe me when I tell you I can't bear to see a chicken being slaughtered. But this was for my country, and I didn't hesitate to take off alongside men" (Kıvanç 1998, 62).

In another interview in 1987, Sabiha Gökçen suggests that no bombs were dropped on civilians, and that the government was well informed about the whereabouts of "the bad people" who were their targets: "To bomb areas with children around would have been an inhumane act. That was not done" (*Nokta*, 28 June 1987). On another question concerning the displacement of the Dersim population to other parts of Turkey (mainly the West), she says:

> That happened, of course. For some time, they were sent to other places for a better life. As I told you before, they lived in primitive quarters that could hardly be called housing. They were moved to other places for a better life. That was Atatürk's purpose. He wanted them to live in more humane conditions. (*Nokta*, 28 June 1987)

Along the lines of Prime Minister Ismet İnönü's descriptions of the Dersim campaign, Sabiha Gökçen regards the change from Dersim to Tunceli as "necessary" to "raise" a primitive life style to a modern one. Modernity in the form of proper housing, roads, bridges, schools, military outposts, and police stations was to bring a primitive population—who, according to some, had forgotten their mother tongue (i.e., Turkish)—in line with the nationalist state and with secular, national time. Literary critic Anne McClintock's insightful analysis of the "colonial journey" holds for the hegemonic perception of the Dersim operation in that it is "figured as proceeding forward in *geographical* space, but backward in *racial* and *gender* time, to a prehistoric zone of linguistic, racial, and gender degeneration" (McClintock 1997, 101). Kurdishness exists at best as a backward identity and language, and at worst as a nonidentity, nonlanguage—out of time. And the ultimate mark of modernity on the side of the Turkish state is the fact that a Turkish woman has become a pilot, a military pilot, a combat pilot, equipped to make this national journey into inaccessible land and suppress this backward rebellion.[11]

Although Kurdish was recognized as a language in 1991 by the Özal government and is no longer illegal,[12] this belief in Kurdish as a nonlanguage has maintained its hegemony in Turkey until very recently. At a meeting in Istanbul in June 1998, a well-intentioned, progressive-minded Turkish feminist lawyer told twelve Kurdish women from different parts of the Southeast that "unfortunately Kurdish is not a language. I have listened to experts explain that in order for it to be a language, you need at least three thousand words, and Kurdish does not qualify."[13] She was comfortable telling this group of women who work in women's community centers in the region (at that time, a war-zone since 1984) that their mother tongue, the language that they have used all their life except when they converse with state officials and Turkish speakers like us, was *not even a language*. Next to me sat a Kurdish friend whose uncle, a prominent scholar and linguist, had published a number of books on Kurdish, including a Kurdish dictionary that contained more than fifty thousand words. Yet, when she raised her hand to make a comment, she referred to a prestigious English dictionary that listed language groups in its back cover, where Kurdish was cited as a major language. An international reference, she must have thought, would be more convincing. She was wrong. It would take much more than a reference from a Kurdish woman from the Southeast to convince this lawyer.

Moreover, in the 1930s, when the discourses of denial and contempt for Kurdishness were being formulated in Turkey, the views expressed by Turkish state officials were in line with international discourses on nation-states and modernization. International sources had given the news of the rebellion, the operation, and Sabiha

Gökçen as part of the same story following the days of the release of information by the government on 14 June 1937. *The New York Times* reported on 17 June that Atatürk's adopted daughter was a "war hero" and that she had received "the highest honor for an aviator in Turkey" for her "bravery and resourcefulness throughout the operation." It was also suggested that she had dropped "the final bomb, which virtually ended the insurrection." Yet Gökçen's story was not the only surprising aspect of the Turkish state's military campaign in Eastern Turkey:

> Details of a campaign in the Dersim region, one of the most secret military operations in history, in which 30,000 Turkish troops and a fleet of airplanes were required to subdue an insurrection in an almost inaccessible region, were disclosed today. Although 5,000 were killed in bitter fighting in rough country where there were virtually no roads, and ladders had to be used to drive the rebels out of mountain caverns, it was not known that anything was going on. (*The New York Times*, 17 June 1937)

Three days later, on 20 June, there was an anonymous commentary in *The New York Times*, again, where the secrecy of this campaign and the success of Sabiha Gökçen were treated as contradictory elements that marked the modern times:

> That a war lasting three months and costing 5,000 lives could be kept completely secret in the contemporary world is the startling thing about the revolt of the Kurds, disclosed for the first time when the Prime Minister announced to the National Assembly on Wednesday that the rising had been crushed...The effect of the shaken Kurds of the appearance of a woman military flier must have been a bombshell in itself. The advance in little more than a decade from the veil and the harem to the air pilot's helmet and the battlefield is a leap that makes even the Western imagination reel. In the juxtaposition of phenomena like SABIHA Hanoum, the Turkish act, and censorship that revive the conditions of the Dark Ages, the strange whirl of progress and reaction in which we grope is fantastically illuminated.

The author of the commentary juxtaposes what he sees as progress in the position of women in Turkish society (i.e., he is willing to replace his Orientalist perspective with a militarized one) and revival of the conditions of the Dark Ages in the acts of the government through censorship. In other words, this critic views militarization as progress (especially when it is embodied in a woman), but the censoring of military acts as a sign of reaction, and their coexistence in the Turkish state as a situation that creates a "strange whirl." This perspective proves Atatürk right in his assertion that Gökçen, as a woman military pilot, would set an important example not just to the Turkish nation, but to the whole world, especially the West. The "Fying Amazon of Turkey" (*The New York Times*, 19 September 1937) would be an international celebrity.

Women aviators in the United States were also trained for wartime service in the late 1930s, but faced different gender anxieties. *The New York Times* reported in 1936, the year Sabiha Gökçen had joined the Air Academy, that women pilots were preparing "to serve if war comes":

> One of the nation's outstanding women aviators, Mrs. Theodore "Teddy" Kenyon, revealed today that she and several other women were preparing for wartime service, should they ever be needed. Mrs. Kenyon, who holds several flight records and has been

a regular contestant at the National Air Races, said that the women pilots did not expect to do any actual fighting. Rather, she added, they would pilot new planes wherever needed, transport wounded soldiers, carry dispatches and relieve male commercial pilots for fighting service. She agreed, she said, that women could not compete with men as fighters. "By nature and temperament", she asserted, "my sex can never compete with men in that line. We haven't the strength. But we can make good in other branches of the service." (*The New York Times*, 30 March 1936)

The gender anxieties that Mrs. Theodore "Teddy" Kenyon had to address were obviously very different from the ones that surrounded or awaited Sabiha Gökçen. One difference, among many, between the circumstances that these women faced was that Sabiha Gökçen was the only woman in the military and she was, after all, the daughter of the President. Her presence in the military could be contained under her special positioning as an icon, a symbol of women's achievements, without the immediate implication that other women would soon be joining the Air Force, the Army, or the Navy. Or could it?

The Military Daughters of a Military-Nation

About five months after Sabiha Gökçen was rewarded the Special Medal of the Turkish Aviation Society, during the Republican Day celebrations on 29 October 1937, Gökçen's status within the military once again became an issue. During the day, Gökçen participated in the celebrations by performing acrobatics with her plane. After a successful show, Gökçen joined Atatürk to go to the Republic Ball: "Atatürk used to take me everywhere in my military uniform. That night, too, I went to the Ball in my uniform" (Gökçen 1996, 227). However, there was also a good reason why Atatürk wanted her to come to this Ball in her military uniform: He had asked Gökçen to talk to Marshall Fevzi Çakmak about the issue of women's participation in the military (227). Following Atatürk's advice, Gökçen approached Marshall Çakmak, kissed his hand and opened up the subject:

> This issue of women's participation in the military. . . . You know that my position in the military is [unclear] because there is no specific law on this issue. Atatürk has asked me to talk to you about this and ask for your help. Your decision and permission will determine whether women can become soldiers or not. Turkish women would be grateful to you if you were to pass this law. There are so many young girls that I know who are ready to sacrifice the best years of their lives to wear this honorable uniform. (Gökçen 1996, 228)

Despite his remarks during Gökçen's medal ceremony that he wholeheartedly appreciated and congratulated Gökçen for having written "the competence and heroism of Turkish women into world aviation history" (*Havacılık ve Spor* [1937], 3115), Marshall Fevzi Çakmak was strongly against opening the barracks to women soldiers:

> You expressed your feelings very well, Gökçen. I am also aware of the fact that Turkish girls want to be soldiers and wear this honorable uniform. But, please child, don't ask me [to let that happen]. Because I do not at all agree that our girls and women should become soldiers. For a nation to exist, its women need to live. (Gökçen 1996, 228)

Apparently, this was an unexpected response for Sabiha Gökçen. To avoid crying in front of the Marshall, she kissed his hand again and left his company. In her memoirs, she refers to her feelings at that moment as follows:

> I had convinced myself that, after all that work and all that success, we would have rights equal to men in the realm of the military as well. Yet, as usual, dreams and reality had been opposed to one another and reality had reigned over dreams. (Gökçen 1996, 229)

Gökçen had proven what Turkish women could do in their country's defense by participating in a real combat situation. Yet, she had not managed to gain the right for women to participate in the nation's military. This disappointing encounter forced Gökçen to, once again, come face to face with her gender identity. This time there was no room for negotiation.

This disappointment finds its reflection in Sabiha Gökçen's language. The above quote is one of the few moments in her memoirs where she claims the voice "we, women." Perhaps more importantly, she does not define military service, here, as a "duty for the nation" but as a realm where "we would have rights equal to men." These slippages in Gökçen's account reflect the gender tensions embedded in the nationalist project. At least momentarily, she changes her position from a nationalist one alongside men to one alongside women against (at least, certain) men. However, as expected, Atatürk is there to console Gökçen after her disappointing dialogue with the Marshall: "There will come a day when the Marshall, too, will be willing to have Turkish women become soldiers. But let us not offend the Marshall now. Let us be patient and wait" (Gökçen 1996, 229). According to Gökçen, if Marshall Çakmak had agreed on the law that would allow women to become soldiers, Atatürk "would have passed that law immediately" (228–229). Atatürk's view of women was very different from the Marshall's:

> For Atatürk, it was not enough for women to be mothers and housewives. . . . They should become doctors, judges, engineers, architects, journalists, and policewomen. . . . and of course, they should take their place among the fliers and become aviators. How about women becoming soldiers? *The Turkish women were the military daughters of a military-nation.* Hadn't they proven this in a number of wars, as Atatürk suggested? Especially during the War of Independence. In which case they certainly had a place in the Republican Military as well. (Gökçen 1996, 223, emphasis added)

Women did not take their place in the Republican military until eighteen years later—and then only for a short period. They would have to "be patient and wait" much longer for a long-term presence in different branches of the military. Sabiha Gökçen herself resigned from her military post after Atatürk's death, and no woman was admitted to military schools and academies until 1955. In 1955, several women wanted to register for the Army College (*Kara Harp Okulu*), referring to the article in the law that specified who was eligible. The article said "Turkish students" were eligible for the academy, and not "Turkish *male* students." Not dissuaded by the school officials, these women opened a court case and won. According to the law, the school had to admit qualified female students. A number of women entered the colleges of the Army, Navy, and the Air Force in the following years. But in the early 1960s, the entry regulations for military colleges were amended to include "being male" as a requirement for the applicants (Kurtcephe ve Balcıoğlu 1991, 172–173). After that, it took more than thirty years for the military to open its gates to women students and officers as part of what appears to be a long-term policy. It was in the early 1990s that women were, once again, allowed to apply for the military colleges and academies.[14] In other words, "military daughters of the military-nation" remained related to the military only symbolically or as exceptions in the first seventy years of the Republic.

Women, Wars, Military Service

Yet this symbolic identification should not be taken lightly. All nationalist projects involve a remaking of femininities and masculinities, with an ambivalent set of opportunities and restrictions for both. In Turkey, too, questions of gender were central to all debates in the early days of state-formation. This was a time of intense questioning and reform of virtually everything, including women's role in the nation's defense. Are women to be men's equals as they fight and vote? Or is their identity to be limited to one of motherhood? These are important questions that have shaped policies and women's lives throughout Turkish history, starting with the early years.

Sabiha Gökçen was not the first Turkish woman to have fought in war or even the first woman to have joined the military. The continuity between the late Ottoman period and the early years of the Republic regarding women's relationship to the military (as in other realms) is worth noting. In February 1913, the Women's Commission of the Society for National Defense (*Müdafaa-i Milliye Cemiyeti Hanımlar Heyeti*) organized two meetings in Istanbul where more than four thousand women gathered to talk and mobilize around the ongoing Balkan War (Kurnaz 1993). These women consisted mostly of educated, middle to upper class women of Istanbul who referred to themselves as "Ottoman women," "Muslim women," or "Turkish women," sometimes interchangeably, and without any reference to the non-Muslim minorities within the Ottoman Empire. The following speech by one of the participants, Gülsüm Kemalova, summarizes the overall tone of women's frustrations and position in the room:

> Our enemies should not think that we are slaves living in cages. They should see that when it comes to matters of homeland and honor, Turkish women are not less able than men. . . . Since women are half of a nation, if we start acting, the whole nation will have started acting. If we remain in silence, half of the nation and the most important part of it will be paralyzed. (Kurnaz 1993, 27)

She also suggested that women's units be formed to go to the battlefront in order to look after the wounded, cook and, if necessary, die for the defense of their country (Kurnaz 1993, 14). At the end of the two day conference, the participants agreed on three sets of action: (1) To write a telegram to the military as "Ottoman Women," (2) to send telegrams to Muslim women in Turkistan, Russia, India, etc. to ask for support against the massacres that were happening in the Balkans, and (3) to send telegrams to the European Queens to ask them to protest and stop the war (Kurnaz 1993, 18). In other words, these women, while challenging the passive role given to women and asking for an active role in the battlefields, also imagined and acted upon the possibility of global women's solidarity that would encompass women from a vast geographical area including Russia, India, Central Asia, and Europe. A claim for an active part in the national imagining and war was accompanied by a call for women's solidarity across national/empire boundaries. However, they received no response from the European Queens (Edib 1930, 107), and there is no historical evidence which suggests that their services were used in the battlefronts during the Balkan War.

It was in 1917, during the heyday of World War I, that a special women's unit was formed as part of the Ottoman military (Karakışla 1999). This unit, named First Women's Worker Battalion (*Kadın Birinci İşçi Taburu*), was composed of women soldiers who "worked" for the military in a variety of tasks, including farming, working in road constructions, and sewing. Historian Yavuz Selim Karakışla suggests that as important as this battalion is in military history, it was hardly recognized by either the military or the larger society (Karakışla 1999, 20). Not surprisingly, the battalion was discharged after about a year, on 1 January 1919.

During the Independence War, fought between 1919 and 1923, women assumed active duties at the battlefront, carrying ammunition, providing support services, or at times fighting with the enemy. Halide Edib (Adıvar), a renowned feminist and writer, had accompanied Mustafa Kemal during the war as a journalist, soldier, and nurse, and had been made a Corporal.[15] In *The Turkish Ordeal*, her autobiographical account of the war published in 1928, she would say: "Corporal Halide is almost a stranger to me now. I often turn her soul inside out and stare at it hard. Where did she find the patience to go through that drab misery? Where did she find the strength to endure the sights of so much human suffering?" (Edib 1928, 311). She characterizes her decision to volunteer at the battlefront as the "highest and strongest form" of identifying with the nation:

> The curious way of identifying myself with my nation now took its highest and strongest form. I meant to be among the strugglers who might prevent the imminent disaster or die in the effort. I did not mind how insignificant and absolutely small my part might be. It was a gigantic picture of an unparalleled struggle: let me be the most insignificant detail. (Edib 1928, 283)

Although Halide Edib sees the battlefront as the "highest and strongest form" of identifying herself with her nation, her accounts of the war also help complicate the official stories of the Turkish Independence War in various ways. As feminist scholar Ayşe Durakbaşa suggests, her "fascination" with war is accompanied by a "detached wisdom," where soldiers, including the commander Mustafa Kemal, are demystified and, at times, directly criticized (Durakbaşa 1993). In the words of Hülya Adak, "*The Turkish Ordeal* emphasizes the network of identities, the interdependence of leaders and people in the Struggle. Such a depiction of interdependence contrasts with the myth of the sole hero, the prophet of the republic, instead describing the Struggle as a collaborative effort" (Adak 2003, 520).

Of course, Halide Edib was not the only woman at the battlefront. The main nationalist woman figure of the Independence War, as she is portrayed in the official discourse and in accounts of the war in textbooks and other writings, is an almost mythical figure of an old woman carrying ammunition on her back, or pulling a cart full of ammunition. In Halide Edib's history of the war, there is also such a woman, Fatma Çavuş (Sergeant Fatma), a seventy-year-old "warrior queen" (Edib 1928, 322). The main story Edib recounts about Fatma Çavuş in her book is when Fatma Çavuş is made to have her picture taken with a rifle in her hand by her overzealous commander. Her ambivalence about the rifle and the picture, together with the fact that she hates guns, is an important part of Halide Edib's account, unlike official histories of such moments and of women like Fatma Çavuş (Edib 1928, 322).[16]

When we come to the Republican period (i.e., post 1923), the most striking moment when women's relationship to the military and their role in the nation's defense becomes an issue is during the Grand National Assembly discussions of the Compulsory Military Service Law on 21 June 1927. As I suggested earlier, it was declared in this discussion that women did not "need conscription" to help in the nation's defense. Their participation in the Independence War was seen as evidence of their preparedness to join the struggle if needed. In Sabiha Gökçen's disappointing dialogue with Marshall Çakmak, ten years after this debate in the Grand National Assembly, it is not clear to me whether the issue was women's compulsory military service or their right to join the military as officers—as Gökçen had done. The implications of the two are very different. While the latter can be seen as the right to choose a military career, the former marks the right of the state to ask for women's service without their consent. Many feminist activists and scholars today would agree that militaries should open their doors to women soldiers who want to make military careers, while arguing against compulsory military service for women (and, most of the time, for men). However, as Cynthia Enloe suggests: "Women *in* the military has never been an easy topic. It shouldn't be. Sexism, patriotism, violence, and the state—it is a heady brew" (Enloe 2000, x).

When we look at the public discussions of the late 1930s in Turkey, it is possible to see that both of these options—women as conscripts and women as military officers—are being debated. Following Sabiha Gökçen's medal ceremony, a number of journalists and public intellectuals make calls for more women to become pilots and officers like Gökçen. Server Ziya Gürevin, for instance, closes his introductory essay to the special issue of *Havacılık ve Spor* saying that they "want not one, but one thousand Gökçens from the Turkish Bird" (*Havacılık ve Spor* [1937], 3115). On the other hand, another journal article in the same year, titled "Our Women Will Become Soldiers," announces the government's plan to call women (with certain exemptions) for compulsory military service: "If this project becomes law during this year, 937 [*sic*] will be a historical and blissful year for the daughters of the republic" (Kutay 1937, 9).

As I tried to lay out in chapter one, the discourse on the Turkish nation being a military-nation developed in late Ottoman and early Republican periods and became central to national self-understanding. Women became a part of this discourse not only as mothers and wives of military-men, but also as "daughters" of the military-nation who themselves were warriors. As mothers and wives, they were responsible for "reproducing" and "supporting" the nation's military force; as "daughters" they were invited to participate in it directly. This choice of terminology echoes the treatment of women in other contexts of armed struggle where married women are organized to "perform 'support' or 'homefront' roles, while *un*married women are channeled into the more strictly military roles" (Enloe 1983, 164). As Gökçen's story as the "first daughter" demonstrated, *some* women would be allowed to become active agents of "the military-nation," while the majority were assigned the role of motherhood. Moreover, the unmarried position of the "daughter" was a temporary position. Not surprisingly, Sabiha Gökçen's actual presence in the military was short-lived (three years between her entry and resignation). Nevertheless, it was enough for her to embody what Atatürk described as a military-nation: "From ages seven to seventy, women and men alike, we have been created as soldiers" (Gökçen 1996, 125). Even to this date, women's entry into the military forces is often announced with references to Sabiha Gökçen.[17] She remains the legendary woman icon of the Turkish military-nation.

Sabiha Gökçen and Atatürk

After I came back from New York in early 1999, I started looking for Gökçen's memoirs. The 1982 edition was already out of print and was very hard to find. However, I soon learned that another publishing house had recently reprinted the memoirs, which was available at bookstores. I checked a number of bookstores, but had no luck. Finally, I went into a large bookstore in Ankara and asked for the book again, without much hope. The name was not the same as the original memoirs and I did not have the full reference with me. So, I said: "I am looking for Sabiha Gökçen's autobiography." The reference person looked at me suspiciously and said: "We don't have that and I don't think she has an autobiography, but we do have her book on Atatürk." I did not even know she had written a book on Atatürk! Together, we walked to the Atatürk section in the bookstore and there it was. I had finally found the book I was looking for, but not *where* I was looking for it. It was not placed under autobiography, oral history, or women's history; it was in the Atatürk section . . . Was it simply because Sabiha Gökçen was Atatürk's daughter that this book would be regarded as part of the Atatürk collection? Or was it the way Sabiha Gökçen herself had chosen to write about herself and Atatürk that had produced this outcome?

The uncertainty about this question also sheds light on how we know very little about Sabiha Gökçen's long life after 1938. In her introduction to her memoirs, Gökçen provides a temporal framework for her life—and for her memoirs:

> How many years have I spent on this earth? You can calculate it yourself, starting from 1913 . . . But if you ask me, how much of this I have lived; my life is short . . . It is indeed very short . . . I would turn to you and say: "calculate the time from 1925 to 1938!" But now I have a better understanding of how much I was able to squeeze into this short life. (Gökçen 1996, 6)

In other words, there are two different concepts of time in Sabiha Gökçen's life story. The first is the time she has spent on this earth, starting from her birth in

1913, and the second is the thirteen years she spent with Atatürk (1925–1938). Gökçen defines her "life" as corresponding to the second one and defines the rest (forty-three years up until the time of her autobiography) as "serving time"; in describing Atatürk's death in the final chapters of her memoirs, she also describes her own death (Gökçen 1996, 306).

Yet it is not only this temporal framework of Gökçen's "life" that marks Atatürk's centrality in her memoirs. In Gökçen's account, everything she did in her "short life" is related to Atatürk and she owes all her success to him. She contributes to the official historiography by giving the sole agency to Atatürk, erasing the stories and agency of women, including herself, from the history of the period. According to Gökçen, "Women in Turkish society have gained their respectful status thanks to Atatürk and his reforms" (Gökçen 1996, 77). She is content with her *designated agency* and, in fact, designated life. It is not surprising, then, that her memoirs ended up in the Atatürk section of a major bookstore.

Feminist Historiography and the Question of How to "Write Women in"

The Turkish Republic was founded in 1923 and the rest of the 1920s, together with the early 1930s, are seen by many as the formative years of Turkey. I agree with Sylvia Walby, who uses Doreen Massey's concept "rounds of restructuring" for nation-building to suggest that "rather than this notion of one critical period of 'nation formation' it is more appropriate to talk of 'rounds of restructuring' of the nation state" (Walby 1996, 246). It is important to see nation formation as a continuous process, but looking at early years of state-formation (I would say, of any state) is particularly important because a close look almost always reveals the existence of competing alternatives for envisioning the nature of the nation or state in formation and of a multiplicity of social groups and actors as taking part in this process (Verdery 1996, 228). Official historiography usually silences these "other" voices and presents its own version as right and inevitable, which make it necessary for us to revisit this period and relocate these other voices—particularly women's. As feminist scholar Nira Yuval-Davis (1997, 3) reminds us, "women did not just 'enter' the national arena: they were always there, and central to its constructions and reproductions!"

In Turkey, there is a long history of nationalist teaching that women's rights were presented to us, almost on a golden plate, by Atatürk and the secularist Republican regime. Even in the West, women had to organize to gain their basic rights, but not us! This suggestion has two implications: One, that our rights were given from above, and two, that women had not organized to demand their rights. As Yeşim Arat notes, "Until the 1980s, there was a consensus in society that Kemalist reforms had emancipated women and that this 'fact' could not be contested" (1997, 103).

Until recently, this approach remained unquestioned by scholars of Turkey, including feminist scholars who had limited access to the historical record on the first wave feminist movement at the beginning of the century. Kamari Jayawardena, for instance, opens her discussion of feminism and nationalism in the Third World with an epigraph from Atatürk and suggests that "the Kemalist reforms in Turkey were cited all over the world as successful attempts at achieving women's emancipation by decree from above" (1986, 41). Halide Edib's reaction to these citations, back in 1930, was quite straightforward: "The prevalent journalistic stuff published in the West about Turkish women, declaring that they were freed from harems in thousands, their veils lifted, and they themselves thrown into public life by a decree in 1926, is both absurd and false" (Edib 1930, 130). Unfortunately, she was not heard—neither in the West, nor in Turkey—and the stories of women's struggles and organizing in the late Ottoman and the early Republican periods were buried under heavy nationalist teaching until a new generation of feminist scholarship in the late 1980s started digging into its holes.

Anne McClintock, in her discussion of Franz Fanon's writings on the Algerian revolution concludes that, in Fanon's account, women's agency is a "*designated agency*—an agency by invitation only. . . . Feminist militancy, in short, is simply a passive offspring of male agency and the structural necessity of the war" (McClintock 1997, 98). I agree with McClintock's assertion that "nations are contested systems of cultural representation and limit and legitimize people's access to the resources of the nation-state" (1997, 89). One of the important discursive moves in limiting this access may be the designation of women's agency as one that is constituted by invitation only. In this construction, women need to be *invited* by the male elite to become part of nationalist cadres and part of nationalist historiography. The analogy of *invitation* can be extended to talk about women who remain *uninvited*, those who later become *unwanted guests* and most importantly, their precarious position as *guests* even when they are *invited*. As guests, women never fully belong to the national center and are always asked to go along with the rules of their (male) hosts. As Neluka Silva notes, "While feminized images define the *iconography* of the nation, the *practice* of nationalism is reserved for the masculine" (Silva 2003, 37).

Halide Edib's story is revealing in this regard. She was a well-known writer and public intellectual long before the War of Independence. She was one of the active participants of the women's meeting during the Balkan Wars. She is known to have gathered thousands in Istanbul before the Independence War making effective speeches "inviting" men and women into the nationalist struggle. She joined the independence war alongside Atatürk, as *Corporal Halide*, but was later denounced by Atatürk himself for having been a traitor. She was, after all, a critical mind whose "detached wisdom," to borrow Ayşe Durakbaşa's term, was at odds with Atatürk's expectations of the people around him (see Parla 1991a and 1991b). Halide Edib spent long years in (voluntary) exile, outside of the new Republic she had fought to establish. Using McClintock's analogy, it is possible to read her story as the history of women's positions changing from those who are doing the *inviting* (their organizing during Balkan Wars, Halide Edib's speeches in Istanbul, etc.) to being the ones *invited* into the struggle and into politics by the new leader of the Turkish Republic, to becoming *unwanted guests* (at times, being forced to leave the country).

Halide Edib was not the only woman with this trajectory. Recent scholarship has revisited many unopened pages in the history of the late Ottoman period and the early days of the Republic, revealing a long history of women organizing for their rights, as well as for the nationalist struggle. According to Ömer Çaha, ten out of the fifty nationalist organizations formed in Istanbul prior to the Independence War were formed by women (Çaha 1996, 100). In the period 1908–1923, there were at least forty women's organizations and twenty-seven women's journals, some of which had three thousand readers (Çaha 1996, 98–101). A number of these journals discussed feminism openly and asked for universal suffrage (Demirdirek 1993; S. Çakır 1994). As Nükhet Sirman (1989, 8) suggests, "What transpires through these journals is an attempt to produce norms to regulate the different aspects of women's lives, an attempt indeed to define a new, Ottoman womanhood."

This activism later turned into organized support for the Independence War and continued into the first years of the new Republic. On 16 June 1923, *Kadınlar Halk Fırkası* (Republican Women's Party) was established, under the leadership of a leading feminist, Nezihe Muhittin. This was the first party to be established in the new era, even before Mustafa Kemal's *Halk Fırkası* (People's Party). The Women's Party was short-lived because the nationalist government, under Mustafa Kemal's leadership, did not approve its establishment, with the fear that it would lessen the support for the People's Party (see Toprak 1988; Tuncay 1989; Zihnioğlu 2003).

Unable to organize under their own party, the same group of women established *Türk Kadın Birliği* (Turkish Woman's Union) on 7 February 1924, again under the leadership of Nezihe Muhittin (Zihnioğlu 2003). Starting with the elections in 1925, the Union organized petitions and demonstrations asking for women's suffrage (Toska 1998, 84). In 1926, they became a member of the International Women's Union (established in 1902) and in 1935, organized the twelfth congress of this Union in Istanbul, less than a year after women's suffrage was granted by the Grand National Assembly. This international feminist conference had women's suffrage as its theme and the Turkish Post Office published fifteen different stamps with women's pictures on them in recognition of it. Soon after hosting this conference, the Turkish Woman's Union was asked to dissolve itself and it did. The reason was that they had "fulfilled their task"; women had gained suffrage. Their time as *guests* (as marginalized as they were) was over. They had to leave. There would be no women's organizing until the late 1970s. As in the West, there was a serious time lag between first wave feminism in Turkey, and the second wave.[18]

Historical records reveal unexpected witnesses to this silenced history. Parliamentarian Hakkı Tarık Bey's question in response to the military service law in 1927 is a good example. Seven years before women were granted suffrage with a "decree from above," and nine years before Sabiha Gökçen joined the Air Force, he feels the need to address the question of women in the military as part of women's citizenship rights (and duties) and starts his speech with reference to women's organized call for their suffrage. An article written by Hıfzı Veldet (Velidedeoğlu), a leading intellectual of the time, in 1935 is also revealing of the male elite's gender anxieties during these formative years of Republican Turkey:

> In Turkey, women do not constitute a separate group or class. The Turkish woman is also a member of the nation. And she is, naturally, entitled to the same rights that man has. Just as Turkey is dealing with all the issues that were not dealt with, or ignored, in the past, it is also dealing with this issue of womanhood. *There is not, has not been, and cannot be a struggle between womanhood and manhood in the new Turkey. Women's rights have not been granted to women, nor have women gained them with their own struggle.* (1935, 268, emphasis added)

What is most striking in this short passage is the recognition of the fact that women were *not granted* their rights from above. What later became official nationalist discourse does not appear to be *the* hegemonic discourse in the 1930s. It is also interesting to see a member of the male elite write a text in the same year that the Turkish Woman's Union organized an international feminist conference in Istanbul and was forced to dissolve itself, and argue against what appear to be feminist positions. What was it that had forced Hıfzı Veldet to make a strong claim that "there is not, has not been, and cannot be" a gender struggle in the new Turkey?

Despite the growing literature on women's activism in those years by feminist scholars, the view that women's rights were given from above is still very strong in Turkey. As Ayşe Saktanber (2001, 333) notes, "the obedient/grateful positionality" demanded from women by Kemalism continues to serve as one of the guiding pillars of "the founding principles of the Republican regime." An interesting example of how central this idea has been in shaping women's (and men's) consciousness comes from one of the "thousand Gökçens" in Turkish history. Şenay Günay is one of the first woman officers of the Air Force and Turkey's first woman jet pilot. After retiring as a colonel from the Air Force in late 1990s, she made the following statement to journalists:

> Women in Europe went into social life as a result of their organizing. Our rights were presented to us on a tray. I feel that we are going backward each day. For instance, we are able to go into the military and become a combat pilot in 1956, and in 1961 that right is taken away. Until the 1990s . . . In other words, we were more advanced fifty years ago. We are going backward each day and I miss the past. (*Radikal*, 5 June 1997)

Şenay Günay has already forgotten (or consciously silences) the fact that her own entry into the Air Force was made possible through the stubbornness and struggle of only a few women a year before her. It was not a right presented to women by the state in a "golden tray," women had had to open a court case to gain this right, and had lost it soon after. Yet the discourse that Turkish women were "given" their rights by the state (in fact, Atatürk), without having to organize around women's rights (like European women), has gained such a strong hegemony since the 1930s that even what might be considered as "hard facts" cannot unsettle this perception. Many women, instead of recognizing the struggle of other women (or even themselves), remain "indebted" to Atatürk and the Republic for having "given them" their rights as women.

"Feminist Margins Have Their Own Margins"

Nationalist history in Turkey is not a history without women in it. On the contrary, women in their varied roles (as mothers, warriors, career women) are central to this history. The overall attitude of the Republican reformers, including Atatürk himself, was based on contradictions and ambivalences regarding the liberation of women and the designation of gender roles. On the one hand, women were seen as mothers and housewives who needed more education mainly to raise their children in new ways (Z. Arat 1998, 176). On the other hand, progressive laws were passed and women were *invited* into the nationalist project, not just as mothers, but also as active participants in the public realm with their newly acquired professions. As Yeşim Arat (1997, 100) suggests:

> All reforms that helped secularize and westernize the republic... encouraged women to play new public roles in society. They could now become professionals expected to be equal to men in the public realm, embodying the universal ideals of equality of humankind. Women assumed their new roles with a vengeance. Theirs was a nationalist mission.... The purpose of the professional work expected of women was service to the modernizing nation.

Zehra Arat highlights the same phenomenon with her observation that "girls were... encouraged to believe that they could study everything and pursue any career. Atatürk himself adopted several girls and encouraged them to study and participate in activities such as aviation that had not been previously open to women" (Z. Arat 1998, 117). The woman in question here is, of course, Sabiha Gökçen.

As I tried to show above, there is also a parallel history of silencing feminist voices, closing the women's party, as well as a large women's organization, and writing out women's organizing from the historical record. This history is being brought to light by feminist scholars. In fact, following Joan Scott's (1986) famous call to treat gender as an analytic category, recent feminist historiography of Turkey does not simply "add women into the historical record," but challenge the basic tenets of the historical record and rewrite it from a gender perspective.[19]

Yet feminist historiography is not without its problems, either. In the words of Catherine Lutz (1995, 251), "the feminist margins have their own margins." While recovering the feminist voices silenced by nationalist historiography, feminist histories in Turkey have produced their own silences. As Kamala Visweswaran suggests, silences among women can be viewed "as the central site for the analysis of power between them" (Visweswaran 1994, 51).[20] Kurdish feminist scholar Rohat Alakom reminds us of one of these silences in her review of the *Kürt Kadınları Teali Cemiyeti* (Kurdish Women's Organization) established in Istanbul in 1919:

> Scholars who have recently written on the Ottoman women's movement, for some reason, have not mentioned this first Kurdish women's organization.... We see a serious body of scholarship in Turkey in women's studies, an area whose importance has been recognized in recent years. It is possible to foresee the disclosure of new documents and information in this field, considering the speed of current studies. This will be the case for the *Kürt Kadınları Teali Cemiyeti* as well. (Alakom 1998, 36–37)[21]

Yelda, another feminist critic who emphasizes the necessity of digging into new and unconventional sources, opens her 1998 essay titled "Mothers of Fathers (*Babaanneler*) are Turks, Mothers of Mothers (*Anneanneler*)..." with a question: "Recent works bring to light our history. How happy we are as women. But who are 'we'? Which women?" (Yelda 1998, 139). Her answer to the question is "Turkish-Muslim women" and she continues the essay by drawing the reader's attention to "other" women: "Women have, of course, struggled on the land we live on today. Jewish, Assyrian, Greek, Kurdish, Turkish, Gypsy women..." (1998, 139). Digging into Armenian sources, Yelda is able to tell us the story of an Armenian feminist, Hayganuş Mark (1883–1966) who was the editor of a women's journal called *Hay Gin* (meaning Armenian Woman in Armenian) for fourteen years between 1919 and 1933.

We learn more about Hayganuş Mark from a recent article by three young Armenian-Turkish scholars, Melissa Bilal, Lerna Ekmekçioğlu, and Belinda Mumcu (2001), who show that Hayganuş Mark was a prolific writer, critic, activist, publisher, and public intellectual. In 1927, Hayganuş Mark writes a daring essay responding to a statement by Istanbul's Mayor that women are not equal to men and, thus, cannot vote, and likens his attitude to a "dish so cold that it cannot be brought to the table" (Bilal et al. 2001, 48). In her definition, feminism is a "cry for justice." Her "courageous rebuttal" is noted in many of the newspapers the next day. We also learn from this essay that Hayganuş Mark feels marginalized by the Muslim Turkish feminists, spends the last thirty years of her life away from the public eye, and dies alone in a hospital in 1966 (Bilal et al. 2001, 55).

Are there other Hayganuş Marks? Does she have Greek, Assyrian, Jewish, Gypsy sisters? How were their relations with each other? How did various nationalisms shape the lives and struggles of women from different ethnic and religious backgrounds in the transition from the Ottoman Empire to the nationalist Turkish state? We still know very little about the struggles of such women as members of their communities, or as feminists participating in the Ottoman women's movement.

What we do know, according to Fatmagül Berktay, is that "the dominant paradigm in Turkey since the nineteenth century was nationalism. Of course, there are important differences between nationalism in an empire context and nationalism in the context of a nation-state; however, what is important for our purposes here is that Turkish feminism and Turkish nationalism have developed hand in hand" (F. Berktay 1998, 1). This observation is important in two related ways. First, it highlights the importance of differentiating between a multiethnic empire which regards its people as "subjects," and a nation-state which is based on the idea of a single culture, a single language and of "citizenship." Second, despite this difference, it recognizes the close connection established in the last decades of the Ottoman Empire between nationalism and feminism, between the discourses of nationalist independence and of women's rights. Contemporary works and critiques sometimes fail to take into account the fact that nationalism *was* the dominant paradigm of the times, not just in Turkey, but in most of the world. Moreover, nationalism created desires that enabled rapid changes, and some of these changes have greatly benefited women. As Partha Chatterjee warns us, "the emancipatory aspects of nationalism" (1993, 3) and the "creative results of nationalist imagination" (1993, 5) should not be undermined in contemporary critiques.

Official historiography helps us see the nationalist desires and energies of this period. Feminist historiography challenges nationalist historiography on a number of major issues and helps us see feminist women's desires, energies, and struggles. Yet feminist scholarship has created its own margins and silences, reflecting the exclusionary cultural politics in Turkey throughout Republican history. One way to work against these particular silences is to follow the leads of recent scholarship and dig into unconventional sources looking for "other" women and the processes of their "othering."[22] Another one is to diversify feminist scholarship by looking into, not just women's activism, but also the stories of women who were not a part of the women's movement. For instance, The Women's Library and Information Center in Istanbul has been collecting such stories since the early 1990s through oral history and archival projects. Yet another way to unsettle this silencing is to ask the more difficult questions about women's efforts in the silencing of other women and their active participation in the making of nationalist histories and of militarized identities. Sabiha Gökçen's story is an important reminder in this respect. Not all Turkish women have been involved in the women's movement; other Turkish women have silenced the women's movement, sometimes along with their own agency as women. Moreover, taking seriously the linkages between nationalism and militarism (Walby 1996, Enloe 1995), we should also write women into the history of their mutual making.

Sabiha Gökçen's success in undertaking an unorthodox career for a woman in the 1930s leaves much to comment on regarding the opportunities opened up for (some) women in the early years of the Republic. However, it also opens the Pandora's Box regarding women's active participation in the development of militarism as a means to solve ethnic and political problems in Turkey. Sabiha Gökçen, as the world's first woman combat pilot and the national hero of the Dersim operation, forces us to look into the militarization of women's identities throughout Republican history and their participation in the construction and perpetuation of the myth of the "military-nation."

In addition to Gökçen's story, the debates regarding women and military service in the early years of the Republic reveal the processes through which national identities were constructed—as gendered and militarized, yet never fixed—through "decisions, many decisions, decisions made by both civilians and people in uniform" (Enloe 2000, 289). We need to better understand the dynamics of these decision-making processes. Feminist scholarship in Turkey has already challenged official historiography on a number of its key assumptions. The task ahead is to write new histories of the period from a more pluralist feminist perspective, paying equal attention to different groups of women, analyzing their relations with one another, and discussing different forms of marginalization.

Another key task in rethinking the making of gendered national identities is to pay as much attention to men and masculinity as to women. As I argue in this chapter and the next, military service is one of the most important sites through which citizenship becomes gendered and militarized, and the state becomes masculinized. As Joanne Nagel (1998, 252) argues, "Masculinity and nationalism seem stamped from the same mould—a mould which has shaped important aspects of the structure and culture of the nations and states in the modern state system." Yet, this has neither been an automatic connection, nor one that cannot change. In Turkey, as elsewhere, any attempt to de-gender nationalism and citizenship needs to incorporate a discussion of universal male conscription. Different from other contexts in which this discussion has been or is being held (see Feinman 2000), there is an added task in Turkey of demythologizing and deculturalizing military service. Part II will look into the making of military service as a disciplining, nationalizing, and masculinizing practice, while at the same time exploring the (marginalized) efforts of conscientious objectors to demythologize military service.

PART 2
MILITARY SERVICE

Chapter Three
Becoming a Man, Becoming a Citizen

Toward the end of 1999, at a dinner gathering with friends, someone told me a story: A friend of his—who happened to have an anthropology undergraduate degree—had done his military service in Western Turkey, in what he called "a bizarre unit where there were a lot of lunatics." On one of his first days in the barracks, this young man's commander gathered all the soldiers and asked the ones with university degrees what they had majored in. Upon hearing that this man had an anthropology degree, he said: "It would have been better if you were a psychologist or a sociologist, but anthropology will do." For the rest of his days in the barracks, this young anthropology graduate was ordered to operate his own office for consultations with soldiers who had psychological problems. His orders were to make sure that no one hurt themselves (e.g., by cutting their arms with razors) or committed suicide. Suicide was the commander's major concern. He was waiting for a promotion and did not want anyone to kill themselves under his command. That is why he had decided to seek the "professional" help of this anthropologist.

From the perspective of the anthropologist, not having to partake in the daily chores of life in the barracks and to have a private office in the camp made this order an attractive one. Moreover, he was given a week off to go back to Istanbul and get whatever he would need to set up a "consultation office." According to the friend who told me his story, after this one week, he went back to the camp with a few books and some pictures to hang on the walls, excited about the prospects of spending his military service in an office of his own. However, it did not take him long to become disillusioned and, in fact, afraid. First of all, consulting the soldiers who came in with all kinds of problems had proven to be much harder than he had imagined. He did not know what to say to a man expressing a desire to kill someone just for the thrill of it, or a man wanting to commit suicide. The problems of these men weighed heavily on him and the constant warnings of the commander that he did not want to see any form of self-injury or suicide added to the pressure. Moreover, everyone in the camp started viewing him as an important person. He held the key to their referrals to the hospital, which would allow them to escape from the barracks, at least temporarily. Soldiers, when they saw him, tried hard to convince him that they needed to go to the hospital for this or that reason. The combined pressures of the commander and the soldiers made his office begin to feel like a prison.

As I listened to the story of the young anthropologist/psychologist/doctor, I reflected on my own research experience. On the one hand, I would have loved to have been in the shoes of this young man, "being there" and talking to other soldiers about their experience on military grounds. Not having access to the barracks has been a major limitation of my research and, perhaps, of my analysis in this chapter. On the other hand, I knew that it was not a coincidence that I was not in his shoes. First, as a woman, the barracks are off-limits to me, a "reality" I seek to unravel in this chapter. Second, my project is not about "the military" as an institution. We would learn tremendously from anthropologists of the military doing ethnographic work inside the barracks. Yet, ethnographies of military service and militarism need to look into other sites in which *ideas* about the military are naturalized and contested. This chapter will explore some of these sites in an effort to (1) examine military service as a disciplining, nationalizing, and masculinizing citizenship practice, (2) highlight the contradictions and silences it embodies, and (3) inquire into the recent changes in its conceptualization and experience.[1]

Discipline

In 1910, British General Sir Ian Hamilton wrote of compulsory military service as "the greatest engine the world has yet seen for the manufacture of a particular type of human intellect and body" (1910, 44). It was a machine that turned out:

> sealed-pattern citizens by the hundred thousand; backs straightened, chests broadened, clean, obedient, punctual, but on the other hand, weakened in their individual initiative. Yes, conscription is a tremendous leveler. The proud are humbled; the poor-spirited are strengthened; the national idea is fostered; the interplay of varying ideals is sacrificed. Good or bad, black or white, all are chucked indifferently into the mill, and emerge therefrom, no longer black or white, but a drab, uniform khaki. (Hamilton 1910, 44)

Almost ninety years later, in 1999, a young man I interviewed in a small town near Istanbul, defined his view of military service in very similar terms:

> [In military service] you learn all about discipline, you learn what discipline means, how to respect someone and all that. [After you come back], even if you don't show respect to a civilian friend or a total stranger, you at least think about it. If you haven't been through military service and learned about paying respect, you simply don't care. At any rate, *esas duruş* [the main military posture] is the position that shows the highest level of maturity in a soldier—spiritually (*ruhen*) and bodily. In other words, during military service you [change] your spirit/soul and your body; you learn a lot.

Although these two utterances by Sir Hamilton and this young man I will call Ali,[2] share a particular amazement with what Michel Foucault (1979, 137) defines "the art of the human body," their basic assumptions about military service are quite different. To the extent that Sir Hamilton recognized this "great engine" as a recent innovation in human and military history, which Britain might or might not consider using in the near future,[3] for Ali, compulsory military service was a rite of passage to citizenship and manhood, an aspect of his "culture" that he took for granted. He believed that the saying that "you become a man only after you have done your military service" had much truth to it and that people did indeed change as a result of having completed that service.

Ali liked the changes he recognized in himself. When I asked him: "So you are saying that you are glad you have done your military service?," his answer was straightforward: "First of all it is an obligation that has been given to you. You have no other choice but to do it. But you also learn a lot there." I will come back to the links between military service, citizenship, and manhood in the later sections; for the moment I would like to concentrate on Ali's recognition of the changes in the soldiers' minds and bodies and expand on the disciplinary aspect of military service, that is, its connections to the development of the "art of the human body" in modern history.

I agree with Sara Helman (1997, 309) that military service "should be conceptualized as an array of disciplinary practices constituting the subjectivity of participating individuals." Contemporary theorizing on the body and discipline, including Helman's, draws heavily on Michel Foucault. In his works, Foucault attempts a critique of the modern forms and techniques of power that work not "on" but "through" bodies. Foucault's discussion of "docile bodies" in *Discipline and Punish*, starts with a description of the changes in the body of a soldier from the seventeenth century to the eighteenth:

> Let us take the ideal figure of the soldier, as it was still seen in the early seventeenth century. To begin with, the soldier was someone who could be recognized from afar; he bore certain signs: the natural signs of his strength and his courage, the marks, too, of his pride; his body was the blazon of his strength and valour . . . By the eighteenth century, the soldier has become something that can be made; out of a formless clay, an inapt body, the machine required can be constructed; posture is gradually corrected; a calculated constraint runs slowly through each part of the body, mastering it, making it pliable, ready at all times, turning silently into the automatism of habit; in short, one has "got rid of the peasant" and given him "the air of the soldier" (ordinance of 20 March 1764). (Foucault 1979, 135)

In Foucault's analysis, it is through the new microphysics of power, the new art of the body and the development of disciplines as general formulas of domination that this change occurs. Along the lines of what he calls "relations of docility–utility" (137), "discipline produces subjected and practiced bodies, 'docile' bodies. Discipline increases the forces of the body (in economic terms of utility) and diminishes these same forces (in political terms of obedience)" (Foucault 1979, 138). What we have, then, is a productive body that is obedient. Foucault's discussion of discipline and the making of docile bodies abound with references to two institutions: education and the military. In other words, the schools and the barracks, for Foucault, are the main sites where modern disciplinary techniques were developed and perfected.

In my conversations and interviews with ex-soldiers, I was given different interpretations of discipline in the barracks. One recurrent theme had to do with the "irrational" character of the "military rationale." According to this approach, things that soldiers have to do during their military service do not necessarily follow a rationale—they are just done because they are orders and it is useless to look for an explanation. One ex-soldier told me about a dialogue he had had with his commander: "The commander was angry because I had done something wrong. I started a sentence by 'Sir, I thought that...,' but he stopped me right away: 'You don't *think*. I do the thinking for you!' What can you say to that? I am not supposed to do any thinking." According to this young man, the reason behind this was the unique character of soldiering: "The soldier's task is not a good one. It is basically to fight, kill, or die. In order to motivate people to do this, you have to break their spirits. You cannot tell a normal person to shoot at people; he won't do it. That is why there are orders, physical and psychological violence... otherwise, that person will *think*."

Although the stress in this explanation is on violence, there is, nevertheless, recognition of the productive aspects of military service, that is, the enhancement of the soldier's utility through obedience. Baron von der Goltz's description of discipline in 1880s was along the same lines: "Discipline demands more than mere negative services. She demands of the soldier that he stakes his life in order to vanquish the enemy, she expects from him something extraordinary, and she makes this extraordinary demand so familiar to him that he considers it unavoidable, and more than this—even natural" (1887, 134). In other words, discipline, for Goltz, renders natural a subjectivity based on obedience, even in the face of death.

In Foucault's "relations of docility–utility," discipline produces docile bodies as they are made more useful. The notion of utility in the case of military discipline is not confined to the naturalization of killing and dying, as Goltz suggests, but has much wider resonance to economic and political realms because conscription is not only about violence or about defense. In Turkey, the connections between the post–World War II notion of "development" (see Escobar 1995) and military service became more pronounced with increasing military cooperation with NATO and the United States. In a 1960 article, two political scientists Daniel Lerner and Richard D. Robinson wrote about the ways in which American assistance was used by the Turkish military to "modernize" society. They commended the military for providing an "overpowering materialism" to "illiterate and impoverished boys" from villages: "Consider the impact upon these young men of their first exposure to the wider world outside their village, as they undergo training in this rapidly modernizing and democratizing army" (Lerner and Robinson 1960, 34). "In the absence of definitive case studies," Lerner and Robinson could not make general observations about what happened to these village boys when they returned home after serving in the military, but they nevertheless made speculations:

> the young discharged soldier is likely to find his traditional society inadequate to sustain his new level of expectations. A sense of frustration stimulates the young man to apply his army-acquired skills to promote civil innovation and "progress". He has been exposed to the machine concept and is aware of the advantages accruing to those with mastery of mechanical skills. Furthermore, the prestige of his military service has become identified in all minds with the new technology. Hence, it is likely that the soldier returning to his native village will resist falling back into the premechanical era. (Lerner and Robinson 1960, 34)

Thus, they believed that "if the young man returning from the army... remains within the village, he may be the driving force behind both technical and social innovation" (Lerner and Robinson 1960, 35). Moreover, such innovation was taking place, with U.S. guidance, at the level of decision-makers as well:

> One should not discuss the impact of the army on the total economic and social structure of the country without reference to the highway development program, initially considered almost exclusively as a military matter. The U.S. Highway mission dispatched to Turkey in 1948 was placed first under the Military Aid Mission. Not until sometime later was the highway program related to the economic aid mission. (Lerner and Robinson 1960, 37)

The linkages between the military and economic development in countries like Turkey was explored by these analysts as a characteristic of "underdevelopment" and lessons were drawn for securing maximum impact in other countries through U.S. military assistance:

> Indeed, the army, the public school, the industrial enterprise, and the economic planning organization of an underdeveloped country tend to converge on common objectives ... Perhaps, learning from the Turkish experience, we can help other countries to harness their national motivation to be strong, via military organization, more directly to the drive for accelerated development. (Lerner and Robinson 1960, 39)

These views present important clues to the linkages between discourses of development and militarization, as well as to the "economic" aspects of global militarization. The role played by militaries and international military assistance programs in the "network of power [that brought] the 'poor', the 'underdeveloped', the 'malnourished', and the 'illiterate' ... into the domain of development" (Escobar 1995, 89) has been understudied. In cases like Turkey, it was not only the state and the military that gained universal access to the young population for increasing their "docility-utility," but various foreign (particularly American) "aid missions" as well.

During my research, I was given numerous examples of how the military experience increases the *economic* utility of a soldier beyond the barracks. A peasant—I will call him Mehmet—who had done his military service between 1967 and 1969 in Kahramanmaraş and Mersin (in Southeastern and Southern Turkey respectively), talked to me extensively and favorably about military discipline: "There is a lot of education, training, and discipline in military service. Discipline is a must. There can be no military service without discipline" and continued to describe the state job he was able to get after military service along the same lines:

> I got a state job (*devlet işi*) soon after military service, which was like another military service. Just like in the military, we would work with orders, time constraints (*saatle*), and with disciplinary committees and supervisors above us. All were civil servants. State job. I was working there as a *kahya*. In the military, I was a sergeant (*çavuş*) commanding privates, in the farm, I was a *kahya* commanding other people. Just like military service. We slept in the same kind of bunk beds and had to be ready for muster (*içtima*) in the mornings. We ate the same kinds of food—*bulgur* and *hoşaf*. Just like military service. There was one difference: You could go home if you wanted. And there were no guns.

If one aspect of this narrative is the similarity drawn between the military and other state institutions, another one is the expression of the knowledge of a capitalist work place having its origins in military service. In other words, according to Mehmet, his two years in the barracks had prepared him for a job in the state farm by teaching him discipline. He knew the daily chores of living in a disciplined environment, with strict management of time and bodies, thanks to his two years in the barracks. Moreover, having been a sergeant in the military, he was given a job as a supervisor, as *kahya*.

As in Mehmet's narrative, my aim here is to draw attention to two aspects of the relationship between military service and discipline. First, I believe that the development of military service as a disciplinary practice that aims to "make" productive, yet docile, bodies out of male citizens needs to be analyzed in relation to how similar disciplinary techniques are used in other realms of economic and political life.[4] Second, I take seriously Mehmet's perception that military service prepared him for his post-military life, particularly the job that would give him his livelihood for the next twenty years. I wonder what would have happened if he had actually worked in the farm for some years before he served in the military. Would he have talked about military service in relation to his earlier work experience? Would that have helped him make sense of the military or would his expectations of "productivity" and "rationality" have been sources of dissatisfaction with life in the barracks? Or what would have happened if he had gone through eleven or fifteen years of disciplined schooling before his military service?

My interviews with university graduates, most of whom have had both long years of education and some work experience before serving in the military, suggest that Mehmet would most probably feel differently about his days in uniform were these not his first introduction to modern disciplinary techniques. "So I went for military service and started participating in the daily routines. Something was strange. It was almost like déjà vu. As we exercised, or did roll call, I felt a strange sense of familiarity," a man in his early thirties told me. "Then I realized that I knew about all that from school. In our physical education classes, we had learned to walk like soldiers, you know, get in line, turn right, turn left. And the roll call was just like the Monday morning and Friday afternoon flag ceremonies."

Moreover, many peasant men who have not received higher education, like Mehmet, typically leave home for the first time to serve in the military. Being away from their family, friends, and familiar surroundings also adds to their sense of "learning," "becoming mature," and "changing spiritually and bodily" through military service. The mother of a twenty-four-year-old young man was complaining to me about the irrelevance of military service for his son:

> My son left home when he was a high school student. He went to a boarding school for his high school and has been away ever since. He even went to America to study. He does not need to do military service. He has already learned to manage his own life because he has been away and on his own for so long.

Ömer, a thirty-year-old university graduate, made the same observation in similar terms: "It is the first time when a lot of people are separated from their families. It is the first time they are on their own. That is one reason why it is so important for them." He was excluding himself from this observation, because he had spent many years living away from home as a university student before joining the military.

Yet there are other reasons why military service is important in the lives of young men, their families, and friends, reasons that Ömer and Mehmet share. First of all, regardless of geographical or educational background, there is still a widespread belief that a young man will not be ready for life before doing his military service. Marriages are typically postponed till after military service, and it is very hard to get a stable, well-paying job before it. The majority of job advertisements state: "Military service is a prerequisite for male candidates." As one employer explained to me: "No one wants an employee that will leave after a year, just when he is learning the job, to do his military service. We prefer people who are ready to make long term plans and take the job seriously." Almost all of my interviewees mentioned the direct linkage between marriage and military service: "You cannot get married before doing your military service, it is as simple as that."

Ömer and Mehmet may not share the same cultural understanding of military service, yet financial concerns, family expectations regarding marriage, market discipline, and traditional values have come together and, until recently, defined similar prospects for Ömer and Mehmet in relation to their lives before and after military service. Moreover, despite the differences in their experience of military service, Ömer and Mehmet shared a common understanding that it was a kind of education. For Mehmet, it was discipline, for Ömer, it was knowledge of the "reality of Turkey." Ömer further believed that the military had an important "civilizing" effect.

Ömer and Mehmet, along with the large majority of soldiers, shared one other aspect of barrack life: beating. Discipline in the military does not only work "through" bodies, as Foucault suggests, but also "on" them. Punishment through beating in the military exists as a "public spectacle,"[5] rather than being a hidden, non-corporal process. The military is not only an institution that *exercises* "legitimate violence," but it is also an institution that *embodies* physical violence in its everyday operations. Use of physical violence in the military by higher-ranking soldiers is both legitimate and routine. There was no ex-soldier that I talked to who did not bring up the issue of beating, especially in relation to the initial training phase.[6] It was also a difficult issue for some men to discuss: Abdullah, a thirty-year-old man, turned red and looked down when he talked about the beatings in the barracks: "Everyone gets beaten without exception. Of course I did, too." Embarrassed looks and hesitation accompanied other narratives of physical violence as well. Some cut them short; others elaborated on them to explain the context in which they had been beaten. Several of them warned me not to believe anyone who suggested that they had not been beaten. In Mustafa's words: "People find it hard to admit to beating, but the truth is no one can escape it. Don't believe them when they tell you they were not beaten. They are lying!"

As Jacolyn Cock remarks, "military training involves stripping young men of their individuality and molding them into soldiers. During 'basics' soldiers are taught two major requirements: to be submissive to authority and to be aggressive to the enemy" (Cock 1991, 56). Regular beating seems to be one of the major strategies through which young men are taught submission to authority. "Before I went, I was warned against the pervasiveness of beating during military service. And it *was* pervasive. You get used to it. The sergeant beats you, but then you see the sergeant getting beaten up by a higher officer. Then, after training, you become a sergeant and you start beating others. I beat people, too. But only when I had to do it!" was how one soldier explained his experience with use of violence in the ranks.

Yılmaz, a former leftist militant who had spent some time in jail before going for his military service, contrasted routine violence within the ranks in the military with torture behind close doors in police stations: one is public and legitimate, whereas the other is hidden and illegal. "When you are faced with physical violence by the police, you can at least call it torture" he said, "but in the military, it is a part of the system. It is out in the open and you cannot speak against it. It is normalized."

I was told many stories of how recruits were hospitalized after being beaten severely by their commanding officers or how, for instance, sergeants would be taught the "art of beating" by their commanders (i.e., how to avoid inducing permanent damage while beating the soldiers). Cenk told me of the beating of a sergeant by a lieutenant because the sergeant had had one soldier hospitalized: "The lieutenant was mad *not* because the sergeant had hit someone, but because he had hit him in the *wrong* way. He demonstrated how the sergeant should beat soldiers without causing injury by beating the sergeant himself with these techniques." For many soldiers, direct physical violence is a central and painful memory. If the aim of military discipline is to make productive, yet docile, bodies, use of direct violence as public spectacle seems to be a crucial tool in this process.

National Identity and Citizenship

Much like Foucault, historian Eugen Weber, in his 1976 book *Peasants into Frenchmen*, pays specific attention to schools and the barracks. E. Weber's analysis is not restricted to discipline; he also highlights the ways in which students and soldiers gain "a sense of nationality" (1976, 298) in these institutions, that is, how peasants turn into Frenchmen [*sic*]. In Weber's analysis, military service in early years of the French Republic *was,* in many ways, a school, "the school of the fatherland" (1976, 298). By teaching the French language, literacy, civilization (diet, lodging, bedding, hygiene, dress, etc.), as well as "what it meant to be a French citizen" (1976, 298), the army "turned out to be an agency for emigration, acculturation, and in the final analysis, civilization, an agency as potent in its ways as the schools" (1976, 302). This is the second aspect of military service that I want to highlight: its connection to national identity and citizenship. The political side of discipline is not only about increasing the soldier's utility in political terms through obedience, but it is also about increasing his utility as a new political body, a national one. In other words, the category of the "citizen-soldier" does not only involve soldiering; it is also about being a proper citizen.

If the new conscript army composed of "citizen-soldiers," put to use during the French Revolution and established as a nation-state practice by Napoleon in the years to come, turned peasants into disciplined national citizens, it also provided a model for thinking about the whole nation as a unified body. There are two senses of national identity developed here (Verdery 1996): First, there is the individual person who is given a sense of national self, and second, there is the national collective self as represented by the "men in uniform," that is ready to fight the nation's enemies. The terms "nation-in-arms" or "military-nation"[7] are expressions of this relationship.

In the words of historian George Mosse (1993, 14), "the modern nation at its birth was a nation in arms" and there is nothing that illustrates this relationship better than the militarist content of most national anthems (Mosse 1993).

According to historian Alfred Vagts: "If the members of a whole nation are to be made soldiers, they must be filled with a military spirit in time of peace" (Vagts 1959, 134). As I discuss in chapter five, nation-states initially had two main tools to create citizens with a military spirit: universal compulsory military service and universal compulsory education. These were the two institutions through which the state had direct contact with its citizens and, in early years of nation-state formation (and during times of war), there was a close link in the way these two institutions were perceived. The military was seen as a school, in Eugen Weber's terms "the school of the fatherland," and the schools were given a nationalizing and militarizing role. Military historian Michael Howard argues that the purpose of "national education after 1870 in most West European countries was to produce generations physically fit for and psychologically attuned to war. It was a necessary part of citizenship" (Howard 1978, 10). During and after World War I, there were debates about militarism and education in the United States and Britain. Educator and philosopher John Dewey, for instance, was vocal in his critique of military training in schools:

> Military Training in schools cannot be defended on the ground of physical training. All authorities agree that so far as the health and development of the body are concerned, there are many better methods. From the military standpoint, it is entirely negligible. Its real purpose is to create a state of mind which is favorable to militarism and to war. It is a powerful agent in creating false standards. Now that war has been outlawed by agreement among the nations, it ought to be recognized that it is criminal to produce in the young, emotional habits that are favorable to war. (Dewey 1990, 124)

In Britain, John Langdon-Davies wrote a book titled *Militarism in Education: A Contribution to Educational Reconstruction*, and argued that schools were being configured as the thresholds of conscription. He urged the public to "beware of the insidious advance of industrial and military conscription" and suggested that they "must cease to educate for war, and to inculcate the doctrine of force" (Langdon-Davies 1919, 149).

In the 1930s, similar connections between conscription and education were developed in China, as part of Chiang Kai-shek's New Life Movement (Dirlik 1975). As Arif Dirlik argues, this movement had "militarization" (*chün-shih-hua*) as its ultimate goal; by which was meant the "replication of military organization in society": soldiers were seen as the "most suitable models for the population" (Dirlik 1975, 972). The use of military training and attitudes were regarded as central in education, as well as at work and in everyday living. Moreover, militarization was also seen as an effective tool for increasing "uniformity" among citizens (Dirlik 1975, 973). "For teachers and students, it also included obedience and the wearing of uniforms. In addition they were to receive military training, participate in athletics, and to foreswear smoking, drinking, and dancing" (P'ei-te Chu quoted in Dirlik 1975, 973).

In Turkey, education and educators have been given a nationalizing and militarizing role from the early years of state-formation. As underlined by the Ministry of Education in 1933: "Republican Education is an instrument to raise nationalist citizens" (*Maarif Sergisi Rehberi* 1933, iv). Mustafa Kemal Atatürk, in a speech to a group of teachers in 1923, suggests that the educational army (comprised of teachers) is just as important as the real army because it fulfils a sacred responsibility by teaching "the army, which dies and kills, why it dies and kills" (quoted in I. Kaplan 1999, 141). An almost logical extension of this view of education is uttered in a publication of the Ministry of Culture in 1938: "Just as the army is a school, so is the school an army" (Yaman 1938, 40). The terms "*öğretmenler ordusu*—army of teachers" or "*milli eğitim ordusu*—army of national educators" are still widely used today.

Conversely, military service was and *is* seen as an educational practice. An article in the magazine *Ülkü* in 1933 refers to it as a "*milli terbiyetgah*—a national school" that cannot even be compared with any other school or institution. In the same vein, Atatürk, in 1937, refers to the military as "a great national school of discipline" (*Atatürk'ün Söylev ve Demeçleri I*, 421). To give a more contemporary example, a 1995 high school *National Security Knowledge* textbook defines military service as follows: "Military service, the most sacred service to the nation and the homeland, prepares young people for real life situations. A person who does not do his military service is no good to himself, to his family, or to his nation" (*Milli Güvenlik Bilgisi* [1998], 20). In other words, the stress here is not on the need for military service for the defense of the country, but on its role in the life of the individual male citizen. To prepare for real life situations and to become somebody in relation to himself, his family, and his nation, he needs to serve in the military. In this formulation, military service does not appear as an obligation to the state, but an obligation to one's nation, one's family, and one self.[8]

With universal military service, the apparatuses of the state reached an increasing percentage of the adult male population. Very soon, every single citizen of the new nation-state would be "connected" to the military, either directly (by serving in it) or indirectly (by sending their sons, husbands, brothers, lovers, friends for military service). It would take the school system much longer to reach every household and village. How does military service turn young men into national citizens? What does this education involve? I have already talked about the making of productive bodies that can function in a capitalist or a capitalizing economy through discipline. At the same time, there is another kind of process occurring, namely a positive "imagining" of a national self and community, to use Anderson's (1991) phrase. One sentence I have heard over and over again from the men I interviewed was: "During military service, I met people from all over the country." One ex-soldier listed his friends from other places: "Now I have friends from Antalya, Alanya, Ankara, Afyon, Adana, İzmit, Edirne, İzmir, Aydın . . . I have their addresses. I mean, I have friends from all regions of Turkey." Others talked in excitement about the places they had seen thanks to military service: "I felt like I was in a different world. I saw places in Turkey I would not have seen otherwise." In other words, military service becomes an important experience through which the soldier learns about his nation as a community and his homeland as a territory. It has the potential to contribute to the development and sustainment of a "nationalist structure of feeling" (Anderson 1991; Alonso 1994) that on the one hand defines and disciplines the soldier in a strict hierarchical structure and on the other hand promises the satisfaction of a sense of belonging to the nation and discovering its otherwise unknown territory.

Yet this process is accompanied by a simultaneous discovery of the *differences* between people from different regions of Turkey with different ethnic, religious, cultural, or linguistic backgrounds. As Corrigan and Sayer (1985, 197) suggest, "social integration within the nation state *is* a project; and one in constant jeopardy from the very facts of material difference ... whose recognition official discourse seeks to repress" (Corrigan and Sayer 1985, 197). All integration projects involve a hierarchy of values based on various hegemonies. Almost all of the ex-soldiers I interviewed emphasized the differences they witnessed in other soldiers. For some, differences were embedded in ethnicity or religion, for others, it was in "manners." Several of the soldiers emphasized the role of the military in introducing "backward" populations of Turkey to "civilization." For an ex-soldier in his forties, military's civilizing mission was not limited to military service, the presence of the military in Turkey's small towns was another positive influence. He added, "unfortunately." That is, he found it unfortunate that these towns were so backward, and that there were no other institutions or state agencies that could play the same role.

A significant part of this civilizing mission is expressed through language and literacy training. The military has historically assumed the role of teaching Turkish and literacy to its soldiers. In fact, given the low literacy rates across the country in the 1920s and Turkish being a language much less known and much less standardized, the significance of military service in early years of state-formation as a nationalizing practice becomes more apparent. Through compulsory education, the state had access to the children, but through compulsory military service they had access to the adult male population.

> In the process of nationalization, the military played a very important role. Besides acting as a kind of "national school" and teaching literacy (the military has taught the alphabet to more than half a million citizens and the Turkish language to tens of thousands), the military has contributed to the making of a "national citizen" with a national language, culture, and set of goals. (Bozdemir 1985, 2654)
>
> For the Turkish History Thesis, which was born out of necessity, to be effective, it had to reach the masses. As was the case in relation to other issues as well, the military assumed this role. The military was able to reach half of the population through compulsory military service. Thus, it succeeded in passing on this ideological history through its educational activities with the soldiers. (Şen 1996, 71)

In their 1960 article, Lerner and Robinson note that the U.S. military assistance given to Turkey included support for literacy training: "Special textbooks have been published with the cooperation of an American specialist. Later, over 100 additional titles will appear in simple Turkish for distribution to soldier-graduates to encourage continued reading" (pp. 35–36). The schools set up for literacy were called "Ali schools" and although they were officially closed down in the 1970s, literacy training, in a more informal framework, has continued to this day.

Several of my older interviewees had become literate in these schools. When I asked them what they thought about having learned literacy in the army, they all said that they were "happy about it," reminding me that they were not the only ones.

Many other soldiers had gone through the same training. Although numbers have gone down,[9] the military continues to educate the conscripted soldiers. Among the seven functions of the military, as they are explained in the current *National Security Knowledge* textbook, is literacy training. Two university graduates shared with me their experiences as "teachers" for other conscripted soldiers. Ersoy, who had served in the early 1980s, was one such teacher: "In the first week, the commander called me to tell me that my task for the next months would be to teach those soldiers who were illiterate how to read and write. There were about fifty soldiers in our unit who were in that category. It was difficult because some of them did not even speak Turkish. They were mostly Kurdish boys." The other "teacher" mentioned the same difficulty. What they perceived more of a challenge was to teach the language itself.

"Illiteracy" and "ignorance" were often presented to me in direct association with Kurdishness. One ex-soldier shared several stories along these lines. One was about a Kurdish soldier who had participated in a political demonstration organized by the pro-Kurdish party HADEP (*Halkın Demokrasi Partisi*—People's Democracy Party) with his uniform. Apparently, the demonstration was taped by the police and this man was identified in his unit. The Turkish ex-soldier who told me this story described this act as "ignorance" and "pure stupidity." He said: "I would empathize with him for being a supporter of the party, but he should at least have had the brains not to go there in his uniform." Similarly, he cited "not knowing Turkish" as an example of ignorance. He told me about the Kurdish soldiers in his unit who did not speak Turkish—or pretended they did not—when they were given orders. They spoke back to the commander in Kurdish. This was either due to their ignorance ("not knowing Turkish") or due to an attempt to escape doing work: "If you don't understand the orders, or pretend that you don't, of course, you do not get to do them!" Moreover, he was contemptuous of the soldiers from the East and the Southeast for not having been to a movie theater before in their lives.

All of these comments came from a university graduate whose politics I would call liberal. He recognized the political and cultural rights of the Kurds and other non-Turkish groups that are a part of Turkey. He went further to acknowledge and criticize the exploitation and bad treatment of migrant workers from the ex-Soviet bloc in recent years. He was highly critical of political and cultural discrimination. Yet, his military service narratives were framed by the military's "civilizing mission." He did not even consider, for instance, that the Kurdish man in uniform at the HADEP demonstration or the ones who insisted on talking to their commanders in Kurdish might have done so as political acts—as acts of civil disobedience. Or instead of questioning *why* there were few movie theaters in the Southeast of the country, or why the existing ones could not function because of state control and censorship, he easily identified this lack as a sign of being "uncivilized". This approach is in line with other comments I have heard from people of different backgrounds on the Kurds or the "people from the East," as well as with state policy on the Kurdish issue since the 1930s. As I discuss in other parts of the book, the framing of the Kurdish issue as one of "civilization" has been a major strategy for avoiding its recognition as a political or cultural issue. In the words of sociologist Mesut Yeğen, this has led to the silencing of the *Kurdishness* of the Kurdish issue (see chapters two and six).

If one differentiation and hierarchy implicit in popular and official conceptions of Turkish nationalism is based on ethnicity and language, another one is based on religion. Despite the fact that the Turkish military defines itself as a secular institution (in fact, as the vanguard of secularism against the Islamicist threat), the discourse inside the army is based on the assumption that all soldiers are Muslims. The non-Muslim soldiers in the military bear the mark GM (which stands for the first letters of *gayri-Müslim*/non-Muslim) on their nametags. This practice was explained to me by several people as a way of knowing what kind of burial to give to the soldiers if they die. The problem with this explanation is that what is written on the nametags is not the soldier's religion (Jewish, Christian, Muslim, etc, each indicating a different kind and place of burial), but the fact that the soldier is NOT a Muslim. This mark suggests that he belongs to one of the recognized "minority" groups in the predominantly Muslim Turkish Republic: Jewish, Greek, or Armenian.

This practice, rather than having a utilitarian function, reflects the systematic discrimination against non-Muslim citizens of Turkey. They are perceived first as negations of the norm, ("non-") and thus as potential threats, later as Turkish citizens.[10] Greeks and Armenians, in particular, are met with great suspicion by their commanders, as well as by their peer soldiers. Moreover, civilian education (see chapter five) as well as training during military service involves the inculcation of highly negative views regarding the Greeks and the Armenians in the Ottoman Empire and during the War of Independence. Indoctrination of official ideology on what it means to be a Turk is a direct form of educating the young soldiers into proper Turkish nationals, where not all are equal. Minorities are reminded of their history of "treason" and Kurds are told that they are indeed Turks. One ex-soldier who served in 1994 told me that his commander cited Kurdish as the East Anatolian version of the Ottoman language, and not a language of its own.

This does not mean that the minority soldiers are universally discriminated against in military service or that they do not participate in the construction of hegemonic Turkish nationalism. Several of the Greek, Armenian, and Jewish men interviewed by journalist Yahya Koçoğlu suggest that their commanders during military service paid special attention to them and made sure that they were not discriminated against by the other soldiers.

> I had no problems during military service. But I noticed that the commander was watching out for me. He did not say anything directly, but I could sense it. (Koçoğlu 2001, 77)

> I was not discriminated against even during military service. In fact, one officer came and asked me if I had any problems. They feel the need to be extra sensitive with us. (188)

> I had no problems as an Armenian during military service. I heard that they had a special policy of protection towards Armenians and other non-Muslims. (214)

Two Armenian-Turkish men talked to me about their active participation in the operations against the PKK during their military service with explicit pride. One of them had taken active part in a commando unit that was involved in direct combat. The other one remarked how suspicious his commander was in the beginning but that his attitude had changed as they got to know each other. "The commander realized," he said, "that I was just like the other soldiers!" The big smile on the face of the twenty-year-old young man who uttered these words was testimony to the pleasure he felt in being "just like the other soldiers." I met him on the plane from Diyarbakır to Istanbul in 1999. For me, it was the end of an intense research trip and for him, the beginning of a short vacation. He had not told anyone from his family that he was coming and was excited about the prospects of surprising them. After telling me his reason for being on the plane, he asked mine. We were still on the ground at that time in the military-controlled Diyarbakır airport, which was heavily guarded, and I was nervous about being there for my research on militarism. Moreover, I did not know who this man was. So I just told him that I had visited friends in Diyarbakır, which was also true.

As our conversation progressed, we talked about politics. He told me that everyone in his unit, including himself, wanted Abdullah Öcalan's death sentence[11] to be carried out. He had done too much harm and caused the death of too many people. I asked him if he did not fear the consequences of such an execution, especially in the Southeast. "That I do not know much about," he said. He did not want to talk about the politics of the situation. So I changed the subject and asked him if he had spent time in Diyarbakır itself. He was doing his service on a remote post in the mountains and had not seen much of the cities in the region. I told him that there was a lot to see in Diyarbakır and gave him a couple of suggestions. One of those suggestions was the small museum called "The Diyarbakır House," which was an old stone house, bought and renovated by a local woman intellectual, Esma Ocak. "It is an old Armenian house," I added. "I am also Armenian" was his excited response. That was the first time I saw his big smile.

It was after this moment that he told me about the suspicious attitude of his commander and some of the other soldiers during his early days in the barracks. His remark about the commander realizing that he was "just like the other soldiers" was the end of that story. What remained with me after our short conversation were the two big smiles: one upon the recognition of his *difference* as Armenian as nothing to be ashamed of (in fact, I was not only recognizing Armenian presence in the history of Diyarbakır, but commending their contributions to the cosmopolitan culture and architecture of the city) by a fellow passenger on a plane, and the other accompanying an expression of pride that emphasized his *sameness* with other soldiers.

As many scholars have shown, official discourse usually represses the differences in its project of national integration (Corrigan and Sayer 1985), yet not all differences are equally problematic. The separate ethnic identity of the Kurds has been vehemently rejected by the Turkish state, whereas the separate religious/ ethnic identity of Greeks, Armenians and Jews as "minorities" recognized under the Lausanne Treaty (1936) is integral to state ideology. What matters in relation to these differences is not their suppression, but day-to-day management. The individual members of these communities, like the twenty-year-old soldier I met on the plane, participate in this management on a regular basis.

Another difference that defines the military service experience is class. From finding the right "contacts" in the military to have oneself assigned to "a proper place," to meeting the expenses of supplies and food during the service, class differences are reflected onto the military uniform. Not surprisingly, this was particularly emphasized in the narratives of the lower class men I interviewed. One of the most difficult parts of military service, they said, was being out of money (some suggested that they could not even afford snacks or tea between the meals). Unable to make money and receive allowances from their families, they had to rely on what the military provided for them, which was not much.

Education becomes interweaved with class in creating two distinct groups of conscripted soldiers. Those who are university graduates are often given the chance of doing a short term (currently six months) as privates or long term (currently twelve months) as noncommissioned officers.[12] Even this long term is shorter than the regular service for those without university degrees (currently fifteen months). Both the short term and the long term have advantages. As privates, they finish early; as noncommissioned officers, they are given authority, a salary, and, depending on where they are placed, the permission to leave the barracks in the evenings and on weekends. One ex-soldier who served his term in Izmir as a naval officer said that it was like "working for the military." He could go to his rented apartment in the evenings and enjoy social life in Izmir, while getting paid to do office work during the day. He reminded me several times that his military service should not be considered "typical." Surely, the advantages of being a noncommissioned officer in smaller towns or in out-of-the-way garrisons are more limited, but they are enough to make it worth it for some people to choose the long service.

Class and educational differences became all the more decisive during the war in the 1980s and 1990s. In addition to the increasing number of conscription evaders (see Sinclair-Webb 2000), there was also a sizeable male population that postponed military service for as long as possible. Education was the main means; going abroad was the other. As long as one remained a student (undergraduate or graduate), his military service was automatically postponed. This meant that many male university students delayed graduation by systematically failing one or two core courses and that many others applied for graduate school. In 1998, a twenty-five-year-old university student who was in his sixth year at school told me, in panic, that due to a change in the curriculum, the course he had failed would no longer be mandatory, and that he would soon be graduating against his will. His lengthy undergraduate studies made it difficult for him to get an acceptance from a Master's Program. This was "terrifying," because he did not want to serve in the military and be forced to fight against the PKK in the Southeast.

Bünyamin, who was a university student at age twenty-eight when I interviewed him in 1998, suggested that for him military service meant war. He had spent his high school and university years in Istanbul, away from most of the fighting and killing, but what he witnessed through the media was enough for him to equate military service with war.

> In my mind, I cannot separate military service from the Kurdish problem. You know, everyone talks about military service being about discipline, not rationality, and so on. For me, this is something about the past. Now, it is all about the war ... Two images are side by side. On the one hand, you have all the news about the dead, the martyrs, and operations on TV. On the other hand, we see loud groups of people going around in cars honking and shouting "our soldier is the greatest soldier!" This is new. We did

not have this kind of fanfare before. They have grown together with the increasing number of dead in the Southeast.

The seemingly jubilant ceremonies for "seeing off" young men for military service marked the streets and bus/train stations of the 1990s. Families and friends of those who were leaving for the military would gather to shout "our soldier is the greatest!" and organize convoys to go around the city with Turkish flags. Anthropologist Yael Navaro-Yashin (2002, 119) argues that in the 1990s these "farewell parties" for soldiers-to-be were transformed into "a show of veneration for the state. The state is exalted, celebrated, and reified in these soldiers' farewells." As Bünyamin points out, it was possible to observe a direct correlation between the increase in the numbers of dead soldiers and the growing popularity and intensity of these farewells. My interviewees from a village in the Thrace region that had given quite a few "martyrs" to the war, shared the same observation with Bünyamin: these farewells were a new phenomenon. Yet, Bünyamin and these villagers were situated differently in relation to this new practice. Bünyamin had never participated in one and knew about serving in the war zone only through the story of the brother of a friend, whereas the Thracian villagers had sent almost all of their young ones to the Southeast for military service.

Bünyamin remarked further that he had no friends who had done military service. In their late twenties and early thirties, they were still "students," studying in Turkey or abroad. There was an added advantage to going abroad. If they found jobs and worked outside of Turkey for three years, they became eligible to do the short term of one month by paying DM15,000 to the Turkish state. With the end of the war, the choice of one month paid service (*bedelli askerlik*) was given to everyone who was born before 1973. This special occurrence in 2000 was interpreted as a revenue-generating measure at a time of economic hardship[13] as well as a means for managing the high numbers of recruits lined up to serve (Sinclair-Webb 2000).

With no education or the opportunity to work abroad, the majority of Turkey's young men had no choice but to partake in the "fight against terrorism" during their eighteen month compulsory service.[14] Many were quite aware of the class inequalities that shaped their experience:

> I never saw the son of a rich person there. They just send the sons of the poor to this region. There were many soldiers who were protesting this when I was there. They used to ask where the rich kids were and I thought they were right to ask this question! (Mater 1999, 41)
>
> Who wants to go to the Southeast? What have we got to do there? We are peasant kids. Peasant kids do not have any influential connection to use to avoid going there. They send those who have no influence, others are saved. It is up to the poor, the disadvantaged to protect the homeland, the rich know how to go about it. (47)
>
> There were no rich kids among us. We were all children of peasants and workers. I did not meet a single son of a doctor there. (238)

In theory, military service is a site for homogenizing all men as "equals" in the same uniform. For Ömer, this was a key characteristic of his military service experience: "There, you are not Ali or Mehmet; you are not the son of your father;

you are not a high school or a university graduate . . . you are there as your bare, unmitigated self." Yet, for many others, various differences—mainly along the lines of class, education, ethnicity, and religion—disrupt that "bareness." As I have tried to show, experiencing these differences during military service may further strengthen, or, at times, rupture the sense of national belonging. Ultimately, it depends on the historical and political context, and the ways in which these differences are managed and negotiated. The big smile on the face of the Armenian-Turkish soldier who told me about his treatment "like any other soldier" with great pride is a sign of successful negotiation. Bünyamin's stories of evasion and questioning in the face of war, the stories about the soldiers who kept responding to their commanders in Kurdish, and the frustrated articulations of class inequalities by Mater's interviewees signal potential tension and rupture in the nationalist sentiment. So do the high numbers of conscription evaders during wartime . . .

There is one difference, though, that is beyond the limits of negotiation inside the barracks: men's difference from women. Despite their ethnic, religious, class, or educational differences, young men share the barracks with other men, as part of a joint obligation to become proper *male* citizens of their state and "survive" through this rite of passage into adult (heterosexual) masculinity.

Hegemonic Masculinity

In chapter two, I discussed the creation of gendered citizenship through compulsory conscription and emphasized the fact that the lawmakers were aware of the impact of their decision when they passed the Military Service Law of 1927. They recognized that military service was a major citizenship practice and that they were about to create a two-tiered citizenship by making it compulsory for men only. In 1933, six years after the short parliamentary discussion on military service, a short (fiction) story published in *Ülkü*, a popular monthly of the early Republican period, reiterated the gender difference created through military service as a cultural given. In the story, Hüsmen, a young peasant from Bergama (Western Turkey), is spending his last day in the barracks. He is very excited that it is his last day, *not* because he is leaving the military, but because he will be able to put to use the things that he learned in the military in his civilian life. He starts daydreaming (*tatlı tatlı hülyalara daldı*):

> After he is back in the village and has his wedding, he will tell Kezban all about the things he learned in military service . . . When Hüsmen says it all to Kezban, she will be dumbfounded (*parmak ısırıp kalacak*); the fascination of his wife . . . will make Hüsmen proud (*gururunu okşayacak, koltuklarını kabartacak*). He will first teach Kezban how to identify herself (*künyesini belletecek*). When he calls "Kezban," Kezban will run to him like a soldier, stand in front of Hüsmen and, after giving the official greeting, she will say "Ali's daughter Kezban, 329 Poturlar [presumably her address] . . . yes, sir! (*Emret, efendim!*)" and will wait for his orders. (Sıtkı 1933, 250–251)

Such was the daydream of a young peasant man as it was narrated by Celal Sıtkı in 1933, a year before women earned suffrage rights. In this story, participation in the military is linked directly to masculinity where military knowledge is power over women. Hüsmen may have been a private accepting orders in the military, or beaten up by his officers, but he is guaranteed the *unconditional* position of the commander at home. As anthropologist Carol Delaney (1991, 109) suggests, "a woman is the prize or reward for having endured the hardships of military service."

One of the soldiers I interviewed, Cengiz, recounted an occasion whereby the commander of his unit initiated a discussion on the "proper role of men and women in the family." There was no controversy among the soldiers that men were "naturally" the ones to decide on important family matters. They were the ones who could tell right from wrong, not women. When Cengiz intervened in the discussion to give his account of women's equality, there was a deep silence in the room. "Everyone was listening to me with interest and shock. I told them that women were indeed superior to us because they could give life. This was too much for anyone to take." Cengiz had disturbed the unconditional position of all men as commanders at home.

Yet the road to being a commander at home is a thorny one, which involves various levels of masculine humiliation. It is significant that in military training "being like a woman" is often used as an insult and, simultaneously, as a strategy for promoting "docility." Several ex-soldiers mentioned this aspect of military training in the interviews, often smiling while they talked about it. One man in his late twenties, for instance, told me about his astonishment when soldiers working in the kitchen were all given women's names by their commander. "They took a group of soldiers into the kitchen and the commander asked, 'what's your name?,' and the soldier answered 'Hayri.' The commander said, 'No, your name is Ayşe.' He went around telling the soldiers their names: Zeynep, Semra—all women's names. He then asked them to wash the dishes."

In the words of Deniz Kandiyoti (1994, 207), "as conscripts, all men will have known the experience of utter helplessness in the face of total, arbitrary authority, where each man will have been controlled by the whims of another man and where, in the absence of compliance, public humiliation and physical punishment may follow." One of my interviewees mentioned this as the most unsettling aspect of his military service experience: "From a life where you pretty much control everything, you go into one where you have no control whatsoever. You become a part of the large machine." Another described this process in computer language: "It is as if your head is being formatted. They clear out everything that was there before and re-format you." In this process of "losing control," soldiers are made to endure humiliation and femininized forms of hardship (like working in the kitchen). However, as soon as young men leave the confines of the barracks, military forms of hierarchy define gender relations in a different way. Every man is promised the position of the commander by virtue of being a man and of having served in the military. As Bünyamin explained to me: "There is a 'before' and an 'after' of military service. It is often said that you cannot become a man before you do your military service. Just as circumcision is a step into manhood, military service is its proof." In Hüsmen's story, the superiority of the husband is legitimized by "all the things" that he has learnt in the barracks. Women will never have access to such knowledge of the nation, of arms, of machines, of the homeland. Their role will be to express fascination, accept orders, and be dumbfounded.

If this "fantasy" points to the militarization of knowledge (in terms of determining what counts as important knowledge), it also points to a significant gender differentiation that ends up creating various advantages for men. Since the 1930s, among the Turkish-speaking uneducated population, men have gained advantage over women by learning literacy in military service—and thus becoming eligible for better paid jobs and having access to such things as newspapers and the laws. Moreover, lack of schooling in rural Turkey, particularly in the Eastern provinces has meant that while many Kurdish (or Arabic speaking) men learn Turkish in the military, many women spend their lives not speaking any Turkish at all. This means that they have little access to the things going on in the larger society that are having an impact on them (or men become their translators), and it includes having no access to the laws. In Eastern Turkey, where a large part of the population is Kurdish, illiteracy rates among women are as high as fifty percent, whereas in the Western parts of the country this figure is less than twenty percent (see Ilkkaracan 2000).

To clarify, I am not suggesting here that the main source of all gender inequality is military service. But I am suggesting that a certain form of gender inequality is established and maintained through this practice administered *by the state* and through masculinist discourses that define men's and women's relationship to the state. Cynthia Enloe (1995) writes about the discourses of military operations, security, and nationalism that construct the state and the army as male institutions that protect "womenandchildren." When I interviewed Ömer in 1998, he told me the following story while describing his commando training in Tuzla:

> There is a small, reconstructed village (*mezra*) in the training site. One regular aspect of the training is to simulate a *mezra baskını* (a village operation) where the terrorists have gone into the home of the *muhtar* (head of the village) and taken his daughter hostage. The aim of the operation is to save the *muhtar's* daughter and to catch the terrorists.

In this village operation, "womenandchildren" are exemplified in the figure of the girl child. Moreover, she is the *muhtar's* child. The honor of the *muhtar*, of the village, and of the state are read onto the body of this young girl. In this training program, as well as in general discourse, military service is configured, in a developmentalist and patriarchal scheme, as a practice that will turn the male soldier into an adult (as opposed to "child") and into a man (as opposed to "woman"), making "womenandchildren" a category to be "protected" in the name of the nation, binding "masculinism to the state" (Enloe 2000, 127) in multiple ways.

The concept of honor (*namus*) and its links to understandings of sexuality in Turkey have been discussed widely and made a political issue by feminist activists since the early 1990s (Altınay 2000b).[15] Its embeddedness in the discourses of the state in Turkey, and particularly of the military, are nowhere as striking as in the life story of Sabiha Gökçen (see chapter two). But how are we to understand this embeddedness? Addressing this question, anthropologist Ayşe Parla (2001, 83) concludes that searching for the answer in the "incomplete modernization" of the Turkish state would be a mistake: "State controls of women's bodies ... should not be dismissed as merely the traditional lapses of an aspiring nation-state." Instead, she draws attention to the very *modern* aspects of the constellations of power and discipline that provide a context for controls over women's bodies, such as virginity examinations. A related argument is developed by Nükhet Sirman in relation to the formation of the "modern Turkish family." Looking at the discourses of male writers in Tanzimat novels, Sirman (2000, 171) argues that their move away from the "large and complex households that were structured according to conceptions of power that had nothing to do with the private/public dichotomy associated with Western modernism" toward a new kind of nuclear family headed by the husband, signals a desire to construct "all men as equal representatives of households which they can now head" (Sirman 2001, 174). In these households, women are presented as "passive and obedient." In other words, both Sirman and Parla argue that modern structures (like the nuclear family and the nation-state) construct their own patriarchies, building on existing forms of patriarchy, as well as inventing new forms. As the above stories highlight, the citizen-army is another modern institution that creates a sense of equality between (heterosexual) men with an accompanying sense of superiority over all women. In the family context, the men are guaranteed the position of the commander over their wives. Outside the family, they are invited to identify themselves with the state and are given the authority to exercise control over women's bodies and sexuality, through such concepts as honor.

Of course, these rewards come with certain conditions. As R.W. Connell (1987 and 1995) and others have shown, there are hegemonic and subordinated varieties of masculinity. An essential component of hegemonic masculinity almost everywhere is the acceptance of heterosexuality as a norm. This norm closely defines the ideal, or indeed the acceptable, soldier. In many countries today, the question of "gays in the military" is a major issue. What happens when all men are obliged to serve in the military, as in Turkey? The solution offered by the Turkish military is for gay men to get a report which certifies that they are "unfit due to psycho-sexual problems."

In November 2002, a joint declaration by gay organizations protested various aspects of this practice. First, they argued that no institution had the right to define gay identity as "sickness" and asked for "sexual orientation" to be added to Article 10 of the constitution that declares the equality of all citizens before the law. Second, they protested the methods used by the military to certify gay identity: "The military does not accept individual declarations and engages in arbitrary measures such as asking for a photograph or undertaking physical examinations. We ask for these methods to be discontinued" (*Hürriyet*, 1 November 2002).[16] The photograph mentioned in the declaration is a photograph of the applicant in a sexual relationship with another man (Çelikkan 2002b; Leloğlu 2002). One of the spokespersons who stood in front of the cameras that day and explained gay activists' demands was Mehmet Tarhan, a conscientious objector who personally refuses to recognize the right of the state to impose military service in the first place (see chapter four). A month later, an antiwar declaration from the gay initiative *Kaos GL* further articulated the attitude of (some) gay activists toward the military:

> Wars and militaries are organized around a socially constructed masculinity that is defined by discrimination and humiliation of women and gays, and a mentality of conquest. We, as women and men homosexuals, we stand against heterosexism, patriarchy, and militarism, which are closely allied with one another.[17]

With the growing antiwar movement in winter and spring of 2003, these connections between heterosexism, patriarchy and militarism found their expression in the streets for the first time in Turkish political history. A placard used in an antiwar demonstration on 1 March 2003 in Ankara said: "We are not 'unfit', we are gays, and we won't do military service." On the other hand, many gay men do serve in the military, without publicly declaring their sexual orientation. Some even consider it a friendly, homosocial site:

> This society encourages men to be friends with, to have relations with other men. The soccer games, coffeehouses, military service. Turkey has seen men and women walking together in the street only in the last fifty years. It is basically a society where men spend their lives with other men. And of course, women spend their lives with other women. (Hocaoğlu 2002, 61)

Some gay men have no problem with doing military service. For others, especially if they publicly acknowledge their gay identity, military service bears many challenges. The alternative, that is, to a report that they are "unfit due to psychosexual problems," is both humiliating and risky. Berk, a gay university student who was contemplating getting an "unfit" report to avoid the war, was concerned about his future employment. What if he applied for a job where this report would become an obstacle?

There are other concerns men express about not doing military service. A major one is being deprived of "military service stories to tell." The monthly magazine *Max* conveys the widespread expectation that gives rise to such concerns:

> There is no escape from it. Every man should have military service stories to tell. Whatever his level of education, regardless of whether he is a doctor or a professor, he will in the end go under that discipline, do his training, wake up by dawn, experience the standard military food, stand guard, and wear the uniform. Reality. What will remain are sentences that start with "when I was a soldier . . ." (Mançer 2002, 101)

Before I started this research, I had been in numerous social settings where men would talk endlessly about their military service experiences. I remember once being "taken hostage" during a dinner gathering by two men, who were each about ten years older than I was. Our conversation that evening had led to a dialogue between the two on military service—with me as the captive listener. It must have gone on for several hours. In the beginning it sounded funny and interesting. They were both good storytellers and had apparently refined these particular stories over the years. I now wish I could remember more of those stories, but at that time, I remember feeling more and more uncomfortable as the conversation progressed.

It was a dialogue between two men, but I was their intended audience. Or perhaps more like the scoreboard as they registered their funniest, most interesting, and craziest memories from those "good old days." Both of these men were environmentalists and peace activists. The military, in their political discourse, was anything but a romantic or funny organization. What marked their narratives was not nostalgia, but, as I realized by the end of the evening, some peculiar combination of pride, male bonding, and a sense of wisdom. As much as I enjoyed the stories themselves, I remember sinking into my chair as they recited them one after the other. I was very uncomfortable with my designated gender position. It seemed like men would always claim a better knowledge of the country, the nation, and subsequently of politics based on their acquired "wisdom" during military service. At that time I was about twenty years old and had recently become a feminist. In situations such as this I was tempted to reach easy conclusions and sometimes take reactionary positions. I remember thinking that I wished women would do military service as well. I wanted to have similar stories to tell.

More recently, when talking with men about military service, in my interviews or in social interactions, I asked them whether they talked about this experience amongst themselves, and if so, where and how they talked about it. In describing the different settings in which they recite military service stories, my interviewees often focused on three aspects of the experience that are closely related to one another. One can think of these as the different ways in which militarized masculinity is performed in the post-military context.

First, as Ibrahim explained to me, men use having served in the military as a criterion to *judge manhood*:[18]

> If someone has not done their military service because they are handicapped or because they are too young, we always tell them that they should not talk, because they know nothing yet. You do not become a man until you serve in the military. It is a sacred obligation. And people make fun of those who have not served. I, for one, did it just because I would feel a lack without it. I am flat-footed. If I had wanted, I could have been excused from military service. But I did not want to be excused. So I did it.

In this context, military service is not only, or perhaps not even primarily, seen as a service to the state, but one that defines proper masculinity. It is a rite of passage to manhood and those men who have not been through it are made to experience a "lack." It is used as a way of exercising masculine authority over the young and over those who are not able to serve due to a particular "disability." The potential masculine humiliation in such contexts was strong enough to prevent Ibrahim, who was flat-footed, from asking for an exemption from military service. Several others I interviewed had also considered getting medical reports for other conditions (like severe eye problems) in order to evade military service, but feared the social and economic consequences. Like Berk, they were concerned about the reaction of their future employers.

A second way in which men perform their masculinity as ex-soldiers is simply by *reciting stories of success* to each other about their barracks days—particularly stories about their use of arms. This time the main differentiation is not between those who have served and those who have not. Instead, a sense of proper masculinity is reinforced by the achievement of each man in shooting or handling other tasks. Moreover, the retelling of these stories serves to both create a sense of sharing and differentiate between those who have stories to tell and those who do not. According to Ömer:

> If you listen to men in those conversations, everyone is a great shooter! They all hit the target right at the center! They are so proud of their shooting performance.

> The truth is that during basic training not many people learn to shoot. Neither the training, nor the ammunition are enough. Usually there are one or two men with previous shooting experience who can hit the target at the center. There are five or six others who also hit it. Others are just shots in the air. The majority of the privates cannot shoot. Of course, that's not how they talk about it afterwards.

Ömer had done his military service as a noncommissioned officer and had come into little contact with privates after his basic training. During our interview, he admitted that he sometimes felt bad about not having many military service stories to tell. He was bored when his friends went on and on about theirs. My feelings of uneasiness in similar situations in the past helped me empathize with his position. Moreover, as a "man," he was expected to produce interesting military service stories, a pressure that would never be put on me as a woman.

A third theme that comes up frequently in the conversations on military service is *complaint*. Ex-soldiers complain about the conditions in the barracks, the absurdities of military logic, the strict hierarchical structure, so on and so forth. Both before and during my research period, I found myself in many situations where complaints about barrack life were publicly articulated. In one instance, a young woman in the group interrupted the ongoing criticisms of an ex-soldier who had done the short service of one month: "You should be ashamed of talking this way. How about the ones who do not have the money and need to go through the same things for eighteen months? You have not done real military service." This remark was met by visible discomfort by the young man. He was suddenly put in the position of a spoiled rich kid, as opposed to a man who had survived the difficulties of long-term barrack life. As another ex-soldier explained to me during an interview, these complaints are usually accompanied by a sense of pride: "All men are proud of their military service experience, whatever their complaints. They are at least proud of having survived it." To put it differently, the difficulties associated with military service and their telling strengthen a narrative of pride and masculine endurance. During her fieldwork in a Central Anatolian village in the early 1980s, anthropologist Carol Delaney (1991, 269) observed the same phenomenon: "Although military service is not remembered with pleasure, it is a common experience undergone and endured, another test and symbol of pride and honor."

Pride was an underlying theme in many of the narratives I listened to during my interviews, although its manifestations differ greatly depending on the person or the circumstances under which military service is performed. One man, for instance, was clearly not proud of all the things he had to do as a commanding officer fighting in the Southeast against the PKK, but he was proud of having protected all his men in the course of their numerous operations: "No one under my command died" was a sentence he kept repeating throughout the interview. He himself had come back alive, which was in itself a success considering that he had spent close to two years in the war zone.

For many others who have survived military service in the Southeast, the sense of pride is almost nonexistent. The majority of Nadire Mater's respondents in *Mehmedin Kitabı* complain about not being able to talk to anyone about their military service/war experiences. Their stories are hardly funny or interesting to recite in dinner conversations. Success in shooting their (live) targets does not necessarily translate into a proud narrative, either. As the father of a soldier, whose son was jailed after having hijacked a plane in the aftermath of his military service, suggests, "It was in our times that people would talk about their military service memories (*askerlik anıları*). Now nobody does" (Mater 1999, 251). Another soldier explains why:

> People ask things like, "How are you doing? Were you doing your military service? When did you return?" . . . What are you saying? I experienced the rupture of my life there, I can't tell you about it in a couple of words, and even if I do, you won't understand. (Mater 1999, 195)

Here, military service is certainly not seen as a rite of passage into manhood, but a life defining "rupture" that is almost unspeakable. What happens to their sense of masculinity when their military service stories cannot be shared with others and when they see little pride in having killed or having seen their buddies killed next to them? As one soldier puts it to Nadire Mater: "Why would I think of myself as a hero? I am against people fighting and dying . . ." (Mater 1999, 142).

When I read or hear expressions of this kind, I remember my grandfather's reluctance to talk about his service in the Korea[19] war. He would simply say "it was bad" and change the subject. When I once pushed him for more details, he said: "it was war. You walk without knowing whether you are stepping on a landmine. That might happen any minute. You face death all the time. That is war." For him, there was nothing glorious about war and he refused to talk about it at all.

Many of my interviewees had not been in combat, yet they still found it difficult to talk to me about their military service in the interview setting. I was often met with questioning eyes, and sometimes with explicit questioning, when I explained my interests in this topic. They all had many stories to tell about military service; in fact, many of them believed that "military service stories can never be exhausted, there is always more to tell" ("*Askerlik anıları anlatmakla bitmez*"). Yet they also wondered why I, a young woman scholar, was interested in hearing and analyzing them. It was easiest with older people who were in their sixties and seventies. But with everyone else, I experienced a certain mutual unease. Some respondents opened up later in the interview or when I saw them for a second time, but many did not.

Nadire Mater, while describing her interviewing experience suggests that most of the soldiers had taken her as a "mother," and talked about even the most difficult issues with some comfort. She was close in age to their mothers (and she had a daughter around the age of most of the men she interviewed), yet their ability to talk about their pain and suffering was also based on her not being their biological mother. Many mothers complained to Mater about not being able to make their sons tell them about their experiences in the military and many sons explained that they did not want to burden their mothers with all that they had suffered. Nadire Mater's position as a journalist and a woman who was the age of their mother facilitated these interviews. Similarly, Anne Allison talks about how her research on male sexuality in Japan was sometimes aided by her being obviously pregnant at the time: "Because to them I was already almost in the category of mother, it seemed easy for them to speak to me about sexuality" (Allison 1994, 174).

While doing the major part of this research, I was an unmarried woman trying to talk to men, some younger than me, about an experience that was constitutive of their gender identity. It was not easy. In the beginning, I was surprised that the same men who would just keep going on and on about their military service stories in social settings refused to talk to me when I defined it as a research interview. I realized much later that this difficulty itself spoke to gender dynamics. Especially for some of the men who saw me as their equal (because of age or educational/class background), it was unacceptable that their stories of pride, male-bonding, and wisdom turn into research material in my hands. By deciding to research military service, I had transformed the position of a passive listener "who hasn't been there" to one who was willing to listen to all that they had to say in order to analyze and write about it. Moreover, I came to realize that as much as military service marks a passage to manhood, it is *after* the fact and mostly in the *story telling* in all-male as well as mixed groups that many rituals of militarized masculinity are performed. In many ways, I was unsettling the dynamics of those rituals by determining the setting of the story telling.

Many were confident that I could never replicate their wisdom simply by listening to their stories. After all, I had never "been there" and would never be able to go behind the well-guarded gates of the barracks into the all-male space.[20] A male sociology professor, upon learning about my research topic, put it very bluntly: "What can you tell me about military service that I don't already know about? Nothing!" As intimidated as I was by such responses during the early phases of my research, they also helped me better grasp the gender dynamics related to this experience, and most importantly, to be curious about the various performances of hegemonic masculinity related to military service.

Divorcing "the Cultural" from "the Military"?

Military service, as a practice that defines the contours of hegemonic masculinity, offers various rewards for heterosexual, Muslim, Turkish men. Hüsmen's fantasy of being the commander of his home is a vivid example of how these rewards are conceptualized. They unequivocally entail an "othering" of women and legitimize men's authority over them. But it is not only women who are the "others" of this hegemonic masculinity. Diversions from the norm are strongly discouraged by a variety of political, social, and economic mechanisms. Sinan, who graduated from high school in 1983 told me the following story:

> During my junior year in high school, in the *National Security Knowledge* course, we learned about the term *bakaya* (conscription evader). I could not understand it. How is it possible for someone not to do military service? So I asked the teacher, "Sir, why don't these people do their military service?" It was an honest question, but the teacher was very angry with me.

As I have argued in chapter one, military service was not a taken-for-granted, culturally and politically accepted phenomenon for the first citizens of the Turkish Republic. They first had to be persuaded about its *necessity*. Part of this persuasion process involved mythologizing about the "Turkish military spirit." Military service became divorced from wars and citizenship, and redefined as a cultural/national/racial characteristic. As Yael Navaro-Yashin (1998, 15) suggests:

> Where the generation of the 1920s and '30s was conscious of construction (in the sense of building something anew), for the generation of the 1980s and '90s "Turkish culture," as grown old and ingrained, is common sense and common place. What was political was in time transformed into tacit knowledge.

Sinan's inability to imagine any man evading military service is testimony to this change. In the past seventy years, military service has successfully become normalized as a cultural practice.

Without necessarily challenging its cultural value, the fifteen years of warfare between 1984 and 1999 has nevertheless unsettled this taken-for-granted nature of military service. With at least 200,000 conscription evaders and additional numbers of "students" in Turkey and abroad who "legally" postponed their service, what was once unimaginable became everyday reality. Moreover, the established performances of militarized masculinity have been disturbed by the silences caused by the traumatic experiences of those who fought against the PKK. Military service stories are no longer funny and empowering. The soldiers' farewells have replaced them as the new rituals for masculine and national pride. Yet they are one time occurrences that take place before the actual service. It is often trauma and silence that reigns afterwards. In addition, there are thousands who have not even survived the war.

As a result of this rupture, many men and women, like Bünyamin, have begun to associate military service more with war and politics than with culture. This new association has resulted in personal resistance, mainly through evasion and postponement; the kinds of resistance that anthropologist James Scott (1985) has called, "weapons of the weak." Yet, such resistance has not translated into a public debate on the nature of military service;[21] nor has it found a political expression, except for the small and marginalized conscientious objection movement.[22] The next chapter will examine this movement, highlighting both the risks and the new openings created through political dissent to military service.

CHAPTER FOUR
THE ROAD LESS TRAVELED:
CHALLENGING MILITARY SERVICE

May 2001. We are in a café on the second floor of an old levantine building in Beyoğlu, the cultural and political hub of Istanbul. There are about thirty-five people, mostly young, gathered to discuss "conscientious objection" in this small student-run café. I realize later that those who identify themselves as "anarchists" form the majority of the group, but there are also curious observers of various political inclinations. It is quite obvious that many people in the room already know each other. Despite the fact that this is a public event in a city of more than twelve million people, it feels like a closed meeting of friends. I feel more at home when I see a couple of familiar faces in the room. A feminist activist I know from years back is there as one of the core participants. She has become an antimilitarist anarchist supporting conscientious objection as a way of "disembodying the war machine." Similarly, I come across someone I have not seen for more than ten years and start chatting. Finally, everyone finds a place to sit and the room is silent. We are gathered in this small café to observe and discuss 15 May, the International Conscientious Objectors' Day.

The setting is quite informal. No platform, no formal speakers, no fanfare. Several of the organizers discuss how they should begin, and finally, Uğur Yorulmaz, a conscientious objector since May 2000, starts telling us his reasons for refusing military service and recites stories of his transformation from being a student in the Naval Academy to declaring conscientious objector status as an individual political act. His stories are weaved with humor, self-reflection, and human connection. There are no slogans, and no agitation, and no attempt to convert. He gets help from the audience to enact some of the turning points in his stories as theatrical scenes. A young woman becomes the commander of his military school and scolds Uğur for having ruined the sense of discipline in the school. Uğur, in return, demands proper punishment for his acts of disobedience. His undeclared goal is to collect enough disciplinary points so that he can be discharged. The commander is furious because he realizes what Uğur is trying to achieve by these disciplinary punishments. During one of their encounters, the commander shouts at Uğur, "Are you not ashamed of what you are doing under this uniform?" Uğur's response is straightforward: he starts unbuttoning his uniform, saying, "If it is the uniform that is a problem, I can take it off." After much struggle, Uğur manages to have himself freed of all military obligations and starts a new life as a computer programmer in Istanbul.

In the meantime, there are a series of tragic as well as funny incidences where Uğur tries to convince his family of this "bizarre" choice. For instance, during a certain period, he has to postpone his acts of disobedience because his mother becomes sick (with his actions as the main cause of her sickness). A "funny" scene acted out theatrically is of Uğur visiting his grandmother. The grandmother insists that he drink the hot milk she has prepared for him. When Uğur refuses, she offers tea instead. Faced with another refusal, she gets very disappointed and tries hard to get him to drink *anything* hot. The more Uğur resists, the more insistent she becomes. Finally, she asks that he at least eat the cubes of sugar she has prepared for him. Why? Because there are spells on the cubes aimed at bringing some sense to her grandson so that he does not quit military school. The reactions from the group, mixed with much laughter, signal a sense of familiarity with such scenes of family resistance.

How does an antimilitarist, let alone a conscientious objector, explain himself or herself to others? Two years later, when I interviewed Coşkun Üsterci, an anti-militarist human rights activist in Izmir, he explained this phenomenon as follows:

> For many people, we are marginals who stand for naïve, if not absurd and crazy, ideas. Why? Because military service has an important place in the eyes of ordinary people. Ours is a country where a man who has not done his military service is not regarded as a human being. When you look at the polls, you see that the military is the most trusted institution in this country. I mean, in a country where the military enjoys immunity in all realms, from the constitution to the budget discussions in the parliament, who are you to stand up to the military and talk about not doing military service? This is not something people can make sense of.

What I would like to do in this chapter is to discuss how this less traveled road in relation to military service makes sense to the people who have carved it with hope and resilience on the one hand, and pain, suffering, and despair on the other. What are the possibilities and difficulties of challenging the widespread acceptance of military service as a given? What does the short history of conscientious objection in Turkey tell us about the myth of the military-nation and its futures?

The Beginnings: From *Sokak* (the Street) to the Izmir War Resisters' Association

The term "conscientious objector" entered the political lexicon in Turkey for the first time in 1990, only 12 years before the above mentioned meeting in Istanbul, when two young men, Vedat Zencir and Tayfun Gönül, declared their conscientious objection through the weekly magazine *Sokak* (The Street) and the national daily *Güneş* (The Sun), both published in Istanbul.

> My name is Vedat Zencir. I am determined to lead a life free of violence and free of any chain of command. . . . Since age 20, whenever I think of myself as a soldier, I have cramps in my stomach. Living in a chain of command is something that goes totally against my character and my feelings. Moreover, I find it utterly unthinkable to prepare myself to kill people I do not know. Human beings are not sacred beings for me for religious reasons, but, without any religious connotations, I do approach each human life as sacred. That is why I cannot see myself under any structure or institution that is

organized around killing human beings. It is my natural right to live a life based on my own values. Moreover, my values are very simple. I do not want violence. I do not want to live in a chain of command. I do not believe that I should be forced to go against these values.[1]

Soon after the declarations were published, two court cases were opened on the charge that Vedat Zencir and Tayfun Gönül were "alienating the people from the institution of military service," based on the Article 155 of the Turkish Penal Code. Both were tried in civilian courts, with Vedat Zencir being acquitted and Tayfun Gönül sentenced to three months in prison. The verdict was turned into a fine, setting Tayfun Gönül free. The trials raised further discussion and initiated greater interest in the concept of conscientious objection. Osman Murat Ülke, who would later become the first conscientious objector to be forced to report to his unit and serve in military jails for "insubordination," followed the cases of Gönül and Zencir closely as a university student in the southern city of Antalya:

I learned about their conscientious objection through *Sokak* and supported the campaign to set them free . . . Nevertheless, conscientious objection was not a familiar concept for me at that time. It was just something to support. I mean, I did not think about it as something that had to do with *me*. I did not even think about what I myself would do about military service in the future.

It was only in 1992 that Osman Murat Ülke (Ossi[2] hereafter) started thinking about conscientious objection as a choice that stood in front of him as a young man eligible for military service. He was not alone. A small group of friends, who were publishing an anarchist magazine in Antalya, decided to declare their objection to military service and militarism and create "as much noise as possible."

At that time, there was no organized opposition. Yes, Vedat and Tayfun were there as legendary figures for us, but their objection was already a "past" phenomenon, despite the fact that it had only been two years. Moreover, we did not know them personally. We thought to ourselves: We are only a small group of young people and there is no way something like conscientious objection will hold in a country like Turkey. So, the best we can do is create as much noise as possible from where we stand.

As this "small group of young people" was struggling to find ways to publicly express their conscientious objection in Antalya, Vedat Zencir and Tayfun Gönül were working with a small group of antimilitarists and potential objectors in the Aegean city of Izmir to set up the first War Resisters' Association (*Savaş Karşıtları Derneği*, SKD hereafter). Established in December 1992 and closed down by the governor's office in November 1993, SKD was the first attempt to institutionalize the objector movement. It was quickly followed by ISKD (*Izmir Savaş Karşıtları Derneği*-Izmir War Resisters' Association), established in February 1994. For the rest of the 1990s, this association would be the main "hub" of the small objector movement in Turkey.

When Ossi and his friends made contact with Vedat Zencir to get his advice about their activities in Antalya, he invited them to join the SKD in Izmir, where they were planning to organize "waves" of objector declarations. The Antalya group took this invitation seriously and joined their efforts with SKD. The first group to declare their objection was composed of six young men, two of whom were from Antalya. Ossi was persuaded to postpone his objection until a later date when it would make more of an impact. In January 1993, the War Resisters' Association (SKD) organized a public event for the joint declaration of these six objectors. These would be the first organized, institutionally supported objector declarations. To everyone's surprise, no police or legal action followed. The state had turned a blind eye.

In the meantime, SKD was busy preparing to host the International Conscientious Objectors Meeting (ICOM) in Izmir. Organized since 1981, by a group originally formed around the War Resisters' International (WRI), ICOM provided an international forum for discussion and political strategizing for conscientious objectors worldwide. The marking of 15 May as the international day of action for conscientious objectors was born out of these annual meetings in the early 1980s. It would soon gain widespread international recognition. The ICOM in 1993 was a "first" both at the international and at the local level. Internationally, ICOM was for the first time moving out of the confines of Europe, and locally, it was the first forum organized around conscription and conscientious objection.

With close to 90 participants from 19 different countries, the International Conscientious Objectors Meeting in 1993 is remembered as "a success," a significant "learning experience," and a timely "catalyst to the objector movement" by many of its Turkish participants.[3] The most important outcome of ICOM was a sense of empowerment. The objectors may have been few in Turkey, but they now knew that they were part of an international movement that had been there throughout the century. Ossi remembers:

> We had never seen so many people thinking along the same lines with us. We were introduced to many different schools of thought, distinctions, and discussions. It was a condensed learning process for us, both in terms of the discussions on conscientious objection and those on violence in general.

Besides learning about the international history and outreach of the political direction they were taking, the Turkish participants also found themselves challenging much of their received political wisdom. According to Coşkun Üsterci, one of the most transformative experiences about ICOM was meeting with the conscientious objectors from such countries as Israel:

> Getting to know the members of the objector group Yesh Gvul from Israel was a very striking experience for us. At that time, I was an anti-Israeli at heart because all we saw on TV and read about in newspapers was Israel's atrocities: the Sabra-Shatila massacre, all those things that the Palestinians had to endure...All of this persuaded me that there was a strong militarist regime in Israel. And there in the meeting, I learned about how soldiers in the Israeli military were developing strategies to work against the occupation. This was very surprising for us.

Surprises of this kind signaled the formation of new political alliances and revised political sensitivities that went beyond the classical analysis of international and national politics. "Militarism" and "antimilitarism" were new concepts that generated much discussion and self-reflection. Coşkun continues:

> We realized during these discussions that Turkey was indeed an important laboratory for analyzing militarism. It was, in many ways, a safe haven for militarism. I made a presentation in ICOM which reviewed the history of militarism in Turkey, going back to the Ottoman times and the Prussian influence. This was a first attempt at coming up with such an analysis. It was rather long and we had problems translating it to others, but we all sensed that we were pointing our fingers at something really important. Later, we were proven right about this hunch.

If Turkey was a kind of "safe haven for militarism," ICOM proved to be a safe haven for the first systematic analysis of militarism and a shared expression of antimilitarist sentiments for its participants. They were able to address even the most critical issues that preoccupied the Turkish political agenda (the Kurdish issue, the Cyprus problem, and the heightened "Aegean crisis" between the governments of Greece and Turkey) under an international framework enriched by comparative cases such as the Bosnian situation or the Palestinian–Israeli conflict. A new antimilitarist language and a motivated antimilitarist group, empowered by international solidarity, was in the making. The individual acts of conscientious objection, which had started with Tayfun Gönül and Vedat Zencir, were now coming together under a new framework.

Defining Antimilitarism at the Height of the War

It was one thing to put antimilitarist ideas on paper, and yet another to implement them in daily life and render them intelligible through political action. Antimilitarism was not only an unfamiliar concept, it was also highly anxiety provoking. Coşkun reflects on his introduction with the concept in the early 1990s:

> I came out of prison in 1991, having spent 12 years in different prisons around Turkey. I had started questioning militarism and the use of violence in leftist politics while in prison. It was a gradual process of questioning and self-critique. When I met Tayfun and Vedat in 1992, I had a strong sense that the best way to confront the ongoing (Kurdish) war in Turkey was through antimilitarism and conscientious objection. However, despite the fact that I had a certain background in political activism, this was all new and challenging for me. I mean, how can you organize a political movement against the Turkish military? How can you be successful with such political action? After a few brief discussions, I was persuaded that this made a lot of sense. A critique of militarism is something that the leftist movement in Turkey has left unexplored. I came to realize that any serious oppositional movement in Turkey had to base itself on antimilitarism. Learning about conscientious objection came a little later.

It is quite striking that one of the spokespersons for antimilitarism in Turkey today recites his difficulties in accepting this concept merely ten years ago. Antimilitarism was not embraced readily and easily even by those who would later be its champions. Besides revealing the long and difficult personal journeys to the development of this "marginal" movement, this self-narrative also points to other important aspects of the movement: self-reflection and critique, humility, and the willingness to share and learn from personal experiences. Ferda Ülker, one of the most active antimilitarist activists to this day, discusses the initial years of their activism in similar terms:

> Nobody is immune to the effects of militarism. I mean, we define ourselves as antimilitarists, but even we are having a very difficult time trying to define the contours of this road. We question militarism in various ways, but it is so embedded in our everyday lives that it is very difficult to free ourselves of its effects and to start talking with a new language. Take the term *şiddetten arınmışlık* (nonviolence). It was not even in our vocabulary seven or eight years ago. There are so many ways in which we ourselves reproduce violence in our everyday lives, in our language.

For many people who have been associated with the objector movement, defining a new political language based on antimilitarism has been the major challenge. Having come out of leftist political organizations or having close ties with such organizations, one of their major struggles was confronting the militarism embedded in these political organizations. According to Coşkun Üsterci:

> The main weakness of the Turkish left is that it has left militarism unexplored and unquestioned. We experienced this problem quite starkly in relation to the Kurdish war. Many people in the Turkish left, directly or indirectly, ended up supporting militarist responses by the Kurdish or leftist opposition to the war. They were also influenced by [Kurdish] nationalism. This is something that the left in Turkey has to re-evaluate if it wants to re-structure itself and create a new political culture.

Yavuz, a conscientious objector from Istanbul since 1993, pointed to the ironic history of the left being "bulldozed over" by military interventions and still believing in the military road to social change. The final intervention in 1980, he believed, had resulted in some questioning, but still "militarism is deeply embedded in the [leftist] culture. In that sense, our political messages are quite new." For Ferda, too, the challenge from the Left has been one of the most important obstacles in their organizing:

> We always said "no to the military, no to the mountain!" We were against militarism of all kinds. So we had lots of problems with the left, with the very people we protested with. Still, in Turkey, people do not see a third way. It is either Saddam or Bush; you either have to support Irak or America.

Coşkun posed the question of violence in the Left as one of "self-critique":

> Especially because there is a long tradition of armed resistance in the Turkish left, it is essential that we undertake a serious critique of militarism. How is it that we have used a major tool of capitalist exploitation, that is militarism, in such an unquestioning manner, and turned ourselves into small militarized political groups? It is essential that we ask ourselves this question.

This emphasis on self-critique and the quest for a new political language was at the center of the political activities of SKD and ISKD from their inception. Both in group meetings and in public events, they were searching for ways to develop a nonviolent response to militarism in general, and the ongoing war in Turkey's southeast, in particular. Ossi explains:

> Our main goal was to create an antimilitarist language. We wanted this radical antimilitarist language to create a new political tradition. We knew that it would not turn into a mass movement right away. It had to start small. But we hoped that putting one stone on top of another, we would slowly build a solid tradition.

Their work would entail two lines of activism. On the one hand, they sought to create alliances with leftist groups, human rights organizations, and Kurdish nationalist groups, to establish platforms for peaceful response to the ongoing war. On the other hand, they confronted the military establishment by challenging conscription and the trial of civilians in military courts. For them, this latter line of activism was *also* about the war; it was about "diminishing the human resources of the war."

Conscientious objection was being formulated as an individual choice and as a line of political activism, just when the war in the Southeast was reaching a peak. As the Human Rights Watch[4] suggested in 1995:

> The Turkish government's ten-year battle with the Kurdistan Workers Party [PKK] reached new heights of violence in 1994. Of the 13,000 civilians and soldiers estimated to have been killed between 1984 and 1994, half died in the past two years. Both security forces and the PKK continued to violate basic human rights of the civilian population in the southeast, with police targeting those suspected of collaborating with the PKK, and the PKK in turn striking at those whom it considered state supporters, such as teachers, civil servants, and village guards.

The government in Turkey had changed during the November 1991 elections and despite the fact that the members of the coalition had come to power promising to "recognize the Kurdish reality," the fighting had intensified. Violence escalated after Spring 1992.

It was at this juncture that the Izmir conscientious objection group was born. One of their actions in 1993 was to help form a "Peace Platform" in Izmir, with representatives from various nongovernmental organizations and trade unions. Coşkun remembers this platform to be "the first antiwar platform in Turkey" and suggests that they were able to "squeeze in a sentence about the necessity of non-violent forms of political action into the joint statement." The platform organized a big delegation to participate in the Spring celebrations in various Southeastern cities on 21 March 1993. What members of the platform did was to bear witness to the human rights violations during these events and raise a voice against the war. Until SKD was closed down (in the fall of 1993), they were quite active in this platform.

In mixed platforms of this kind, what most members remember is a constant struggle to recognize the use of violence by nonstate actors, alongside the violations of the state. Their antimilitarist stance was not welcomed by members of the (mostly leftists) oppositional political groups and human rights organizations in these platforms. Violence was either openly defended as part of "revolutionary struggle" or silently ignored when it came to its use by non-state actors. That is why Coşkun remembers the one sentence about the need for nonviolent political actions they were able to "squeeze into" the statements of the Peace Platform with surprise. In the midst of this political athmosphere of heightened fighting in the Southeast, a notable increase in human rights violations by state and non-state actors alike, and antiwar coalitions that remained ambivalent about the use of violence for political aims, it was no easy task to open up a space for antimilitarist politics.

Precisely because they did not define antimilitarism as anti-Turkish-militarism, the War Resisters' Association (SKD) was also active in developing new forms of expression against *all* wars and forming international ties with conscientious objectors around the world. For instance, in August 1993, they used street theater to remind people of *their* responsibility in wars around the world on the anniversaries of the Hiroshima and Nagasaki atomic bombs. They exploded a fake bomb in a central park dedicated to 'human rights' and lay down on the ground as "dead" people, with their faces painted in black and white. They also stopped passersby and asked them to reflect on their responsibility in "the war machine."[5] Ossi remembers this event as one of the most creative of their activities:

> We were constantly testing new forms of expression and action. Stopping people on the way, putting a piece of writing in their hands and saying "You are responsible!" was very provocative and effective. I remember an old lady who came to us and said, "Son, please tell me why I am responsible."

By fall 1993, SKD was closed down by the governor's office. The objector movement was going into its second phase, which would be marked by more controversy, more action, and more contact with the authorities.

Having faced their first blow from local authorities, members of SKD decided to reformulate their line of action and establish a new association which would be more difficult to close down. In the meantime, they wanted to strengthen their ties with the international antimilitarist movement. Ossi, who had grown up in Germany where his parents were migrant workers, was sent to Germany to build connections and inform people about the initial steps of the objector struggle in Turkey. A trip planned for a few weeks lasted four months:

> I traveled from one city to another, one village to another, giving talks and engaging in intense discussions. This trip formed the basis of a series of relationships that would continue for more than ten years. There were many positive outcomes, many new ideas, and new inputs. For instance, we first learned about nonviolence training during this trip and have been developing and practicing it since then.

In the meantime, things were heating up back in Turkey. In December 1993, the former president of SKD and a conscientious objector from Izmir were interviewed in a mainstream national TV channel (HBB),[6] which resulted in an investigation initiated by the General Chief of Staff. Providing a legal turning point, the resulting court case was tried in a military court. The charge was "alienating the people from the institution of military service" (Article 155 of the Penal Code) and it encompassed the interviewees, along with the reporter and the producer of the TV program. The reporter and producer were given two-month imprisonment sentences, while Aytek Özel, the former president, was sentenced to one year and fifteen days. All would serve as civilians in military jails.

This case provided an important precursor for future trials. It was now made possible for civilians to be tried in military courts during 'normal' times (as opposed to times of Emergency Rule or war).[7] This development was testimony to the heightened anxiety within the military ranks created by the acts of even a few conscientious objectors. It was also testimony to the high price one would need to pay to engage in any action to declare or support conscientious objection.

This first military trial may have discouraged future reporters from covering the actions of conscientious objectors or discouraged potential objectors themselves, but it provided a renewed commitment on the part of the Izmir objector movement. On 25 February 1994, a new association under the name *Izmir Savaş Karşıtları Derneği* (ISKD-Izmir War Resisters' Association) was established. Ossi had come back on the day of its establishment together with a group of supporters from Germany. The goals of the new association were cited as follows:

- To struggle against wars, militarism, and racism;
- To bring together and create ties of solidarity among people who share these goals;
- To contribute to the creation of a new culture based on peace and freedoms, replacing the hegemonic culture of racist-militarism.[8]

War was defined as an "act against humanity, an act of aggression by the male world towards women, and an initiator of ecological disaster." The group paid special attention to differentiating themselves from those who talked about "dirty" wars or "just" wars. For them, all wars were dirty and "just war" could only be an oxymoron.

> We are asking you a simple question: Is there a war in our country today? We are not saying "dirty" or "just"; we are not saying "terror" or "fight against terror." We are just saying war…A war that is experienced in "Kurdistan", "the region," or "the Southeast."…We know that there are very few people who would be able to answer this question without using the qualifications in quotation marks cited above. This means that there are very few people who think about wars independent of the political positions that create these qualifications in quotation marks.[9]

The emphasis was on the need to create an antimilitarist line of political action that would refuse the militarism embedded in state practices (which, for them, included military service) alongside the militarism embedded in oppositional politics (including the armed Kurdish struggle). The solution was not "pacifism," but an engaged activism that included acts of civil disobedience, nonviolent action, and conscientious objection:

> ISKD welcomes all individuals and groups who are interested in working on such topics as antimilitarism, the women's movement, nonviolence, anti-chauvinism, ecologism, and solidarity with the victims of war.[10]

This multifaceted approach to social change distinguished ISKD and its activists from the majority of existing political organizations in the 1990s. They were not after a "revolution" and there was no "basic contradiction" that defined political reality. As Ferda points out, during this time, there was a prevalent perception of antimilitarists as "sweet, little marginals" who were too idealistic, thus not to be taken seriously. This attitude would change with Ossi's indefinite imprisonment. Conscientious objection was not to be taken lightly in the land of the "military-nation."

"Osman Murat Ülke: Conscientious Objector Imprisoned for Life"

This was the catchy title of an Amnesty International Report in 1998.[11] Osman Murat Ülke (Ossi) spent more than two years in military prisons between 1996 and 1999 (with eleven trials and two "releases" in between). A year after declaring his conscientious objection on 1 September 1995 (International Peace Day), he was taken under custody and sent to his military unit to "become a soldier." Refusing to wear the military uniform and comply with other "orders," and declaring that he refused to be a "soldier," Ossi was sent to prison. After some stations in between, he ultimately found himself in the Eskişehir military prison, in Northwest Turkey. In the absence of the legal recognition of conscientious objection, his charge was "insubordination." After he served his time, he would be sent back to his unit, again refuse to wear the uniform, and find himself in the same prison cell. This was a vicious cycle with no legal way out. Hence the title "imprisoned for life." With the existing laws, no one could tell if Ossi would stay in prison for 20 days, 2 years, 20 years, or, indeed, all his life. He was the first conscientious objector to experience this vicious cycle, and until Mehmet Bal's case in 2002, he would remain the only one.

The first months of Ossi's imprisonment were marked with confrontation and negotiation. After spending two days in the nearby Buca Prison, four days in the Ulucanlar Prison in Ankara, he was transferred to the Mamak Military Prison, again in Ankara. His first concern in Mamak was that he was asked to wear the "prison uniform."

> I told them that the reason I was there was because I had refused to wear the military uniform. Therefore, it was impossible for me to accept to wear the prison uniform.

His refusal resulted in solitary confinement in a small, dark cell below the ground, which did not even have a bed to sleep on. Ossi formulated his demands from the prison authorities and started a hunger strike. On the twenty-fourth day, he had reached an agreement with the Colonel commander of the prison. His demands were accepted, but only days before he was released. Therefore, he "did not have enough time to enjoy the gains of this hunger strike." Upon release, he was transferred (with soldiers accompanying him) to his military unit in Bilecik. The vicious cycle had begun. Since he refused to wear the military uniform, he was sent to the nearby military prison in Eskişehir for "insubordination."

When I asked Ossi what kinds of responses he received from the soldiers and officers who were involved in the various stages of this journey, he said:

> Many of the soldiers and officers were astonished. But they often refrained from expressing their ideas. After all, their superiors were always nearby. Still, many of them approved of my objection; only a few were critical. I mean, there were all kinds of

reactions, covering a wide spectrum. I cannot really generalize. . . . There were even young officers who would wake me up in the middle of the night to talk to me about my political views. They were particularly curious about my views on the military. They would often tell me that things inside the military were different from what I imagined. We had discussions on the role of the military in a democratic society. It was exhausting, but also interesting and fun.

Wherever he went, Ossi was becoming an object of curiosity. Who was this individual who dared to take on the whole institution of the military as an adversary? What kind of political motivations did he have? Was he really "sincere" about his objection, or was he doing this for some other political aim? When Ossi was sent to the Eskişehir Military Prison, he found himself going through the same discussions with his prison-mates. Yet, the conditions had changed radically. From facing the military as an institution, and various officers and soldiers as individuals processing his case, he had now become a part of a "social unit."

The prison, like many others in the 1990s, was composed of cells each of which had a different make up and a different "head." Ossi had been assigned to a cell of 12 prisoners headed by a young man, Mehmet Bal, who was known to be tolerant for differences. His cell was more "peaceful," despite the fact that it housed people from many different backgrounds. Yet, some differences weighed heavier than others. Ossi remembers religion being a major difference between himself and the rest of his cellmates. As an atheist among a group of pious believers, he remembers sticking out as an oddity that needed to be explained. For this reason and others, including his objection to military service, he was soon marginalized in the cell.

> I was now living in a social unit. I had to survive and resist at the same time. At the same time as I was trying to relate to others in the cell, I was also trying to resist their perceived wisdom. The first month passed with this tension.

Soon, Ossi became friends with someone else who seemed marginal and solitary. From the outside, they looked like mirror opposites. Ossi was an atheist anarchist; his new friend was a devout Muslim who belonged to the *Aczmendi*[12] sect and hated leftists and anarchists. Their life experiences were very different from one another. Yet, there was one quality about this man that helped him share Ossi's marginal status: he was gay. In Ossi's terms, he was "ruptured inside." He knew well that he was gay and could not be otherwise, and he also knew that his religion regarded gay identity as abnormal. He was serving in this military prison because he had shared his gayness with his commander, asking to be assigned tasks that would not involve close interaction with other soldiers. Nevertheless, no one else in the cell knew about his gay identity, except for Ossi and Mehmet Bal. As they became friends, they found other ways of relating to one another, other than being the marginals of the cell. Ossi remembers that when he told his friend about "civil disobedience," it immediately made sense to him: "He saw his own refusal to pray in state mosques as an act of 'civil disobedience,' although this terminology was very foreign to him and his politics." Later on, Ossi would go through a similar process of long, engaged, and, at times, tense discussions with the head of the cell, Mehmet Bal. Like his other friend, Mehmet was also a devout Muslim who prayed five times a day and came from a conservative, inner Anatolian background. He had further been involved in the ultra-nationalist (*ülkücü*) movement. As they tried to understand each other on the long days and nights inside the walls of the Eskişehir prison, Ossi and Mehmet had no idea that they were not only sharing the present, but carving a joint future as well.

The Objector Movement and Its First Campaign

Ossi was the first conscientious objector to be taken to his military unit and to be forced into military service. From its inception, the Izmir War Resisters' Association was preparing itself for campaigns to set conscientious objectors free. Ossi was their first case. Moreover, he was one of the most active members of the Association, a close friend to many, boyfriend to another core member. It was a personal campaign, as well as a political one.

When I asked Ossi how he was able to endure the conditions in the various jails, the hunger strike, and the looming uncertainty about how long he was going to be "inside," he reminded me of their previous preparations as a group and of the strong support coming from the "outside."

> I was very lucky because I had come to that point well-prepared from years of organizing around this issue. I mean, I was psychologically equipped, and politically ready to face the consequences of my objection. We were also ready as a group. We had been expecting one of the objectors to be taken in and we were prepared to give him support. My friends never left me alone. At any given moment, there were more than enough people who were actively giving support. Every week, they came to visit me in Eskişehir. . . . I never felt alone when I was there.

It was also important for Ossi that he was able to get six or seven new books every week. In his words, he was able to "create his own island inside the prison" with the help of these books. He read constantly, mostly books in history, anthropology, and science fiction, his "passion since childhood." After the initial days of adjustment, his relations with his cellmates, especially with Mehmet, had improved significantly, but he still felt very different from everybody else and, "ultimately, alone." The books were his "saviors." In time, they became other people's saviors, as well. Ossi's cellmates, particularly Mehmet, had become dedicated readers of his rotating library collection.

The support Ossi received was not limited to weekly visits, the provision of books and other needs, and group attendance in his trials. Izmir War Resisters' Association, as well as other antimilitarists around Turkey, was campaigning hard to draw attention to Ossi's case in particular and the right to conscientious objection in general. Their efforts were not in vain. Osman Murat Ülke soon became a familiar name to many people both inside and outside Turkey. The Amnesty International took on the issue in 1998 and issued a report in May, depicting Osman Murat Ülke as "a prisoner of conscience" and asking for his immediate release.

> Amnesty International believes that everyone should have the right to refuse to perform military service for reasons of conscience or profound conviction arising from religious, ethical, moral, humanitarian, philosophical, political, or similar motives. . . . The right to refuse to perform military service for reasons of conscience is inherent in the right to

freedom of thought, conscience, and religion as recognized in Article 18 of the Universal Declaration of Human Rights, Article 18 of the International Covenant on Civil and Political Rights, and Article 9 of the European Convention for the Protection of Human Rights and Fundamental Freedoms. (*Turkey: Osman Murat Ülke— Conscientious Objector Imprisoned for Life* [1998])

Besides asking for Ossi's immediate release, Amnesty International also called on the Turkish government to issue "alternative civilian service" for all conscientious objectors, citing the recommendations of the United Nations Commission on Human Rights and the Council of Europe. As Coşkun, one of the key figures in this campaign, suggests, "international support was truly crucial in this process. If Ossi was able to go through all that with no serious consequences, in a period that was much more complicated and risky than today [due to the war in the Southeast], it was thanks to the international support and solidarity we received, as well as the national campaign we undertook."

It was a small group of less than fifteen antimilitarist activists who had coordinated this multifaceted campaign. According to Coşkun, the effectiveness of the campaign was due to a combination of factors:

> Ossi had developed a course of action that was truly nonviolent. He was very careful, calm and controlled. Therefore, he was able to tie the hands of militarism. On the other hand, we undertook a truly effective campaign. . . . We constantly wrote articles and letters to draw attention to the issue. We went from door to door, visiting writers and journalists, including people like Orhan Pamuk, Ali Kırca, and Oral Çalışlar, giving them files on Ossi's case. We also organized antimilitarist events; for instance, a group of women demonstrated outside of the Eskişehir Military Prison. We also alerted the human rights organizations about this issue. Of course, the political situation was in our favor. Because of the war, the Kurdish groups and their supporters were very much interested in this campaign. Kurdish newspapers, pragmatically, did not publish the parts of our statement that called on people not to become "soldiers, nor guerillas," but they did contribute to making our campaign visible.

It is this visibility that remains from years of activism around Ossi's case and conscientious objection. With this campaign, the term "conscientious objection" had reached the masses and was identified with the name Osman Murat Ülke. An ex-soldier interviewed by the journalist Nadire Mater notes that he learned about this concept through Ossi's campaign:

> At that time, I did not know [about conscientious objection], because the campaigns against compulsory conscription carried out by people like Osman Murat Ülke and Vedat Zencir were not there yet. . . . So the solution I found on my own was to lose weight. If I had known about such campaigns, I would have joined them. In our society, there are very few people who support the campaign against compulsory conscription; one person here, three others there. Why? Because no one gives you a girl to marry unless you have served in the military. You are not treated as a man. (Mater 1999, 35)

Coşkun Üsterci remembers a remark made by Nadire Mater, with a smile on his face: "She said, 'you were a small bunch, yet you managed to shake up Turkey as a whole.' And she was quite right." Despite the fact that the campaign was successful in making conscientious objection visible and intelligible in Turkey, that Ossi enjoyed support, solidarity, and empowerment in this process, that a "small bunch" of antimilitarists were able to "shake up Turkey," it also had its toll on its organizers. Izmir War Resisters' Association was closed down for about seven months in this process due to a statement they had made against the trial of civilians in military courts, which resulted in the loss of their limited infrastructure. Coşkun has vivid memories of this period, "This happened in the most intense period of the campaign and made life all the more difficult for us. We had to meet in coffeehouses to coordinate the campaign. It became very difficult to communicate with one another." The small group of supporters was already exhausted from months of organizing and constant travel to Eskişehir (a distance of approximately six hours by bus). They all had jobs to attend to and money to raise in order to cover the various court, travel, and other expenses. Ferda remembers both the excitement and the exhaustion resulting from this process: "We experienced everything in fast track. We did a lot; we indeed did a lot in a short time. Yet we also consumed a lot. In the end we were burned out."

For Ossi, too, the campaign was exactly as they had imagined it to be. In fact, "it could not have been better." This was exactly what enabled him to keep his calm throughout his years inside military prisons.

> The walls around you are physical. I mean, in the face of your struggle, their static power is really insignificant. When you also consider the historicity behind it . . . I mean, the fact that things were not always this way, and that they will not be this way in the future. . . . This is only a moment in history, and it is a historical moment because you are playing with certain principles, shaking them up. Realizing this gives you incredible power. All your problems, all that you lack in this particular moment become meaningless. You are empowered by the whole process because things are going exactly as they should. Indeed, [the campaign] could not have been better.

Yet, what did all of this mean for the future of conscription practices in Turkey, the future of antimilitarist activism, and the future of the Izmir War Resisters' Association? The years following the campaign would be dedicated to the in-depth, and at times painful, evaluation of these questions.

Mehmet Bal: The Second Objector in Prison

Between 1996 and 1999, Ossi was taken to court eleven times and released twice, spending up to four months outside. He remembers this vicious cycle as being very "exhausting:"

> You set up a certain life in prison; you start doing your translations, reading your books, having conversations with your cell-mates, and so on. Then, suddenly, you are released, but instead of going home, you are sent to your military unit and the whole thing starts over. You are put in a cold, solitary cell; you face humiliation in your unit. Each time, you spend about ten days going through this procedure, and then you find your calm in the prison. It lasts for about three months, and then it starts all over.

In other cases, Ossi was able to go home, only to attend a court case after a month or several months, and be taken to his military unit, to "start all over." His final release was on 9 March 1999, and he has been "out" since then.

Ossi was tried for continued acts of "insubordination" and currently has the status of a "deserter." From the beginning of this long process, he has denied all charges:

> I kept refusing the charge of insubordination, because I had refused to be a soldier. If I am not a soldier, how can I be guilty of "insubordination"? And I am not at all a deserter. I never accepted those charges and asked for my release.

As the 1998 Amnesty International Report demonstrates, Ossi told the court:

> I maintain that the military court has no legal right to try me. I never became a soldier. Therefore, I have won the trial from the start: it will not change my attitude and thus will fail in its purpose.

His position has not changed since 1999. He still identifies himself as a conscientious objector, refusing to perform any kind of military (or other state) service. His life is limited in various ways. From opening a bank account, to getting a legal job with social security,[13] to applying for a passport or a new I.D. card, he has to stay away from all kinds of procedures that will bring him face to face with "the list of conscription evaders." If he insisted, he would at the very least be denied these services. More likely, he would be taken into custody to be sent to his military unit. Ossi believes that the state authorities are officially keeping him on their "search" lists, while making no attempt to find him. "They know where I live and work. If they wanted, they would find me right away." Then, why is Ossi (and other conscientious objectors) not taken under custody? According to Ossi,

> It is because they have no interest in arresting me. Yet they also cannot not search for me, because that would contradict with the rule of law. So, this is the perfect solution. They both search for me and leave me alone at the same time. I don't think the state wants the international campaigns such an arrest would initiate. They won't gain anything by taking me in. They know that they were not able to weaken my resolution in those two years. What would the Turkish Armed Forces gain from keeping someone like me inside military jails?

Whether this is the main reason or not, one thing is certain: the state authorities have consistently turned a blind eye on conscientious objectors (whose numbers are currently around thirty) since Ossi's release in March 1999.

What has this meant for the objector movement? The number of objectors has kept increasing, though at a slow pace. Each year, on 15 May, the International Conscientious Objectors' Day, various events are organized in Istanbul, Izmir, and Ankara. Some of these events involve new declarations, others (like the one I recited at the beginning of this chapter) are days for sharing and remembering of past declarations. In the meantime, the movement has lost its "Izmir-based" quality and has become more dispersed. An anarchist, antimilitarist newsletter, *Oldsletter*, prepared by a small group in Ankara has been running since 2000. A web-based discussion group (the "*savaskarsitlari*" Yahoo Group, which had 142 members in

January 2004) and an antimilitarist website (*www.savaskarsitlari.org*) were initiated by conscientious objectors from Istanbul in 2000. With these web initiatives and the establishment of the informal Istanbul Antimilitarist Initiative (IAMI), Istanbul has become the new "hub" of antimilitarist organizing. As a consequence, it was the Istanbul group that stood out in the solidarity campaign for Mehmet Bal when he declared his objection in October 2002, in the midst of intensified discussions on the U.S.-led war on Iraq.

Mehmet Bal's declaration came as a great surprise to many. First of all, no one from the objector movement (except Ossi) knew Mehmet. More importantly, however, his background did not fit anybody's expectations of conscientious objectors. Mehmet was born in 1975 in a small town in the Inner Aegean province of Uşak, as the sixth of seven children in a lower-middle-class family. In his own words, his family possesses the "typical Anatolian rural characteristics." They are highly religious and "moderately conservative." Mehmet graduated from a vocational high school and then started working as a mechanic. In the meantime, he became active in "ultra-nationalist" (*ülkücü*) politics, with friends from the same circles. He does not remember this involvement to be a "conscious choice;" nationalism in these circles was simply a fact of life.

After three years of working as a mechanic, Mehmet had reached the age of military service.

> I had no intentions to go for military service. Despite the fact that I was a nationalist, I did not. No one wants to do military service. Everyone wants to find a way to evade it.

However, he became involved with two of his friends in a robbery that resulted in murder and changed his mind about military service. Since no one knew that they were responsible for these crimes, the three friends decided that it was a good time to join the military and stay away from Uşak for a while. From May to September 1995, this plan worked. In September, one of Mehmet's friends was arrested, providing the police the names of his accomplices. The trial went on for five years. Since Mehmet was being tried when he was officially a "soldier," he had to stay in the Eskişehir Military Prison during this time. After his verdict was given (16 years imprisonment), he was transferred to a civilian prison, where he would stay for two more years until his release through the 2002 Amnesty Law.

> If you ask me if I had killed that man? No. But I was there as an accomplice. That is why I did not want to pull myself away from the case [saying I was not guilty].... Of course, I wish that this incident had never happened. But remorse does not change the reality that a human life was taken. I don't see those seven years in prison as a loss, because they provided a turning point in my life.

Mehmet remembers the first couple of years in prison as being marked by confusion and depression. The trial was going on and on, and he was not able to find all the answers to his questions in religion.

> I gave myself to religion first. I was doing all the necessary rituals on a daily basis. But the more I asked questions, the more difficult it became to find satisfactory answers.

Mehmet's questions would increase and diversify with each new person coming into the cell. During his five years (ages 20 through 25) inside the Eskişehir prison, Mehmet got to know approximately 2,000 people. The cell accommodated 12 people, but there was very rapid turn around. Moreover, all the "problem cases" were sent to Mehmet's cell as it was known to be peaceful. As a devout Muslim, he spent days and months with Jehova's Witnesses, gays, leftists, and an anarchist conscientious objector, Ossi. With each acquaintance, his ideological and religious worldview would be challenged.

> Everything I knew told me that these were "bad people". That's what I had been taught. Yet, as I lived with them in the same place, eating at the same table, breathing the same air, I realized that they were more "human" than some others I easily identified with. They were able to share, be respectful to others, and so on. All my prejudices were being shattered one by one. Of course, it was an unsettling experience to have everything that I had taken for granted up until the age of 23–24 undermined. No one could have persuaded me about these people being good by talking to me about them. But I was experiencing it first-hand. Especially this guy Ossi who claimed to be an anarchist and an antiwar activist.... He was challenging and resisting what I regarded as the sacred institution in this country, the military.

It was not only Ossi's ideas that had caught Mehmet's attention. He was also intrigued by his way of relating to violence. He observed that Ossi never responded to (symbolic or physical) violence by using violence. This was, at first, counter-intuitive to Mehmet:

> His methods were very different from mine. I would respond in kind when someone assaulted me physically or verbally. Ossi did not. He did not let the other person's framework determine his actions. I was trying to make sense of this...

In his efforts to "make sense," Mehmet had many long conversations and heated debates with Ossi. In the course of their two years of interaction, Mehmet's resistance to new ideas had changed radically. In his own words, he had become more interested in "knowledge," rather than "belief." He reacted strongly to people who tried to make him believe in one thing or another. He wanted to *learn*, not believe. He started reading books, particularly philosophy books. He was hungry for new answers to his questions and for new ideas.

> I slowly began to gain pleasure from learning, and from that point on the prison lost its meaning.... Yes, I was living inside those four walls, but in my thoughts I was elsewhere. It was only my body that was in prison.

His whole routine had changed. He slept less and his interactions with others around him gradually became minimized. He remembers reading up to six hundred pages per day: novels, philosophy, anthropology, history, and other nonfiction. It was difficult to quench his thirst. At the end of his five years in Eskişehir, it had become clear that he would have to spend at least another eleven years in civilian prison.

> I thought to myself: I will spend eleven more years in prison, but in the end I will come out as a totally new person. I wanted to make good use of those 11 years. I was determined to keep changing and fight monotony.

When Mehmet got transferred to a civilian prison in Manisa, he became even more of a recluse. He asked to be put in a solitary cell (which is usually used for punishment) and stayed there for six months, so that he would not be interrupted by others. All he wanted to do was read. After six months, he was forced to relocate to a bigger cell with other prisoners, but his routine did not change much. He would wake up at seven a.m. and keep reading all day long.

Mehmet's sentence abruptly ended at the end of his second year in Manisa when the government passed an Amnesty Law that was eventually amended to include cases like his. On 23 May 2002, he was free, but he still had his military service to complete. He was given only one day to see his family; he had to report to his unit in Mersin the next day. This obligation changed Mehmet's feelings about the amnesty:

> At that point, it was more difficult for me to do military service and to face the military institution than to serve in jail. In that sense, I was not happy to have been released.

In any case, he was determined to go through his fourteen months of remaining service without getting himself into trouble. He spent the first four months avoiding arms training, telling his superiors that he had promised himself not to touch guns due to his criminal past. In return, he was sent for psychiatric treatment to get over this situation. Mehmet received depression treatment and medication until, one day, he had an argument with his psychiatrist. That day he decided to put his thoughts about the military and militarism on paper. Instead of going back to the garrison, he stayed at a friend's place for four days and formulated his ideas. On 23 October 2002, Mehmet Bal faxed his declaration not to serve in the military to the media:

> Militarism, in its essence, sees destruction as a way of solving problems. . . . Another intrinsic characteristic of militarism is unconditional obedience. . . . The wars led by militarism and its supporters do not only harm human beings. The various nuclear and biological weapons possessed by militaries also harm the environment. What can justify such harm? . . . Based on my personal experiences and my nine-and-a-half months of military experience, I have decided that I cannot refuse to listen to my conscience any longer. From this point onwards, I refuse to perform any services given to me, against my will and conscience, by military or civilian, local or universal persons, institutions or structures, and declare my conscientious objection.[14]

Like Osman Murat Ülke, Mehmet Bal's declaration was also in the form of a "total objection."[15] His refusal encompassed much more than "military service," he resisted all kinds of "compulsory service" that would go against his "will and conscience."

The rest of Mehmet Bal's story is also similar to Ossi's. He returned to his unit to turn in his military uniform and identity card. He was sent to the nearest military prison, where the commander forced him to wear the prison uniform, which he refused. He was forcefully dressed and kept in cuffs and shackles for days. As soon as they were removed, he would take off his military uniform, to be punished by solitary confinement. Finally, he started a hunger strike that went on for 33 days.

From 60 kilos, he dropped down to 40 kilos. Unlike Ossi, Mehmet's hunger strike did not end with his demands being accepted by the prison administration. To everyone's surprise, it ended with his release.

Mehmet was charged with several counts of insubordination and desertion, as well as "alienating the people from the institution of military service" under Article 155 of the Penal Code. After attending a series of court cases in Mersin, where he would take off his military uniform as soon as his handcuffs were unlocked, he was transferred to the General Staff Military Court to be tried for Article 155. Since his medical condition was getting worse, he was taken there in an ambulance. However, he never had to appear in court in Ankara, because the indictment prepared by the General Staff Prosecutor argued that there were no grounds to charge him for "alienating the people from the institution of military service." According to the Prosecutor (Major Zekeriya Duran), Mehmet Bal's declaration was protected under the "right of conscience and expression," and indeed, it was everyone's "basic right and duty to preserve world peace." However, it was not realistic for a country to abolish its army and that anyone who declared conscientious objection should take into consideration the outcome of their actions. In Mehmet's case, the Prosecutor found no evidence that he was doing anything more than making public his own act of conscience.[16]

Mehmet was acquitted and released on the condition that he would surrender to his unit the next day. Declaring that he would not "surrender" to his unit because he refused to perform military service, Mehmet went to stay with his parents, after receiving medical treatment in Ankara. His body was weak after 33 days of hunger strike and he had bruises on his arms and legs resulting from the use of cuffs and shackles. He was accompanied by his attorney Suna Coşkun (who had also repre- sented Ossi several years before) to the Human Rights Foundation for medical examination and to the Human Rights Association for a declaration.

"Nobody is Born a Soldier": Supporting Mehmet Bal, Refusing the War on Iraq

In the meantime, antimilitarists in Istanbul, Ankara, Izmir, and Adana had formed "Solidarity Groups" that followed Mehmet's case closely, attending his court cases and publicizing his conscientious objection through various channels. Until Mehmet was released on 27 November 2002, no one except Ossi knew Mehmet personally. This time, they were organizing for an anonymous conscientious objector and not a friend. There were other differences between the two campaigns. Ossi's campaign was coordinated by an institutionalized body, the Izmir War Resisters' Association. By the time Mehmet declared his objection, ISKD had closed down and there was no other institutional infrastructure. Yet, there were "initiatives" around which antimilitarists organized, mainly in Istanbul, Izmir and Ankara, along with a website updated daily, and a vibrant internet discussion group. Much of the organizing and communication during this campaign would take place in these virtual spaces. The Solidarity Groups formed in the different cities would coordinate their actions on the web as they raised awareness of Mehmet's case both nationally and internationally. Mehmet remembers the first time he saw his name mentioned in one of the daily newspapers, *Radikal*:

> It was earlier in the process, before they prevented my access to newspapers. I saw the article written by Murat Çelikkan[17] and said to myself, "that's it; my declaration has reached the right people." You know, I had just sent it out to the press without establishing any contacts with anyone.

It also heartened him to see people he did not even know attend his court cases and give him support. He knew from his lawyer, Suna Coşkun, about the Solidarity Groups formed just for him and felt good about "not being all alone."

Once Mehmet Bal was released, he was able to access the newspaper articles written about him, meet with his supporters, and share his experiences with those who were interested. The media was mostly silent about Mehmet Bal, but occasional news of his condition, the hunger strike, and the international responses to his case were reported in some newspapers.[18] Particularly influential was an article by the renowned writer Yıldırım Türker (2002) in the Sunday supplement of the national daily *Radikal*. He was the first one in national media to mention Mehmet Bal's atypical story of ultra-nationalist-turned-conscientious-objector and publish a summary of his declaration. Following Mehmet's release, more journalists became interested in capturing his story. The following month, a one-page interview with Mehmet was published in the Sunday supplement of one of the most widely read national dailies, *Hürriyet*, which emphasized his transformation from a criminal found guilty of murder to conscientious objector. The title quoted Mehmet saying "When I read *Crime and Punishment*, I thought it was about me" (Sarıbaş 2002). The interview was accompanied by a short explanation of "conscientious objection" and a brief summary of Dostoyevsky's *Crime and Punishment*.

As the antiwar protests against the U.S.-led plans to attack Iraq were intensified, Mehmet Bal became a landmark case of individual action against the war for the small group of objectors and antimilitarists in Turkey. New declarations of conscientious objection followed. About two months after Mehmet's release, four new names were added to the list of objectors.[19] As they made their declarations in front of an audience of more than 60 people at the Istanbul branch of the Human Rights Association on 24 January 2003, these four objectors were accompanied by six "old" objectors, who repeated their resolution to resist taking arms. Their joint statement had a clear message: "We refuse to participate in any army, war, or war preparation.... We will struggle to resist and to prevent the current preparations for war [in Iraq]."[20]

The individual declarations displayed four levels of resistance: resistance to participate in militarism and wars; resistance to define themselves as members of states; resistance to contribute to discriminations based on gender, race, class, ethnicity, and religion; and resistance to participate in the destruction of nature. Resistance to wars and militarism is at the center of all the declarations: "I declare that I refuse to kill" (Erkan Ersöz), "I refuse to harm any human being or to be trained for such harm" (Hasan Çimen), "By asking me to serve in the military, you are asking me to give up my belief in life and my dreams for a free world; but they belong to me, and I am not going to give them up for you" (Uğur Yorulmaz),

"I refuse to partake in the military, which is the state institution for organized violence; I refuse to take up arms, kill human beings, obey orders, and be prepared to die" (Timuçin Kızılay), "I will, in no circumstance, join the military. I call on everyone to do the same and to work, in solidarity, against wars and militarism through nonviolence" (Erdem Yalçınkaya), "I refuse to be an accomplice to the state and the militarist apparatus for any crime" (Yavuz Atan), "I will not be anybody's soldier" (Sertaç Girgin).[21] Some of the declarations address more specific concerns regarding the workings of militarism. For instance, Mehmet Tarhan, the only gay objector, rejects the "unfitness" clause used for gays:

> The state that claims to own me as its citizen, in order to continue its existence, wants me to join the military, to turn into a war machine that kills and, if necessary, dies, and, ultimately, to participate in crimes against humanity. I will stick to my beliefs and not let this happen. Because I am gay, I am presented with the "right" to obtain an "unfit" report [to avoid military service]. I take this "right" to be about the "unfitness" of the state itself.

Although the declarations are mostly written in universalistic language, some of the objectors pay attention to contextualizing themselves in relation to national and international events. Mehmet Tarhan, who had initially declared his conscientious objection in October 2001, refers to the September 11 attacks, the bombing of Afghanistan, and the planned war on Iraq in the same sentence, and states that he condemns "all acts of violence." Mustafa Şeyhoğlu, besides mentioning the workings of militarism and wars in general, also pays specific attention to Turkish militarism:

> Everybody talks about September 11 these days. I want to remind you of another date—a date everybody has forgotten—September 12 [the day of the 1980 coup d'etat]. I also want to remind you of institutions such as DGM [State Security Courts], YÖK [Higher Education Council], and of MGK [National Security Council], which have institutionalized the violence, hierarchy, and militarism that is embedded in every aspect of our lives. It is in our hands as individuals to render these institutions ineffective, just as it is in our hands to devoid wars of their human resources. "Nobody is born a soldier."

The last sentence, in quotation marks, marks a reference to the popular saying "Every Turk is born a soldier" (see chapter one).

At a second level, the conscientious objector declarations mentioned above, refuse to accept the authority of "the state" in organizing their lives. Representing an "anarchist" worldview, the objectors refuse to accept the "imaginary border" (Uğur Yorulmaz) of all states and express a desire to live in a world without states and borders. As a consequence, they refuse to partake in all forms of compulsory service "dictated by the state." As I discuss below, one of the characteristics of the small objector movement in Turkey is that it has so far been dominated by anarchist individuals. The practical implication of this characteristic is that their objection is best classified as "total objection," as opposed to "conscientious objection," because it embodies a latent refusal to accept civilian alternatives to military service. It is marked by a total rejection of the authority of the state on any individual. "I long for a world without any states, borders, authority and violence" (Erdem Yalçınkaya).

A third level of resistance expressed in the declarations has to do with power relations between people. Most of the objectors declare their desire and efforts to overcome all forms of discrimination and exploitation, while also emphasizing the value of nonviolence in all human interactions. "I stand against sexism and other discriminations based on race, religion, and language" (Mustafa Şeyhoğlu), "I believe that human beings could live in a world that does not have borders or authority; a world where individuals only exercise authority over themselves; a world that does not accept violence as a means in any circumstance; a world without money, a world where there is no sexism; a stateless, borderless, flagless world characterized by anarchy" (Sertaç Girgin), "I dream of living in a world based on sharing, not exploitation" (Uğur Yorulmaz).

A fourth level of resistance is articulated in relation to the human domination over and the destruction of nature. In their desire to rid the world of all authority structures, some of the objectors declare their intentions to work against the destruction of all life forms: "I don't exercise domination over nature and its creatures" (Erkan Ersöz). "I will struggle to prevent the destruction of nature, all life forms, in short, the ecology" (Hasan Çimen).

Not accidentally, the public meeting for these declarations took place in an intense period of antiwar activism against the looming Iraq war. The Turkish government was planning to join the coalition forces in attacking Iraq, thereby bringing Turkey into a war. A day after these declarations, the Peace Initiative of Turkey was organizing the Assembly of the 100s, the joint peace declarations of 100 representatives from 100 occupational groups. Two days later, there would be an international peace event that would host representatives from British, American, and Middle Eastern antiwar groups and NGOs. Having come to Istanbul for this international peace event, an African-American objector to the Vietnam draft, Michael Simmons from the American Friends Service Committee (AFSC), was also among the participants in the public declarations of the ten objectors.

If this international context provided one background to these declarations, the campaign for Mehmet Bal was the other. Objector activism had intensified during the previous months of organizing for Mehmet Bal, and his release had provided an added impetus. Yet, they also recognized that this may not be the end of the story for Mehmet, or for themselves. And it was not. Mehmet was taken under custody on 22 January, only two days before the Istanbul declarations. Three undercover officers took him from his home in Izmir and "surrendered" him to the nearest garrison. He was sent to his military unit again, only to be released two days later. As the ten objectors made their declarations public at the Human Rights Association on 24 January, they did not know whether Mehmet was free or not. Their statements were prefaced by an announcement regarding Mehmet's situation and a declaration of support.

Mehmet has been "free" since January 2003. When I met him for the second time[22] in an Aegean town in July 2003, he had recovered some of his weight and had long hair and a suntan from long hours of working in the sun and enjoying the sea. Together with two "older" conscientious objectors, he was running a small kiosk in a coastal town filled with vacationers from Izmir. His future was uncertain, as was his employment status once the summer was over. Nevertheless, he looked very satisfied with his life and with the choices he had made.

A similar sense of satisfaction is also expressed by those who were active in Mehmet's campaign. Although they are all aware that this may be a temporary condition, they are content with the outcome and with their "success" in giving support to a fellow-objector when he needed it. Yet, the larger question of whether one can talk about an "objector movement" in Turkey and whether the objectors and their supporters see themselves as "successful" in the larger political sense, is a different discussion.

From Osman Murat Ülke to Mehmet Bal: "One Stone Next to Another"?

The ten-year-old antimilitarist movement in Turkey is still in its start-up phase. We have not moved on to the development phase yet.... We have not yet managed to put one stone on top of another. We are still strengthening the foundation by putting one stone next to another.

Osman Murat Ülke

The only aim [of our actions] is to leave a question mark.... But it is beyond debate that there is a problem. If seventy million people live on this land, half of them eligible for military service, and if the number of conscientious objectors is still 30, and if I know every single one of them personally, there is a serious problem here.

Uğur Yorulmaz

If you ask me about my dreams, sure I dream about hundreds of conscientious objectors creating a real movement. Unfortunately, this does not look very realistic at this point.

Ferda Ülker

Can one talk about a conscientious objector movement in Turkey? Or an antimilitarist movement? How can one evaluate the last fourteen years of public resistance by this small group of men and women to military service? Ossi, Uğur, and Ferda, who have dedicated an important part of their young lives to creating the beginnings of an antimilitarist movement in Turkey, share a positionality marked by mixed feelings. On the one hand, they feel good about what they have accomplished in the short history of conscientious objection in Turkey, but on the other hand, they are well aware of the weaknesses and limitations of their activism. Ossi is frustrated that the ten-year process of institutionalization in Izmir (through SKD and ISKD) has come to an end, and that the experiences of this first generation have not been conveyed to the newcomers. Uğur emphasizes the "essentially individualized" nature of conscientious objection when he says "If you don't want it, don't do it [i.e., military service]! It is that simple."[23] Yet he also recognizes the need to organize around conscientious objection in order to familiarize the people with this concept and, ultimately, to increase the number of objectors. Ferda, who was one of the founders of both the Izmir War Resisters' Association and the subsequent women's group called ANFEM (Antimilitarist Feminists), now volunteers in non-violence training sessions with political groups in her struggle to demilitarize oppositional politics in Turkey. She recognizes that their activism around conscientious objection needs to be strengthened by other kinds of work that foster antimilitarism.

I conclude this chapter by discussing the various bottlenecks of organized political activism against militarism in general, and military service in particular. My discussion of these bottlenecks focuses on three main aspects of this form of activism: the high price of conscientious objection, the pervasiveness of both state and popular forms of militarism, and the intrinsic limitations of the existing movement.

Everyone that I interviewed for this research, including Ossi and Mehmet who have done prison time for their actions, have emphasized the extraordinary price that a conscientious objector has to pay in Turkey. Conscientious objection, which was outside the margins of political imagination until very recently, is still a legal oddity. Mustafa Şeyhoğlu, an objector since January 2003, sees the reference to the concept in the military legal documents through the cases of Ossi and Mehmet as a major accomplishment of the movement.[24] Others emphasize the recognition of the declaration of conscientious objection as part of the "freedom of conscience and expression" in the Prosecutor's Statement of Mehmet Bal's case in October 2002 as an even more important step. Yet, these references do not change the basic reality that, legally speaking, it is feasible for a conscientious objector to remain in prison for the rest of his life, in the vicious cycle involving forced "surrender" to the assigned military unit, trial and imprisonment for "insubordination," transfer to the military unit upon the completion of the sentence, and further imprisonment for "persistent insubordination." As the cases of Ossi and Mehmet suggest, this process involves various degrees of physical and psychological hardship. As Inci Ağlagül, a very active antimilitarist feminist in the objector movement in Istanbul, suggests:

> The objector is ultimately on his own. Yes, we will be there to give him support, but this will not change the fact that he will be all alone in the process. And there is no limit to what can happen to him when he is taken under custody. In return, what we can do for him is very limited. We might want to think otherwise, but actually there is a limit to what we can do for him. This is a heavy psychological burden for all of us.

The psychological burden of a conscientious objector and his supporters does not end there because imprisonment is not the only price to pay. As the stories enacted by Uğur and his friends at the International Conscientious Objectors' Day events in 2001 suggest, one has to endure social and economic pressures of various kinds: Resistance from family members and friends, staying away from the legal job market, and the inability to undertake any legal transaction (buying or selling property, applying for a driver's licence or a passport, opening a bank account, education, marriage, and so on). In many ways, a conscientious objector has to take on the risks of leading the life of a noncitizen for the rest of his life, which is not an easy price to pay in the world of nation-states. In the words of Uğur,

> There is tremendous social pressure you have to face. You cannot find a job, you cannot go abroad, you cannot get a passport. It is indeed a heavy burden when you think about all this. Then there are all the people around you—your family, your friends—that you have to face and struggle against; and you have to keep doing this every single day. All your life. Numerous times. Nothing will be over once you have made your declaration. It will continue for the rest of your life. You can't just do it and get it over with. It will stay with you.

All of these "prices" become more intensified in situations of political conflict. Inci, who went to Adıyaman in Spring 2003 for a panel on "Women and War," recalls the high-level of anxiety in this Kurdish-dominated Southeastern city that lived under Emergency Rule throughout the 1980s and 1990s:

> We were invited to Adıyaman for a panel titled *Women and War*, which was preceded by the screening of the film *Ret 1111*. There were about 500 people in a conference hall that normally accommodated 300 people. The audience included about 20 undercover police officers and 3 police cameramen. A lawyer was sitting between me and the other speaker, screening the written questions that were sent to us. Even we, the speakers, were not free to speak our mind. The lawyer censored the questions, crossing out certain parts. I still keep those questions, with his censoring marks.... In the beginning, I objected to getting written questions. I wanted people to be able to talk to me directly. Then they warned me that the people would not feel safe about identifying themselves.

This brief anecdote is a clue as to why the objector movement has been confined to the big cities of Istanbul, Ankara, and Izmir. The stakes of talking against military service in a small town, particularly in the parts of the country that lived under Emergency Rule for almost twenty years, can be much higher. Many objectors and their supporters recognize these personal stakes as a significant set back for the expansion of the conscientious objection movement.

Another important stumbling block they identify is the intensity of both state and popular forms of militarism in Turkey. Uğur mentioned a story he had heard from someone else as an illustration of the challenge they face: "Two officers are talking. One of them says, 'There are seven hundred thousand soldiers in Turkey.' The other one intervenes, 'No, there are seventy million soldiers.' This is the main problem we face!" Uğur, Inci, and Mehmet (Bal) were among those who emphasized the role of education in militarizing the population. According to Mehmet, militaristic school practices start shaping people at an early age:

> I would of course want this militarist logic to disappear. I mean, another way of imagining the world should be possible. But the roots [of this militarism] are very deep. A student in first grade has to stand in line like a soldier and sing the national anthem. You start losing something at that very moment. The roots are very deep.

Several antimilitarists are currently working on the militarized aspects of the education system, struggling to make them more visible. Uğur and Inci, who participated in a number of discussions on antimilitarism at university campuses in 2003, recall many of their discussions with students leading to debates on the militarized nature of education in Turkey.

Another institution that is identified for its militarizing effects is the media. The campaigns for Ossi and Mehmet are simultaneously remembered as campaigns against censorship or self-censorship in the media. Uğur notes the overall lack of media attention to conscientious objection or antimilitarism as a major cause of their inaccessibility to the population at large:

> So few people discuss or even use the terms conscientious objection or antimilitarism.... For something to be discussed, it first needs to be known. How is that possible?

Through its use in mass media or through widespread use in the streets. When you are so few in number, you get stuck.

According to Mehmet Bal, militarism in Turkey can most visibly be observed in the media: "Just look at the first pages of newspapers and it is right there." On a rare case of criticism coming from inside the media, writer Yıldırım Türker (2002) suggests:

> Those who listen to their conscience only, those who don't hesitate to sacrifice their social identity for their moral choices are often left on the isolated, soundproof margins of our world. The blind-deaf-mute attitude of the media in the face of the struggle of conscientious objectors, i.e. those who refuse to serve in the military, is a perfect example.

According to many conscientious objectors and antimilitarists, militarism is not only perpetuated by the state or mass media, but also by oppositional political culture in Turkey. Neither the Right, nor the Left of the political spectrum in Turkey is immune to militaristic assumptions and practices. According to Coşkun,

> Militarism is very powerful in Turkey. Its effects are even in the smallest veins, the remotest corners of the society. Therefore, it is difficult for any oppositional movement that grows out of this structure to start questioning its own militarism. One can almost talk about a genetic problem in political attitudes and perspectives.

Ferda has a similar observation. She finds it particularly troubling that the antiwar movement in Turkey has not questioned its militaristic tendencies:

> I could not see much antimilitarism in the antiwar movement. . . . I mean I would have expected the antiwar movement to recognize conscientious objection as a way of disembodying the war machine. What more can you do? This did not happen. Perhaps more people paid attention to conscientious objection compared to the past, but because militarism itself remained unquestioned, it did not take hold. . . . This, I cannot make sense of. I mean, of course one can say that the roots of militarism are very deep, and so on, but how can you question the war without questioning militarism?

Ferda's concerns are shared by Inci, who complains about the lack of discussion on violence or lack of sincerity in calls for nonviolent solutions to problems:

> I have been concerned about the way nonviolence is discussed [in the antiwar movement]: Is it rejected only as a tactic? Or as a way of life? I ask people this question and get mixed answers. Some people see nonviolence as a tactical choice, others regard it as a way of life. You have to have a problem with violence in order to be a conscientious objector or an antimilitarist. That is why there are only 30 conscientious objectors.

Despite these problems, many in the movement have "hope" that they will find new ways of making antimilitarism a more visible and desirable political direction in Turkey.

Yet there is a third set of problems, stemming from the particular history and nature of the movement. From its inception, the movement has been dominated by individuals who identify themselves as "anarchists," in the tradition of Henry David Thoreau, Michael Bakunin, Murray Bookchin, Emma Goldman, and others. This identification may not be shared by all antimilitarists involved or affiliated with the movement, but it has provided a collective political reference for all conscientious objectors to date. This has various implications. Most importantly, anarchism rejects institutionalization, hierarchy, and leadership. This makes political organizing difficult. As Inci suggests,

> Antimilitarism is not something that starts and ends with you. Anarchism is. Anarchism does not necessarily involve a search for social change. On the other hand, antimilitarism can only take hold if it turns into a worldwide movement encompassing everyone.

How is this going to take place when the majority of the movement is composed of anarchists cynical of organized politics? Ossi, who also identifies as an anarchist, believes in the merits of certain forms of institutionalization: "In Izmir, we tried to institutionalize. This went on for about ten years. Now, there is an emptiness."

Another point of debate that marks the tensions between anarchism and antimilitarism has to do with the difference between the concepts of "conscientious objection" and "total objection." Although conscientious objection is a more familiar term, both in Turkey and the world at large, the objectors often remark that they are not "conscientious objectors" refusing military forms of service to the state, but "total objectors" refusing *all* forms of compulsory service. This includes "alternative civilian service," which has been practiced in many countries since the introduction of conscientious objection. In Turkey, no political group, except for the Human Rights Association, has yet voiced a demand to add alternative civilian service to the compulsory conscription system although there have been individual attempts. For instance, in 2003, a young man wrote to *www.savaskarsitlari.org* informing them of his desire to write a petition to the parliament asking for alternative civilian service. This demand initiated a big debate in the discussion group. Some participants rejected this demand as a valid form of political action for themselves as anarchists. Others insisted on the need to give support to this demand even if they would not want to sign the petition. What was striking was that no one claimed this demand as their own.

As I have already shown, Amnesty International and the Human Rights Watch have both mentioned the need for Turkey to add a clause to its conscription law, making alternative civilian service a legal option. Although their call was welcomed as a form of international support for Ossi and Mehmet who were in prison when these reports were issued, their content did not directly match the personal demands of either one of these objectors, or those of the majority of their supporters. When I asked Uğur about this mismatch, he suggested that he did not understand why there were no *other* groups that asked for alternative civilian service in Turkey: "Why is it that total objectors have been the only visible group of objectors?" Ossi's answer to critics who question his total objection takes on a different spin:

> I see demilitarization also as a form of civilian service. The only difference is that it is not registered anywhere. It is not the state that tells you to do this or that for this many hours. If I am involved in demilitarization, I am doing civilian service. This is another interpretation of total objection.

Ossi's inversion of the concept of "service" is an important reminder that the objector movement in Turkey is closer to Gandhian nonviolence than to anarchist pacifism (see Fox 1997). Anthropologist Richard G. Fox differentiates between pacifism as an individual act of conscientious protest and Gandhi's protest methods, which combined "morally informed nonviolence, mass civil disobedience, and courageous suffering" (Fox 1997, 70). Fox emphasizes Gandhi's belief in social change through mass action:

> In Gandhian protest, civil disobedience could begin with individual acts, but always with the purpose of mobilizing mass protest. Otherwise, civil disobedience was an ego-trip, not a moral action. (Fox 1997, 70)

Ferda has not been alone in her "dream" about hundreds of objectors; the movement was initiated with this dream in 1993. SKD and ISKD were planning on "waves" of objectors, hoping that the waves would grow large enough to challenge the compulsory military service system.

Regardless of whether this dream was realized, the fact that the movement *aimed* at achieving mass mobilization based on nonviolent action points to their undeclared departure from the classical anarchist tradition. Although some objectors have said that they "don't care about what the state does in terms of military service,"[25] they have all made public declarations of their conscientious objection, participated in political protests against wars and militarisms, written articles, and coordinated list serves that discuss and promote antimilitarism. In fact, they keep repeating their objection to military service in public meetings on a regular basis. In other words, most of them have done much more than "civil disobedience." Most significantly, they have not had to display civil disobedience because they have not been "recruited" by the military, except in the cases of Mehmet and Ossi. Therefore, one can argue that one of the inherent limitations of anarchist forms of political protest, what Fox defines as "civil disobedience [turning into] an ego-trip," has been overcome in favor of an engaged activism that seeks to initiate mass action, not through preaching, but through example, communication, and sharing.

Richard Fox and Orin Starn (1997) argue that much of political action today occupies the "in between" zone between revolutionary movements and everyday forms of resistance. These "midways of mobilization" (1997, 3) differ significantly from "foot-dragging resistance or all-out revolt," providing independent visions of "opposition and mobilization" (1997, 4). Sonia Alvarez highlights the need to develop new concepts to analyze these movements. According to her, social movements are best understood in terms of the intra- and inter-movement "webs" they create:

> Movement webs encompass more than movement organizations and their active members. When we examine the impact of movements, then, we must gauge the extent to which their demands, discourses and practices circulate . . . in larger institutional and cultural arenas. (Alvarez 1997, 90–91)

The effort to create extensive "movement webs" has been one of the distinguishing characteristics of the objector movement in Turkey. From anti-nuclear activism to feminism to human rights, the activists of the movement have established discursive and practical links between various realms of political action. Yet, despite these efforts, conscientious objection has remained the main focus. Ferda believes that there is need for diversification:

> When I look back on the movement, I only see activism organized around conscientious objection, and, for a while, around military justice. We need to find other ways of making antimilitarism intelligible and accessible to people. The nonviolence training that we have been doing can be one example, but it is not sufficient.

Ferda also believes that the critique of militarism should interact more closely with the critique of the existing gender order: "Militarist thought does not confine itself to the barracks, but envisions a 'male world' in the minute details of everyday life as well. In this construction, women are humiliated or ignored altogether." For her, conscientious objection presents a direct, clear challenge to this "male world" and is relevant for both men and women. Inci elaborates on this connection based on her own choices:

> As a woman, I have also entertained the idea of writing a declaration that would say that I do not want to be used by the military, that I do not agree to send my son or brother to the military, and that I would struggle against militarism for as long as I lived with these principles. As women, we are sanctified as mothers. We are supposed to gain a special status as the mothers of martyrs. What does that mean? I started thinking about all this and entertained the idea of a kind of objector declaration. In many ways, I still believe that this would be the best support I can give to my male friends, to my brother, and to many others I don't even know. I can tell them that whatever they do, I will stand next to them.

For Mehmet Tarhan, a gay activist and a conscientious objector, sexism is also associated with heterosexism, and both are strengthened by militarism: "I refuse to partake in this system and turn into a machine that kills. The only way I can maintain a sense of integrity is by constantly struggling with militarism, sexism, and heterosexism." His approach echoes Cynthia Enloe's argument that "nationalism typically has sprung from masculinized memory, masculinized humiliation and masculinized hope" (Enloe 1989, 44). Mehmet Tarhan, Ferda, and Inci are among the very few who voice such arguments, in an effort to change the (hetero)sexist nature of the state and the military.

If one challenge is to diversify politically and draw attention to the connections between feminist, gay, and antimilitarist struggle, another challenge, which would require very different strategies than the first, is to render antimilitarism intelligible and imaginable to the politically unorganized majority. As Ossi suggests, "Mehmet Bal represented an important milestone in the normalization, or localization, of conscientious objection." The question is whether there will be other Mehmet Bals (or, for that matter, Ossis).

The pervasiveness of various forms of militarism in Turkey, combined with the very high price of taking action against compulsory military service make it difficult for any form of organized dissent to expand beyond a small circle. On the other hand, the disillusionment with military service that fifteen years of warfare has created and the growing antiwar activism in the past two years resulting from the Iraq war provide new openings for antimilitarist work. Moreover, the independent, creative, and nonviolent nature of antimilitarism seems to attract a new generation of activists who are tired of old forms of politics and conflict, and in search of alternatives. The antimilitarist slogan, "I will not be anybody's soldier!" was one of the most popular slogans of the antiwar movement in 2003, particularly embraced by young people of different ideological orientations. The myth that the Turkish nation is a military-nation still prevails in public and popular forms, but the counter argument that "no one is born a soldier" is also at the table now.

PART 3
MILITARIZING EDUCATION

CHAPTER FIVE

"THE ARMY IS A SCHOOL, THE SCHOOL IS AN ARMY": THE NATION'S TWO FRONTS

We were walking down the stairs towards the cafeteria for lunch with Colonel Yılmaz, when he turned to me and said, "you know, there are only two ministries that have the title 'national' before them: National Education and National Defense. That in itself speaks to the significance of the *National Security* course." He said this with great pride and looked at me to see my reaction. I affirmed that this was indeed an interesting relationship between the two ministries. In many ways, this relationship marked him as a person, as well. He was not only a commander, but also a teacher. For years, he had been teaching the high school course, *National Security Knowledge*, in the schools near his command posts.

I was not surprised to hear him make this remark, nor was it the first time I had heard it. In 1994, the Minister of National Education Nevzat Ayaz wrote:

> In the organizational structure of our state, there are only two ministries that have the term "national" in their titles: Ministry of National Defense and Ministry of National Education. The Ministry of National Defense has assumed the duty to protect our Republic and to defend our country from outside forces. And the Ministry of National Education has assumed the duty to raise citizens who are committed to Atatürk's principles and revolutions, and to Atatürk nationalism as it is defined in the constitution; who embrace, protect, and develop the national, moral, spiritual (*manevî*), historical, and cultural values of the Turkish nation; who love their family, country, and nation with a constant effort to strengthen them; *who know their duties and responsibilities towards the Turkish Republic* which is a democratic, secular, and social state based on human rights and the basic principles defined in the Constitution; and who have turned these duties and responsibilities into a behavior. (Ayaz 1994, emphasis added)

As we shall see, the two ministries have been perceived to have a similar mission with different realms of responsibility from the early days of the Turkish Republic. Moreover, these realms are regarded as being closely linked to one another not only by the virtue of being "national," but also because they define each other. Education means defense and defense is always also about education. In the words of an official of the Turkish Ministry of Culture in 1938, "Just as the army is a school, so is the school an army" (Yaman 1938, 40).

Chapter three highlighted the "educational" aspects of military service. In this chapter and the next, I look into the militarizing aspects of education, with a particular focus on the high school military course, *National Security Knowledge*. First, I discuss the ways in which "national education" and "national defense" were conceptualized as the "two fronts" of state-making and nation-building in Turkey. Second, I examine the continuities and changes in the teaching of this military course since 1926, and closely analyze the contents of the current textbook. Classroom dynamics and student responses to *National Security Knowledge* is the subject of the next chapter.

Nationalizing Education

The idea of national education, which was first systematized by Ziya Gökalp in the 1910s, became central to the formation of the Turkish nation-state in its early days: The Ministry of Education was founded on 2 May 1920, only ten days after the formation of the Grand National Assembly. About a year later, in July 1921, as the Independence War was going on, an Education Congress was assembled in Ankara, the would-be capital of the new Turkish Republic. The aim was to "give a national direction to education" (Akyüz 1983, 89). The meeting of the Congress in the midst of heavy fighting was an important sign of the prominence education policies would take in the shaping of the new republic. The first step was to make public education mandatory and free for both boys and girls, which took effect in 1923. In the same year "a month long education convention, the First Convention of Education (*Birinci Heyet-i İlmiye*), was held. Implemented in 1924, the decisions of the First Convention of Education included setting primary education at five years, which was to be followed by three years of secondary school and three years of high school education" (Z. Arat 1998, 157). A year later, on the same day that a bill was passed to abolish the caliphate, another one nationalized the education system by placing all educational institutions in the country under the control of the Ministry of Education. This law, known as the Law of Unification of Instruction (*Tevhid-i Tedrisat Kanunu*), is still in effect and forms the basis for all other educational laws and by-laws.[1]

Another major reform in the first decade of the Turkish Republic was the change of the alphabet from Arabic script to Latin script, which took effect in 1928, aimed at making literacy learning "easier" while severely limiting the access of the new generation to books and documents written before 1928, as well as to the Qur'an and other religious texts. According to Feroz Ahmad: "Perhaps the most iconoclastic reform of this period was replacing the Arabic script by the Latin in the writing of Turkish. At a stroke, even the literate people were cut off from their past. Overnight, virtually the entire nation was made illiterate" (Ahmad 1993, 80)—to be made literate again under a national program administered by the Ministry of Education.

In 1926, the first Primary School Curriculum was adopted with the general goal of bringing up "good citizens by making the young generation adapt actively to their environment" (quoted in I. Kaplan 1998, 186). In 1936, this "citizenship education program" (I. Kaplan 1998, 186) was elaborated. The main goal for primary schooling was set as follows:

> To bring up children who attend the primary school as strongly republicanist, nationalist, etatist, laicist, transformist (*sic*) citizens; to raise students who will assume it their task to inculcate into the entire citizens the ideas which will cause the latter to respect and make others to respect the Turkish nation, the National Assembly and the Turkish State. (quoted in I. Kaplan, 1998, 186)

Citizenship education was not limited to the primary school but was extended into secondary schools and even the university (I. Kaplan 1998). The role of education, as perceived by the founders of the Republic, is stated clearly in the introductory text to an exhibition on education opened in 1933 (the tenth anniversary of the Turkish Republic): "Republican education is an instrument to raise nationalist citizens" (*Maarif Sergisi Rehberi* [1933], iv).

Much has changed in the realm of education since the 1930s, yet there are major continuities in the centralized and nationalized character of schooling. The Ministry of National Education, to date, acts as a centralized body where all decisions regarding schools, administrators, teachers, students, and textbooks are made in Ankara, regardless of the type of school and where it is located. Private schools, minority schools, technical schools, as well as public schools have to act upon the national curricula set by the Ministry of Education, use the textbooks written or approved by the ministry, have their teachers appointed by Ankara, organize their classrooms in the exact way that it is written in the Ministry guidelines (with the picture of Atatürk in the same position above the blackboard, the same speech by Atatürk framed and hung by the picture, etc.) and seek for approval for every decision they make regarding supplies, school events, and so on, either from the Ministry's bureaus in their province or, more likely, from Ministry officials in Ankara.

Another major continuity is that raising nationalist citizens remains one of the main goals of many educators and politicians. Article Four of the current Law of Higher Education suggests that the primary goal of higher education is to educate students so that they:

- will be loyal to Atatürk nationalism and to Atatürk's reforms and principles,
- will be in accord with the national, ethical, human, spiritual, and cultural values of the Turkish Nation and conscious of the privilege of being a Turk,
- will put the common good above their own personal interests and have full devotion to family, country, and nation,
- will be fully conscious of their duties and responsibilities towards their country and will act accordingly,
- will be objective, broad-minded, and respectful of human rights,
- will develop in a balanced way, physically, mentally, psychologically, morally, and emotionally,
- will prove to be good citizens contributing to the country's development and welfare and at the same time acquire the necessary knowledge and skills for their future vocations.[2]

In his review of contemporary textbooks, Tanıl Bora (2003, 68) shows that "nationalism in textbooks is presented as a compulsory ideology, or rather as a 'system of ideas' beyond ideology. The presentation has a *commanding* tone," that rules out the possibility of any critique. A high school book on Atatürk's principles and revolutions suggests that "Turkish existence would come to an end if nationalism were to be abandoned" (quoted by Bora 2003, 69). As Bora highlights, this alarmed attitude reveals a deep sense of insecurity. Due to this insecurity, the 1933 maxim that "Republican education is an instrument to raise nationalist citizens" continues to inform education policies and textbook narratives to this day.[3]

War on Two Fronts

Before the first Education Congress met in Ankara in 1921, *Hakimiyet-i Milliye* (National Sovereignty), the period's leading newspaper, announced the plans for the Congress on 3 June, praising its importance and situating it in the ongoing struggle of the nation for a sovereign state: "The two main elements that make nations triumph are soldiers and teachers" (quoted in Akyüz 1983, 90). When the Congress was assembled, an editorial titled "Two Fronts" elaborated this point further:

> As the army of salvation and independence is fighting in the fronts against the Greeks, the army of teachers in Ankara is preparing a defense program against ignorance. There is activity in both War and Education fronts; the national army will force the enemy out of the homeland while the teachers' army will force out ignorance and darkness. The appearance of both struggles simultaneously is a divine coincidence. (quoted in Akyüz 1983, 95)

What this author defines a "divine coincidence" marks the institutionalization of two activities of the new state, "defending" the homeland and "civilizing" the population, through the formation of a national army and a national education system. It also points to the close relationship established between these activities as the two (related) fronts in the making of a Turkish nation and state.

These "fronts" were later elaborated by Mustafa Kemal Atatürk as he led the constitution and consolidation of the Turkish Republic in the 1920s and 1930s. Mustafa Kemal was not only declared the "Father of the Turks" with his given last name, Atatürk,[4] but had two other titles he is often remembered by: "Commander in Chief" (*Başkumandan*), a title he was given during the War of Independence (1919–1923), and "Teacher in Chief" (or Head Teacher—*Başöğretmen*), a title he received during the education reforms. The importance he gave to both of these titles and the institutions they represented was reflected in his speeches and are often quoted often in textbooks, public documents, as well as in academic works. For instance, in 1931, Mustafa Kemal spoke in Konya, a city in Central Anatolia, to a group of military officers and their families:

> There are very few examples, in the world and in history, of the kind of union established between [our] nation and the military, made up of the nation's heroic children. We can always be proud of this national manifestation. My friends! When I talk about the military, I talk about the bright children of the Turkish nation. The teachers who raise the heroes of tomorrow are surely among those children. The teachers who, when necessary, switch roles and walk side by side with the military, risking their lives are among those children. When I talk about the officers and bright Turkish

children of our distinguished military, I am talking about the Turkish youth who are with them and who are ready to participate in national heroism with their ideas, conscience and knowledge.... As I wrap up my words, I would like to state this with clarity: The Turkish nation loves its military and considers it the guardian of its ideals. (quoted in Parla 1991b, 169–170)

In this speech, the military is given the role of guarding the "ideals" of the Turkish nation while the teachers are given the role of educating "national heroes" and being "national heroes" themselves. The "two fronts" are indeed one. The association Atatürk establishes between the military and education can be observed more distinctly in two speeches he gave at the opening sessions of the Turkish Grand National Assembly in 1937 and 1938 respectively.

> I have no doubt that special attention and effort will be made in order for the military, which is a great *national school of discipline*, to be turned into a grand school where the most needed personnel for our economic, cultural, and social wars will be raised. (*Atatürk'ün Söylev ve Demeçleri I* [1997], 421, emphasis added)

In 1938, he refers to his speech a year before and says :

> As I pointed out and explained last year, efforts have been intensified so that our undefeatable military, which is not only the guardian of our country and our regime, but also a *hearth of education and instruction*, as well as an agent of peace in the largest and truest sense, will be equipped with the latest models of arms and motor vehicles. (*Atatürk'ün Söylev ve Demeçleri I* [1997], 429, emphasis added)

The first thing to note about these speeches is that the military is seen as a guardian of not only the country, but also the regime itself, giving it an internal policing role (Parla 1991, 178). Moreover, it is seen as a "hearth of education and instruction." In other words, the military is given a multiplicity of roles in an expansive manner. Its role is not limited to the defense of the country against outside threats. The military is also equipped to protect the regime in the country against internal threats, as well as to educate and instruct the citizens of the country. But how would this role to educate be realized? Who would the army educate? Part of the answer, as I have suggested in chapter three, is to be found in the practice of universal military service. In this perspective, the significance of military service is not limited to the creation of an armed force for defense, but also encompasses the education of the citizens and the creation of (gendered) citizen-soldiers. The other part of the answer involves the participation of military-officers as teachers in formal education, which is the main subject of this chapter.

From "Preparation for Military Service" to "National Security Knowledge"

In describing his approach to the study of discourse, Michel Foucault talks about the need to substitute "the uniform, simple activity of allocating causality" with an analysis of the "play of dependencies" between different transformations "to render apparent the polymorphous interweaving of correlations" (Foucault 1991, 58). These dependencies can take different forms: *intradiscursive* (i.e., "between the objects, operations, and concepts of a single formation"); *interdiscursive* (i.e., "between different discursive formations"); or *extradiscursive* (i.e., "between discursive transformations and transformations outside of discourse") (Foucault 1991, 58). I find this framework useful in looking at national education and compulsory military service in Turkey. The dependencies between the discourses and practices that define these two realms are both interdiscursive and intradiscursive. The interdiscursive dependency is shaped by the mutual definition of the activities that characterize each one. Military service is partly defined as an educational practice, and vice versa. Moreover, there is an intradiscursive dependency: both education and defense are quintessentially "national" activities and form the "two fronts" of nation-state formation. In other words, these two activities are intricately linked, and together constitute major aspects of another discursive practice, namely nationalism. Particularly in early years of nation-building, the making of citizens and the making of soldiers can be seen as mutually dependent activities (*intradiscursive dependency*) while education and defense develop as mutually dependent discourses (*interdiscursive dependency*).

In Turkey, the mandatory military course taught in high schools by military officers remains one of the most significant sites where the "dependencies" between education and defense are established and naturalized. Taught under different names in different periods (Military Service, Preparation for Military Service, National Defense Knowledge, and National Security Knowledge), the military course has been in the curriculum of high schools since 1926. Currently, it is called *National Security Knowledge* and is mandatory for all students (male and female) in the second year of high school, regardless of the kind of school. As I show below, the content of the course has changed significantly throughout the years, but the overall aim of teaching the students to be proud members of a military-nation and obedient citizens of the Turkish state has remained unchallenged. Let us begin by examining the aspects of the course that have *not* significantly changed since 1926.

The most important continuity is that the course has been taught by military officers (or retired officers) who get paid by the Ministry of National Education or the school that employs them. However, neither the Ministry nor the schools have any say in the choice of these officer-teachers. The officer-teachers are "appointed" by the highest commander of the nearest garrison on an annual basis. There is no requirement (or even expectation) that these officer-teachers have any training in pedagogy. Their qualification for teaching this course is defined solely in military terms: the most preferred category is that of staff officers (Staff Colonels, Majors, and Captains), followed by other officers ranked militarily.[5] The current regulations (in effect since 1980) that outline the parameters of the course differ from previous ones in that they leave room for the employment of a civilian teacher as a last resort *if* the garrison is not able to allocate a sufficient number of officers for the high schools in its province.[6] Of course, this civilian teacher cannot be just any teacher: he has to be a (male) teacher who has performed his military service as a reserve officer.[7]

Another basic element of the course that has not changed since 1926 is that the General Staff exercises sole (or, since 1980, primary) control over what gets taught, at what level and for how many hours. In the current regulations (dated 1980), it is suggested that the General Staff act *in coordination with* the Ministry of National

Defense and the Ministry of National Education in making curriculum decisions. All regulations prior to 1980 assign all responsibility and decision-making power to the General Staff *only*. Moreover, textbooks are written by a commission made up of military personnel in the General Staff. Since 1980, the Ministry of National Education has been given the role of "examining" these textbooks and making "suggestions" (together with the Ministry of National Defense) for the program to be followed in the course. In short, one can say that military officers have been the exclusive authors and teachers in this course in its 77-year history so far. They have frequented *all* high schools in their uniforms[8] at least once a week and educated *all* students (female students since 1937) in military affairs.

Another long-standing continuity in the course is the prominent discourse that governs the textbooks. The most important element of this discourse has been the emphasis on the predetermined role of the military in Turkish history, character, and contemporary politics. In this picture, the military appears as a *natural* extension of national character and an embodiment of the achievements of "Turks throughout history." The students are told that the "eternal symbol of heroism is the Turkish nation and its unmatched military" (*Tipi* 1941, 48) and are called upon to be worthy of their "ancestors" (*ecdad*) by displaying the "heroism that is naturally present [in their character]" (*Millî Güvenlik Bilgileri I* [1965], 13).

The arguments developed in the Turkish History Thesis in the 1930s, as well as its overall framework, closely inform these textbooks with the military at center stage. According to the textbooks: Turks have been a military-nation throughout history (somewhat dropped in the 1990s); Turkish history is written with victories; military service is not only a *sacred* duty, but a necessary rite of passage for young men; military is a school and students are soldiers; self-sacrifice is necessary for the nation (and the state) to survive and all Turks sacrifice willingly and without hesitation; and so on. The Turkish History Thesis, in these texts, is a "fact" that defines the major tenets of Turkish history and characteristics of the Turkish nation. The "aim" of this course, as described by Ministry guidelines, laws, and regulations and as elaborated upon in the textbooks, bears witness to this spirit. In 1944, a publication of the Ministry of Education explains it as follows:

> Turkish youth is hard-working, sportsmanlike, patriotic, and militant.... The art of soldiering, which Turks have inherited from their ancestors, is taught in Turkish education through instruction, training, and practice, under a strict discipline, and in accordance with contemporary war techniques and desires, to all male and female students in the secondary schools, high schools, and higher education institutions. (*Türkiye Cumhuriyeti Maarifi, 1923–1943* [1944], 112)

The high school *National Defense Knowledge* textbook used in the 1950s is more direct in its assertions of the militarist character of the Turkish nation: "The Turkish nation is a healthy, strong, enduring, disciplined, and competent nation. Love for the homeland is very strong in Turks. Turks have a passion for their independence and honor. Turks are soldiers and warriors" (*Millî Savunma I* [1952], 6). It is further suggested that "the military is the essence of the Turkish nation" and that "*Mehmetçik* (Little Mehmet) is a first-class soldier" (*Millî Savunma I* [1952], 6). The textbook used in the 1960s gives a more elaborate list of the characteristics of the Turkish nation/race:

> [One of the aims of national security education] is to instill in students the following
> high (*yüksek*) and historical characteristics of the Turk, with the use of historical
> examples and heroic legends:
>
> (1) Turks are the oldest, noblest, and most heroic race in the world.
> (2) Turkish civilization, which starts with history, is an old and superior civilization
>   and has formed the basis of contemporary civilization.
> (3) The Turk is strong, dashing, combatant, intelligent, diligent, brave, and serves as
>   an example of morality and virtue for all of humanity.
> (4) The Turkish woman is the most faithful and virtuous woman in the world and the
>   Turkish man is the most brave and faithful man. When these two entities come
>   together, they form a force that History has recorded as undefeatable. The Turkish
>   Nation that consists of such human entities, then, is the strongest nation in the world.
> (5) The victories of the Turk begin with world history. Turkish armies have been the
>   creators of honor and glory.
> (6) Turks are advanced human beings who hold respect for their elders, love for their
>   youngsters, and feel joy while helping those in need.
> (7) Turks are very devoted to their homeland and very alert about their independence
>   and freedom. They do not hesitate to face death to protect them. The Turk strikes
>   as lightning those who place their eye on his/her homeland, independence, and
>   selfhood and destroys them.
> (8) In short, the Turk is a superior entity that has a unique place on earth with all these
>   countless characteristics. (Ulubay 1962, 10)

Although this list is used only in the early 1960s and then dropped, for the next two
decades there are frequent references to the "military-nation" idea. In 1965, Baron
von der Goltz himself is quoted and it is argued that the suggestions made by Goltz
in 1883 regarding the nature of modern warfare have been proven by history, and
that the "Turkish" Independence War is the prime example of the unification of the
nation and the military with all the "men and women" of the nation (*Millî Güvenlik
Bilgileri III* [1965], 15). The need for the students to combine an understanding of
the requirements of national security and the "heroic blood" they carry is emphasized in this text and the students are further told that they "will work for this
homeland, live for this homeland and die for this homeland" in bold letters (*Millî
Güvenlik Bilgileri III* [1965], 37).

The textbooks used throughout the 1970s and the early 1980s make similar
claims that resonate with the Turkish History Thesis: "Turks have formed strong
states in all historical epochs. They have won many legendary victories as the greatest
military-nation of the world" (*Millî Güvenlik Bilgisi I-II-III* [1973], 27). For the rest
of the 1980s and early 1990s, the textbooks include passages that define "love for the
homeland" as the greatest "passion" of Turks (*Milli Güvenlik Bilgisi* [1987], 262)
and "heroism" as a spirit that is hereditary:

> The spirit of heroism is inherited from ancestors. If a nation is not heroic this way, the
> few brave ones that come out of that nation cannot live freely on this earth. They cannot
> turn every war into victory. The heroism of our nation has been addressed in many
> works from those of Herodotus to the Old Testament, and by the greatest writers and
> poets. (*Milli Güvenlik Bilgisi* [1987], 259)

Not surprisingly, when I told Major Niyazi, an officer-teacher I interviewed, that I was interested in the military culture of Turkey, his response was: "If your goal is to explore Turkish military culture, analyzing the *National Security* course is not sufficient. In fact, it is not even relevant. To do that you should look at history. Since Central Asia (*sic*), the main occupation for Turks has been military service. War and war-making are essential in our culture."

The current regulations that define how the course is to be conducted list its major aim as "reinforcing the national security consciousness that *naturally* exists in all Turkish youth in line with the requirements of total warfare" (*Milli Güvenlik Bilgisi öğretimi Yönetmeliği*, Article 1-a, my emphasis). In the previous regulations, dated 1968, the term "essence" is used instead of "naturally," but the idea is the same. Although "race" has largely been dropped in official discourse since the 1950s, the linkages that were established among culture, nation, and race with the advancement of the Turkish History Thesis in the 1930s continue to shape the basic assumptions of Turkishness and Turkish history in these textbooks. Terms such as "naturally," "in essence," "blood," and "hereditary" are widely used to define the military character of the "Turks." The myth of the military-nation, in this course, is a historical and sociological fact.

The History in the Present

At present, the course is taught in the second year of all high schools (private, public, technical, or other) for one hour every week. The most recent textbook used in the military course (since 1998) requires special attention not only because it openly discusses the relationship between nationalism and racism, but also because it marks the new turn that this course and its textbooks have taken at the turn of the century. This is the sixth academic year since the current textbook has been used in the high school *National Security Knowledge* course. This means that more than four million students have so far studied this book.[9]

Its first distinguishing characteristic is that there are very few references in this text to the military characteristics of the Turkish nation or race and all of the existing ones are direct quotes from Atatürk's speeches. Instead, there is a sophisticated discussion of "latest scientific theories on nations and nationalism" (*Milli Güvenlik Bilgisi*, 1998, 72). This is significant because, for the first time in the history of the course, "the nation" is treated as a debatable ontological category, one that can be defined in different ways. It is suggested that theories that base themselves on the primacy of "objective" characteristics in defining nations (such as race, language, or religion) have recently been replaced by other theories that emphasize "subjective or cultural" foundations for nationhood recognizing the modern nature of all nations (72). It is then argued that Atatürk's nationalism[10] falls within the latter category:

According to Atatürk, "the natural and historical elements that have played a role in the constitution of the Turkish nation" are as follows:

- Political unity,
- Linguistic unity,
- Unity of the homeland,

- Racial and *menşe* (place of origin, root) unity,
- Historical kinship,
- Moral kinship. (72–73)

This definition of the nation by Atatürk is given as an example of the "subjective or cultural" approach to nationalism with the further suggestion that what Atatürk means by "racial and *menşe* (place of origin, root) unity" does *not* stand for a "racist theory based on an idea of pure races" or a "racist approach to nationalism" (73). Here is the long quote from Atatürk that the authors of this textbook use to *refute* the "racist" aspect of Atatürk's nationalism:

> All members of the Turkish nation, with certain differences, generally look alike. Certain physical differences should be seen as natural. Because: is it possible that every one of the children of such a great and old human community that has spread out towards and settled in the valleys of Mezopotamia and Egypt to start with, Central Asia before recorded history, Russia, Caucasia, Anatolia, old and new Greece, Crete, Central Italy before the Romans, in other words the coasts of the Mediterranean; and that has lived with different kinds of people and in different climates for thousands of centuries, be all alike? ... It is not right to think that the Turkish *kavim* [race or ethnicity] has appeared at a single location or in a limited geographic area. (73)

According to the writers of the 1998 textbook, this quotation "clearly shows" that Atatürk's understanding of the Turkish nation was not based on "race" because he does not believe that the Turks are a "pure race" as seen in German national socialism (74). The fact that the arguments Atatürk is reciting in this quote are based on the Turkish History Thesis, which was "proven" by racist anthropological and prehistoric archeological research on skeletons and living human beings, is obviously written out of this account.

Later in the text, Atatürk's nationalism is defined as rational, unifying, peace loving, humanistic, and secular (73–74). There are other characteristics of this nationalism: it is against non-nationalist ideologies (such as Marxism–Leninism), against racist ideologies based on ideas of pure race (such as German Nationalist Socialism), and against ideologies that seek to divide Turkish society along race lines or along the lines of religion or religious sects (74). These negative connotations give important clues to what "race" (*ırk*) stands for in contemporary political discussions in Turkey and why it has been included as a topic in the current textbook. The first thing to note is that, much like the 1930s, the term "race" has not been differentiated from the term "ethnicity." This conflation is not peculiar to the *National Security Knowledge* textbook. In the constitution, the laws, as well as in public debates, the term "ethnicity" is hardly used and, instead, "race" defines ethnic difference. For instance, Article 14 of the 1982 Constitution rules that basic rights and freedoms cannot be used to "promote discrimination on the basis of language, race, religion and sect." Similarly, the 1998 textbook talks about "ideologies that seek to divide Turkish society along race lines." In both cases, ethnic movements, particularly the Kurdish movement, are in question.[11] This particular clause of the constitution and the laws in the Penal Code that are based on this clause are often used against Kurdish or pro-Kurdish activists. In a peculiar twist, in this textbook and elsewhere, the "racism" of the extreme Right—e.g., Nazism—is associated with the racism of those "that seek to divide Turkish society along race lines." Their shared character is an emphasis on "race" as an organizing category. In opposition to these discourses, Atatürk's nationalism is presented as being nonracial, and thus, nonethnic.

An overall critique of the term "Turk" (*Türk*) that has been launched since the late 1980s by oppositional groups forms another aspect of the background to the detailed discussion of race in the current textbook. According to its critics, the term "Turk" should not be used in place of "citizen of Turkey" because it has an ethnic/racial connotation and not all citizens of Turkey identify themselves as Turks. A popular replacement has been the term *Türkiyeli* (one who is from Turkey), which defines the relationship of individuals to the homeland and the state through citizenship and belonging, rather than ethnicity. In June 2003, Prime Minister Tayyip Erdoğan was echoing this approach when he stated that his government was against "racist nationalisms" and added that "the tie that binds us together is citizenship. When we come to a [shared] consciousness of constitutional citizenship, our relations with each other will change" (*Hürriyet*, 29 June 2003). The response of state officials and others to this approach has emphasized the nonethnic/nonracial character of the term "Turk" as Atatürk defined it. In the textbook, the unifying nature of Atatürk's nationalism is explained as follows: "Atatürkism, accepts as Turks all Turkish citizens who 'share a common history, morals and laws,' embrace the same shared culture and ideals, and have tied their fate to the Turkish nation on their own will" (74). Yet the same narrative identifies Turkishness with Central Asia, draws a racial overview of history, and, later in the text, excludes the non-Muslim minorities from this "shared culture and ideals" altogether (see later).

This discussion of "race" and "nation" in the earlier sections of the book establishes the necessary background to the overall discourse on Turkey's "internal and external enemies." It is argued, over and over, throughout this textbook, that those who claim to belong to a different race are the "divisive elements" (*bölücü unsurlar*) that promote racial discrimination in society and are supported by Turkey's enemies, not by the Turkish people themselves (74–75, 90–100). It is also made clear that the minorities (Greek, Armenian, and Jewish) recognized by the Lausanne Treaty of 1923 are the only minorities that exist in Turkey, that these non-Muslim minorities are regarded as "Turkish citizens" regardless of their religion and race, and that they are treated equally under the law (97). The rest, that is "the large majority comprising more than 95 percent of Turkey have shared the same fate for thousands of years and have blended with the same culture and goals" (97).

One implication of this suggestion is that the 95 percent majority *has not* shared the same fate or blended with Jews, Armenians, and Greeks for "thousands of years," a move that simultaneously denies the coexistence of multiple ethnicities, religions, and sects under the Ottoman Empire and ethnicizes and Islamizes Turkishness.[12] Defined outside of the shared culture of the "majority," these non-Muslim "minorities" are denied an equal standing in relation to the "Turkish nation" and are only recognized as "Turkish citizens," that is, they are given an equal status *only* in relation to the laws. The second implication is that the "95 percent majority" is made up of a homogeneous *Turkish* nation that is thousands of years old. This formulation denies the history of different Muslim communities that fought together in the Independence War, who (Kurds, Laz, Çerkes, etc.) Atatürk himself had announced as "sibling nations" in the early years of the Republic (see chapter one), and denies the contemporary existence of any group or member of society that has not been a part of the "historical" Turkish nation.

As I argued in chapter one, one of the main characteristics of the Turkish History Thesis as it was formulated in the 1930s was its use of race, nation, and culture almost interchangeably. In the 1998 *National Security Knowledge* textbook, as well as in Turkish official ideology in general, a similar position is assumed. Race stands for ethnicity and, despite the arguments to the contrary, Turkish nation/culture is clearly defined by Atatürk and these authors in ethnic/racial terms through its "thousands of years" long history.

Today it is often argued that the Turkish History Thesis was an "extreme" theory that should properly be historicized, that the 1930s were the difficult years of state-making and that race-based thinking was common in the world at large. It is assumed that this thesis is not relevant today. However, historian Etienne Copeaux (1998) has shown that Turkish History Thesis, despite certain changes and mod-ifications, still informs textbooks, as well as the official ideology at large. My research on the military course textbooks leads to a similar conclusion. Furthermore, I suggest that, without even mentioning the name of the Turkish History Thesis, the 1998 textbook assumes its overall discursive and historical framework, while silencing its clear connections to racist ideologies of its time (e.g., eugenics) as well as its racist scholarly basis. This narrative also silences the presence (in Atatürk's times) of alternative voices regarding the nature of Turkish nationalism (such as that of Ziya Gökalp) together with Atatürk's own participation in these alternative formulations (during the Independence War and the early days of the Turkish Republic). Yet it would be simplistic to conclude a discussion of this textbook as being yet another articulation of Turkish official nationalism. It is a *particular* articulation that is situated in the late 1990s in the school textbooks written and taught by officers of the Turkish military. It differs both from the textbooks used in the same course prior to it and from other textbooks used in the education system.

Strategic Thinking as a Way of Life: Textbooks

A historical inquiry into how the high school military course has evolved since 1926 needs to take into account world historical changes (particularly the two world wars and the Cold War), changes in Turkey's internal politics (particularly the three military coups, the Kurdish conflict and the recent tensions between Islamism and secularism), as well as changes in the (self) perception of the military regarding its role in society and politics. A detailed historicity would require another study. Therefore I concentrate on the present textbook and classroom practices, and try to understand their specificity in relation to the past, on the one hand, and to the current political background, on the other.

I argue in this chapter and the next one that the high school military course is at a major turning point, where it is literally changing "face" and overall approach. First of all, the 1998 textbook has been the first one to be printed on white paper (instead of a straw-colored paper of low quality), with colorful pictures and graphics. This development is in line with the changing face of all textbooks in Turkey and is significant only in light of the larger changes that have taken place in this particular course. The 1998 textbook is not only more presentable in its outlook, but in its contents as well. Its language is more accessible and its topics simultaneously more political, more up-to-date, and more comprehensive.

Furthermore, it is different from all previous books in that the issue of "military service" is almost completely dropped and replaced with what I will call "strategic thinking as a way of life."[13] Its emphasis on Atatürkism as a lifestyle and on strategic thinking as a worldview bring about this particular blend of Cold War thinking and nationalism in a post–Cold War Turkey. Its efficacy is increased in the depoliticized, post-coup (i.e., post-1980) educational atmosphere of Turkey where neither the students nor the teachers are allowed to discuss politics in other courses. In other words, at the turn of the new millennium, high school students in Turkey study politics mainly from a textbook written by the General Staff and discuss it mainly in the presence of a military officer.

One of the major changes in the military course since the late 1990s has been the shift from an emphasis on military service and military organization to Atatürk's principles, on the one hand, and strategic analysis of national, regional, and world politics, on the other. The chapter headings in the current textbook are as follows:

(1) The Definition of National Security (4 pages),
(2) Our National Security Strategy (11 pages),
(3) The Establishment of Turkish Armed Forces and Its Organizational Structure (9 pages),
(4) Turkish Armed Forces and Special Laws (6 pages),
(5) The Duties and Functions of the Turkish Armed Forces in Our Country (4 pages),
(6) Atatürk's Principles and National Unity (19 pages),
(7) Games Played on The Turkish Republic (12 pages),
(8) Important International Organizations that Turkey Participates In (8 pages),
(9) Mobilization for War (4 pages),
(10) Civil Defense (6 pages),
(11) Police Forces and their Duties (4 pages)

For the first time in the history of the course, there is no chapter, or even a subsection, in this textbook on military service. It is only touched upon under other topics. Its first appearance is in a short reading piece (*okuma parçası*) where military terms such as military service, soldier, private, noncommissioned officer, military student, officer, commander, subordinate, post, discipline, and duty are defined. The definition of military service is given as follows:

> Military service is the obligation to learn and perform the art of war in order to defend the Turkish homeland, Turkish independence, and Republic. Being the most sacred service to the homeland and the nation, military service prepares the youth for real life conditions. A person who has not done his military service cannot be useful to himself, his family, or his homeland. (*Millî Güvenlik Bilgisi* [1998], 20)

This definition is almost identical with the earlier definitions used in the 1980s textbooks (e.g., *Millî Güvenlik Bilgisi* [1987], 57) but is not backed by the larger framework in which military service was presented in the 1980s, or throughout the history of the course.

As the first title of the course in 1926, that is, *Preparation for Military Service*, attests, military service was central to the idea of the course in the first place. The 1930 textbook written by Atatürk and Afet Inan was devoted primarily to outlining the universal history of warfare and justifying the need for compulsory military service (see chapter One). The rest of the textbooks used in the 1930s and 1940s had several different sections on military service where the compulsory conscription law was explained in detail, history of conscription was laid out, and issues such as discipline, hierarchy, and military virtues were discussed. Practical military knowledge, such as the use of arms, basic topography, and geography knowledge (how to define surface, read, and draw maps, etc.), mobilization for war, and military communication systems were the other topics covered in these textbooks.

The title of the course, together with its content, changed in the 1950s. From 1950 to 1962, the course was called *National Defense Knowledge*. It was the aftermath of World War II and the first chapter of the textbook was simply titled "War" (Aka and Çiçekoğlu 1950a). The discussion of what war was, in its various types as well as its reasons, was followed by a section on national defense and another one on national defense education. Military service was elaborated upon in this section, as the "ultimate form of education" for national defense. Three forms of education were discussed: in the family, at schools, and in the military. The rest of the book was about other aspects of the military and wars. The different branches of the armed forces (army, navy, and the air force) were given ample attention, together with continued emphasis on topography and use of communication systems during wartime. In the course outline published by the Ministry of Education in 1956, it was suggested that "general information is to be given only to the extent that it relates to total defense since military education is given because of the compulsory military service in the armed forces" (*Lise Müfredat Programı* [1956], 93). It was also argued that one of the major goals in the course was to give the "necessary direction to feelings of patriotism" (93). Throughout the 1950s, the course covered issues related to national defense: military service, preparation for war, mobilization for war, the organization of the armed forces (which were now called "war forces"), together with readings on the history of Turkish warfare.

In 1960, the military initiated Turkey's first coup d'etat and wrote a new constitution in 1961. This constitution, which was abolished by another military regime in 1980 and replaced by the current constitution of 1982, significantly changed the political structure of Turkey. Many observers have praised it as a politically liberal document that placed primary emphasis on social, economic, and political rights. However, one aspect of it has rarely been recognized: the institution of the military as a legitimate power structure that was situated above the political system. Although the 1961 constitution was totally rewritten in 1982, this aspect of it was kept in place and, in fact, was reinforced. An important legacy of the 1961 constitution is the National Security Council: a powerful body composed of Commanders of the General Staff, members of the government, and the president (see Parla 1991c).

At the level of international politics, NATO membership and the Cold War were having a significant impact on Turkish official ideology that found its reflections in these textbooks. With its entry into NATO in 1952, Turkey joined the Cold War and rapidly turned into what has been called a "national security state."[14] The 1950s were marked by the development of strong ties with the United States, including those established through military assistance. With the formation of the National Security Council in 1961, the name of the military course was also changed from *National Defense Knowledge to National Security Knowledge*. However, this name change did not amount to significant modifications in the curriculum. The introduction of the idea of Cold War and of security as an all-encompassing concept that defined all peacetime politics was the obvious and expected addition. There was a second addition, which was just as significant: throughout the 1960s, students were also taught the "Atatürk Revolution" as well as the 1961 "Revolutionary Movement" initiated by the Turkish military (see Ulubay 1962, *Millî Güvenlik Bilgileri I* 1965).

In 1973, these two subject headings were dropped, revealing another change initiated by the military in Turkish politics: a semi-coup where the military gave an ultimatum to the government and was able to force new elections and major changes in the political system. The 1960 intervention and the 1961 constitution were no longer seen in a positive light by the new military leadership. Moreover, the language of "revolutions" had been claimed by a growing leftist movement. The 1961 "Revolutionary Movement" would never again be mentioned in any military course textbook. However, Atatürk's revolutions, renamed *Atatürkism (Atatürkçülük)*, would be reincorporated into the textbooks in the 1980s. This was not a simple renaming, though. The discussion of the "revolutionary" changes initiated by Atatürk was no longer an issue. It was replaced by "Atatürk's principles" (Republicanism, Nationalism, Populism, Laicism, Etatism, and Reformism) (*Millî Güvenlik Bilgisi*, 1987). The 1973 textbook, while erasing the subject of revolutions, introduced a Cold War concept: *geopolitics*, defined as "the definition and administration of government politics in accordance with the necessities and inclinations of geography" (*Millî Güvenlik Bilgisi* [1973], 284). Since then the notion of geopolitics has played a major role not only in the military course textbooks, but in Turkish official ideology in general.

Apart from these additions (Atatürk Revolution in the 1960s, Geopolitics since the 1970s, and Atatürkism since the 1980s) to the curriculum and limited modifications in the specificities of the "military knowledge" provided, the rest of the topics covered in these textbooks did not change significantly until 1998. Military service was always a major focus, although with changing definitions and emphases. Since 1998, two other aspects of the previous textbooks, namely the emphasis on Atatürk's principles and the discussion over Turkey's geopolitical positioning, have become the focus of military education in high schools. In terms of page numbers, these two topics make up the longest sections of the book. Moreover, their prevalence in the course has been reinforced in the last two years by special directives from the military to the officer-teachers.

The three officer-teachers I interviewed in 1999 talked passionately about this particular aspect of their teaching in the past two years. "Each year, in addition to the textbooks, we are given classified directives that highlight the issues we need to emphasize in our teaching for that academic year. For instance, this year we have been told to pay special attention to Atatürk's principles," one of the officers explained to me. He himself had gone as far as devoting a whole semester to Atatürk's principles only! He was determined to "make the students understand what Atatürk *really* wanted for this country." For this, he had asked them to do research on these principles and prepare a class presentation. Another teacher had assigned term papers on the principles of Atatürk—which is very unusual in an education system based on exams.

The changing focus of the military course is reflected in the presentation of the 1998 textbook. The Introduction page, which is followed by a picture of the flag, the national anthem, and Atatürk's address to the youth, is short and very clear in its message:

> The Turkish Republic is faced with [political] games that have their origins outside of Turkey due to its geopolitical positioning. The Turkish youth needs to be ready for these games. And the most important requisite of being ready is to accept that a secular and democratic system is the ideal system for Turkey and to have a developed awareness regarding this issue. The way to do this is to embrace Atatürk's principles and revolutions *not only at the level of ideas, but also at the level of life style.* As long as the Turkish youth is aware of these games and accept Atatürk's principles and revolutions as a life style, there is no doubt that Turkey will reach the level of contemporary civilizations. The aim of the National Security Knowledge course is to inculcate these two important behaviors. The Turkish youth will learn these behaviors and, thus, will not let Atatürk down. (7, emphasis added)

There are several important messages in this short text. First, the aim of the course is presented as teaching the Turkish youth how they could live up to Atatürk's *expectations* of them. By implication, students are told that they are educated to fulfill Atatürk's expectations. Second, defense is defined as *ideological* preparedness rather than *military* preparedness, which might explain the absence of "military service" as a topic in this textbook. Third, it is made clear that the teaching in this course will not be limited to *ideas*, but will target *life styles* as well. In other words, to be a good student, one would have to *think, live, and behave* in the way that the officer-teachers of the *National Security Knowledge* course find appropriate. The officer-teachers are given the authority to intervene in their students' life styles and teach them how they should live as good Atatürkist citizens. Catherine Lutz defines the military as a *total institution* that presents a totalistic claim on the life of its members:

> Military is a hierarchical and authoritarian workplace. It is a *total institution*, the sociological term for an organization that makes claims on all aspects of a member's life rather than just, for example, the work or school hours or the time spent in club activity. (Lutz 1999, 187)

What the *National Security Knowledge* course makes possible is the expansion of this *total institution* into the lives of all high school students. Rephrasing Cynthia Enloe's provocative question "who is the military wife married *to*?" (Enloe 2000, 197), one might ask "*whose* students are the high school students taking this course? The military's or their school's?"

All three of these points came up repeatedly in my interviews with the officer-teachers. According to Colonel Yılmaz, good education meant the inculcation of Atatürk's principles. This was his main goal in the course. Lieutenant Ahmet suggested that the Turkish Armed Forces were the greatest leader of Atatürkist thought in contemporary Turkey and that their task was to teach it to young people. In fact, he believed that the teachers in his high school were not "conscious enough" either: "If I get a chance, I want to educate them as well!" For Major Niyazi, too, Atatürkism was central to the course and his teaching: "the most important thing is to teach kids what Atatürkism is. In our education system, it is always what Atatürk did, what he said, etc. That's not it! Students should be able to *feel* and *live* Republicanism!" There was no question in the minds of these officer-teachers that the major responsibility of the students was to fulfill Atatürk's expectations of them by living in a particular way (i.e., based on his principles) and that their own task was to educate them in this way of life.

This teaching involved two major subject topics: Atatürk's principles and contemporary politics. In the words of Major Niyazi: the course was organized around issues

> that matter to people's everyday living. Political science is an important aspect of our task. What is national security? What is strategy? What is political power? These are the issues we teach. We pay special attention to daily politics. If you don't do that, you lose the students' interest anyway.

Other issues covered in the course, such as mobilization for war, national defense, military ranks, and terminology, would only be needed in specific occasions, whereas the political issues were "relevant on an everyday basis." He was critical of the current textbook for not going into enough detail concerning political issues. The fact that the students would ask them questions about politics was both "good" and "normal" according to Major Niyazi. After all, they were the ones most qualified, among teachers, to answer such questions.

Similarly, Lieutenant Ahmet's main goal was to teach students enough politics that they felt confident to argue with their parents: "If they can express their opinion as they listen to the news next to their father and tell him right from wrong, then I consider myself successful." As I will show in the next chapter, the freedom to discuss political issues in class was also raised as one of the defining characteristics of the military course by the students as well. There were conflicting opinions as to whether the officer-teachers were indeed the most qualified to teach these issues, but the lived experience of almost all the students I interviewed was the same: politics was at the center of the military course. Any issue, from the question of whether Abdullah Öcalan should be hung or not to the *türban*[15] issue at the universities, was a legitimate discussion topic in this course.

This is a new development that characterizes the late 1990s. When I was a high school student in the 1980s, there could be no talk of political issues in the *National Security Knowledge* course. It was indeed a course on military affairs and not one on political affairs. This shift is obvious when one looks at the textbooks. The one used since 1998 reads like a political science and international relations book in its emphasis on Atatürk's founding principles, Turkey's geopolitical positioning and discussion of issues that define contemporary Turkish politics: Relations with Greece, Armenia, Iraq, Iran, Russia, and Syria; the Cyprus issue; the minorities in Turkey; the characteristics of "divisive" political movements (i.e., the Kurdish movement); Islamic "fundamentalism"; the political organizations that Turkey has joined (e.g., the UN, NATO, Council of Europe, Black Sea Economic Coopera-tion); and Turkey's relations with the European Union. Both the teachers and the students I interviewed since 1999 talked about the possibility of EU candidacy and its implications, Abdullah Öcalan's death sentence, and the Islamic movement in Turkey as some of the major topics of discussion in the classroom. The overall framework that defined the presentation of these issues, both in the textbooks and according to my interviewees, was the idea that "Turkey has no friends" (*Türkün Türkten başka dostu yoktur*) and that no country or organization in the world (especially the EU) wants Turkey to be a strong country. The overall conclusion of this "strategic" worldview is that "Turkey must always be a strong country" (*Milli Güvenlik Bilgisi* [1998], 90).

The revealing title of the section in the current textbook that discusses Turkey's geopolitical uniqueness, its relations with neighboring countries, and its "internal" enemies, is: "The Games Played Over Turkey." Here, all of Turkey's neighbors are regarded as enemies that play particular "games" over Turkey. For instance, it is suggested that the Greek attitude toward Turkey is based upon the historical ideology of "Megalo Idea" (Great Ideal), which aims at a larger Greece that includes Turkey's western and northern provinces: "Until they obtain these lands, they will continue to fight" (92). Similarly, Armenia seeks to "establish Great Armenia, which is believed to have existed in history but in fact has not" (94). For this reason, Armenia is blamed for supporting all kinds of movements that are aimed at weak-ening and dividing Turkey. Iran's main goal is also to weaken Turkey and to "turn Turkey into a theocratic state" (95). Syria claims that Hatay, "a province that has been Turkish for centuries is part of their land mass and dreams of a weak Tur-key . . . Syria supports all kinds of movements against Turkey" (96). It is further suggested that other countries that are not Turkey's immediate neighbors also feel uncomfortable with the idea of a strong Turkey, particularly because Turkey is a democratic and secular country with a predominantly Muslim population.[16]

The games played by "our neighbors" are followed by a discussion of Turkey's internal threats. The "activities" that seek to divide Turkey along the lines of race, religion, or religious sect are presented as the major threats to the democratic and secular regime of the country. However, it is emphasized over and over again that these "games" are *external* in their origins and that Turkish people have not been fooled by them. Overall, what this section of the textbook suggests is that Turkey needs to be a strong country (because it is surrounded by enemies) and that Turkey's internal problems are indeed external in their origin and are sponsored by its ene-mies. In this approach, all of international relations and internal politics are reduced to issues of "strategy." Being prepared to fight against them, first of all, requires a strong Turkey and, by implication, a strong military: "If our country has not been attacked in many years, this is because our military strength is sufficient. If the Armed Forces did not possess this strength (which is a deterrent force), Turkey would have faced many military offenses" (27). Second, it requires *strategic thinking as a way of life* for its citizens. The kind of lifestyle that this course seeks to inculcate is clearly articulated as one based on an unconditional belief in Atatürk's principles and strategic thinking.

The treatment of the Cyprus question in the textbook is emblematic of the kind of strategic thinking promoted for all Turkish citizens:

> The Cyprus Peace Operation has confirmed certain facts. Firstly, it was a very successful military operation. Secondly, it has confirmed the heroic character of the Turkish military.... As a result of this operation, first the Northern Cyprus Turkish Federal Republic was founded, and later the Northern Cyprus Turkish Republic. (102–103)

These "facts" place other facts out of view. For instance, the students are not informed by the fact that Northern Cyprus is a political nonentity, "trapped outside the international system" (Navaro–Yashin 2003, 108) since the "Peace Operation" in 1974, unrecognized by any other state. Nor does the book mention the diplomatic and political problems this has caused for Turkey, particularly in relation to Greece and the European Union. Moreover, this narrative implies that international problems are best solved by military operations. This view encourages the students to be blind to or suspicious of peaceful efforts, as well as of legal and diplomatic processes.

In short, students in this course are encouraged to view both international and national political issues in *strategic* terms and adopt this thinking as a *way of life*. Instead of developing critical faculties as individuals, they are instructed to blindly follow the principles laid out in their military textbook. They are encouraged to be suspicious of all foreigners, particularly people from neighboring countries; fear all differences, remaining blind to the differences among their Muslim friends and treating their non-Muslim friends as categorically different (in fact, as non-Turkish); regard all dissent within Turkey as having an "external" origin (and thus non-authentic, non-Turkish); and think of international politics as being determined by wars and international politics by the military, accepting the inevitability of the use of force.

The discussion of daily political issues in the classroom reinforce the basic assumption that the right political perspective is the military perspective. This assumption also shapes the positioning of officer-teachers in relation to other teachers. The young Lieutenant Ahmet, thus, feels qualified to "educate" the other teachers in his school on Atatürk's principles. Moreover, in 1999 all officer-teachers were asked to file a report that provided answers to a detailed questionnaire on the conduct of students, teachers, and school administrators in their schools. As a military officer explained to me: "one of the good things about this course is that it enables the state to obtain information about every single high school in the country. There are certain schools, such as religious schools, that are totally closed to the outside. But we are able to get into those schools." In this perspective, the military is identified as "the state" and the officer-teachers who teach the military course as "agents of the state" that collect information. Even teachers in public schools who are employed by the state are inspected by officer-teachers, the *real* representatives of the state.

A similar connection between the military and the state is implied in the discussion of politics in this course. All politics is reduced to state policy that is best understood through a military perspective, i.e. through strategic thinking. As a result, military officers almost by default become political scientists and teachers of politics in high schools. The recent developments in this course point to the "securitization of politics" (see Buzan et al. 1998; Weldes et al. 1999) as a state policy, a phenomenon that political scientist Ümit Cizre (2003, 216) aptly observes in her article titled "Demythologizing the National Security Concept: The Case of Turkey": "Contrary to the global trend, the end of the Cold War did not lead to softer security perceptions and a less securitized domestic agenda in Turkey." To the contrary, the "redefinition of national security from external to internal threats" is closely connected with the "increased political activism and autonomy" of the Turkish Armed Forces (Cizre 2003, 216). Nowhere is this activism better realized than in the "education" of all high school students in matters of national and international politics by military officers.

The implications of this activism for male and female students is quite different. First of all, the *National Security Knowledge* textbook is one without any reference to women. None of the illustrations in the book contain women figures, and there is no mention of women's relationship to the military. Even the women officers in the military are excluded from the narrative of the book. It is not only the practice of military service that differentiates between male and female citizenship, but also military teaching at the high school level. All young women in the second year of high school are required to take this course and go through a year long discussion of military and political affairs presented to them by male officers as "male" issues.

Conclusion

In a 1961 report prepared by the National Defense Committee, it is suggested that both the NATO countries and countries behind the "Iron Curtain" have educational programs that prepare students for their nation's defense.[17] Turkey's need for the National Defense courses in high schools is, thus, presented as a natural outcome of this international system and a "necessity." Whether it has been reinforced by the traffic between nationalism and militarist thinking in early years of state-making, the conditions of a Cold War world, or the continuing perceptions of threat posed by Turkey's "internal and external enemies" in a post–Cold War present, the "two fronts" ideology has persisted to this day.

The words of the Minister of Education Nevzat Ayaz in 1994 and of the *National Security Knowledge* course teacher Colonel Yılmaz in 1998 point to the prevalence of the approach that military service and education still form the "two fronts" of state-making in Turkey today, much as they did in 1921 when the first Education Congress was gathered in Ankara. In state discourse, the military and the schools are still the main sites where the principles of the Republic will be protected and where citizens and citizen soldiers who know their "duties and responsibilities to the state" will be "raised." It is not a coincidence that all three of the military course officer-teachers I interviewed emphasized the intimate connections between the military and the education system. I argue that their connectedness, supported by the idea of "two fronts," is both the raison d'être of the high school military course *and* one of its major consequences.

In other words, by bringing officers-in-uniform into civilian schools and making military knowledge a requirement for secondary education, policy makers and educators have contributed to the blending of military and civilian realms, barrack and school culture. This course and its officer-teachers embody the idea that education and defense are two sides of the same coin, where citizenship is reduced to the willingness to die for one's country. This, I believe, has been the most significant long-term impact of the high school military course since its introduction into the curriculum in 1926. Regardless of its changing content or success, it has been effective in *naturalizing* the "two fronts" idea by naturalizing the existence of military officers in every high school as well as the need for military knowledge for every student. Moreover, this course has provided uninterrupted access for the military to *all* high schools and *all* high school students since the 1920s.

As it was reported in the National Defense Committee report in 1961, the military has been involved in civilian education in other parts of the world as well. Jacolyn Cock writes about the Youth Preparedness Programme and "school cadet system" in white South Africa which began in the early 1970s and suggests that "the military nature of the white educational environment became more marked over time. During 1987 it became known that the Transvaal Education Department had instructed certain teachers to carry guns; and fences, barbed wire, and high walls have been built around many white schools" (Cock 1991, 72). Catherine Lutz and Lesley Bartlett (1995, 14) show that the JROTC (Junior Reserve Officer Training Corp) programs in the U.S. high schools have been expanding rapidly, causing "a proliferation of military influence into what should be a strictly civilian world of education and youth services." What is unique about the Turkish case is that the presence of military officers in schools has remained a constant throughout the past 78 years, despite changes in Turkey's internal politics and changes in the international arena. Moreover, it is significant that this course has been compulsory for all students.

Students throughout Republican history have been told that they are members of a "heroic" race and that they should prove this by being good soldiers. Crucial among the "duties and responsibilities" that students have been asked to learn through education is the one towards the Turkish "military-nation." More recently, these responsibilities have included "thinking" and "behaving" in a certain way, that is along the lines of Atatürk's principles and the requirements of military strategic thinking. The recent developments in the course point to a renewed traffic around politics between the realms of education and the military: (1) the officer-teachers of this course are no longer experts on military affairs only, but on Atatürk's principles, international relations, and contemporary politics as well, and (2) the student-soldiers are no longer educated in the necessities and technicalities of military service, but in developing *strategic thinking as a way of life*. This approach leads to the "securitization," and by extension militarization, of not only politics, but also the concept of "everyday life." The military interprets its authority to reach the level of determining not only how the students "think," but also how they should live their lives. Whether they are successful in their efforts or not, and how the students respond to this authority-claim are questions I explore in the next chapter.

One thing I should note here is that, although a number of students have expressed opposition to the military course, its contents, or its officer-teachers in my interviews, no public debate about the course has existed in Turkey until recently.[18] Nor have I been able to find any critical reference to it or an explicit discussion about it in Turkish history. Surely, individuals must have approached it in different ways. I have listened to stories of personal unease with the course not only from current students and young people, but also from people of all ages. Yet it is very significant that there has not been any public discussion about military's direct involvement in education throughout Republican history and their continued presence as teachers-in-uniform. This, I believe, is partly the result of the intimate "play of dependencies" established between the "two fronts" of state-making: education and defense. This course has both resulted from and contributed to the "two fronts" ideology. It is, no doubt, also a result of the continued influence of the military on the political regime of Turkey, whether in the form of direct coups (27 May 1960 and 12 September 1980), indirect interventions (12 March 1971 and 28 February 1997), or through the constant monitoring of the political process by the high command in the National Security Council. Moreover, at least since the 1980s, other avert interventions of the military into the education realm contribute to the seemingly unproblematic reception of this course by the Turkish public. The country's education system and its schools from the primary to the university level have often been in the agenda of the National Security Council meetings where decisions have been made about the curriculum and proper attire in schools (such as hair styles, beards, *türban*, etc).[19] The military is represented in institutions of higher education and their governing bodies as well. For instance, one member of the Higher Education Council (*Yüksek Öğrenim Kurulu*—YÖK) and one member of the Higher Education Supervisory Board are appointed by the Chief of the General Staff.[20] The military's presence in shaping higher education was pointed out to me by one of the officer-teachers I interviewed: "We also have the university years to mold students." Having shown what this "molding" has involved in the high school military course, I now turn to how the students feel about their "duties and responsibilities" to the Turkish military-nation.

CHAPTER SIX

SILENCING THE PRESENT: STUDENT-SOLDIERS AND OFFICER-TEACHERS MEET IN THE CLASSROOM

Silence itself—the things one declines to say, or is forbidden to name, the discretion that is required between different speakers—is less the absolute limit of discourse, the other side from which it is separated by a strict boundary, than an element that functions alongside the things said, with them and in relation to them within over-all strategies. There is no binary division to be made between what one says and what one does not say; we must try to determine the different ways of not saying such things, how those who can and those who cannot speak of them are distributed, which type of discourse is authorized, or which form of discretion is required in either case. There is not one but many silences, and they are an integral part of the strategies that underlie and permeate discourses.

Michel Foucault

You, the heroic young SOLDIERS of our sacred homeland, which the Turkish Armed Forces have defended and will continue to defend with success, make-up a real ARMY OF EDUCATION. The responsibility of the future has been placed on your shoulders, minds, and wrists.

National Security Knowledge II 1965 (original emphasis)

An analysis of the high school military course solely based on its textbooks and teachers would be incomplete. To rephrase what Catherine Lutz and Jane Collins (1993, 217) have said about the magazine *National Geographic*, there would have been no military course without the millions of students who have taken it. Since Janice Radway's (1984) paradigm-shifting ethnographic work on readers of romance novels in the United States, the issue of "reception" has been central in studies of cultural forms, products, and processes. The "tradition of the docile and imagined" audience (Lutz and Collins 1993, 218) has been replaced with an interest in the agency of the consumers of popular culture in interpreting cultural products in their own way. In this view, readers/viewers/consumers are not assumed to be passive recipients of the meanings intended by the producers of cultural texts, but they attach their own meaning to them. The question of whether possible meanings of a particular cultural form are infinite or whether they are limited by certain dominant themes constitutes a central concern of many cultural studies scholars today.

This chapter indirectly addresses this question and argues that "positionality" is a dominant factor in shaping the different interpretations of the high school military course by the students who have taken it. Based on my ethnographic research, I look into the ways male and female students from different parts of Turkey, with varying socioeconomic, ethnic, and religious backgrounds have experienced being educated into military and political matters by an officer-teacher.[1] What does this course mean for the students who have to take it? Do they think it is necessary? What, according to them, is this course about? As I show below, my questions have stimulated a wide range of responses from students. This chapter seeks to analyze the specificities of various positionalities (or in Haraway's terms "situated knowledges") in relation to this course, while at the same time highlighting the changes taking place in its teaching in the last couple of years from the perspective of students.

As Donna Haraway suggests, "Vision is *always* a question of the power to see—and perhaps of the violence embedded in our visualizing practices" (1991, 192). In chapter five, I have tried to lay out the military vision provided in the current and past military course textbooks and its embeddedness in the discourses of power. This chapter aims to highlight the different visions embedded in the narratives of the young people I have interviewed. The tension created between the hegemonic security discourse that dominates the teaching of both military and political affairs in high schools and the strong insecurities experienced by many students will be the focus of my discussion.

In chapter five, I argued that the major success of this course has been to help internalize the idea that the military has a place in civilian life, including education, and that the latest developments in the course have brought (military) strategic analysis of politics into the classroom as a legitimate topic of discussion and learning. My ethnographic research points to the tensions behind this process and reveals that the "securitization" of political issues, which has dominated both the textbooks and the classroom discussions in this course, has resulted in growing feelings of insecurity in students whose identities have been associated with "threats," particularly Kurdish students in Southeastern Turkey. I show that the relationship of students to "national security" is strongly determined by who they are and where they go to school. In other words, the move away from military service and strictly military issues to "strategic analysis as politics" in this course has intensified the conflict between students and the officer-teachers, and has created "silence" as an expression of insecurity and a form of resistance among students. Therefore, I saw my task as an ethnographer throughout this research as one of listening for "silences," as much as for various articulated interpretations.

Who Cares?

My interest in the *National Security Knowledge* course was met by surprise by many of the young people I interviewed. Many of those who had taken the course in the 1980s (or late 1970s) suggested that this course was "not important at all." Almost everyone remembered it as an (academically) "easy" course that did not "mean anything to the students." Many remembered that the students often made fun of this course and its teacher. The suggestion that the course might have had an impact on them in any way was "absurd." "No one took the course seriously. Poor guy, he never established the kind of discipline he was looking for" was Alp's response to my question about the course. I heard similar remarks over and over throughout my research.

At the same time, many of my interviewees had not questioned why this course had been in their curriculum. After hearing me raise this issue, some of them first reflected on the lack of earlier questioning on their part. In Mustafa's words: "I am sure I can speculate on the reasons for why they would want students to take this course, but why have I not asked this question to myself before?" Asude, who was a leftist student in high school and is now a history graduate student, recalled having been uncomfortable with the right-wing ideologies that dominated the teaching of history in high schools, but never having given serious thought to the *National Security* course: "Of course, when I look back now, I realize that this course should be seen as part of the right-wing hegemony created in schools. But we never discussed it at that time." The same was true for Kader: "This course is like the flag ceremony on Mondays and Fridays. You just do it but never think about what it means. It is interesting that you would ask this question. When I think back at the kinds of things we learned in that course, it is shocking!" None of my interviewees remembered questioning why this courses existed in the first place. Simply, it had always been there.

According to Leyla, who had gone to high school in Izmir in the early 1980s, it "was interesting that a guy with a uniform would come to class every week. He wanted us to call him 'commander' (*komutanım*) instead of 'teacher.' It was so weird to call someone 'commander' as a young woman. It seemed like a game." Only a couple of my interviewees had found these practices "interesting" or "weird" like Leyla. For most of them, they were normal. So was the military greeting they had to give to the "commander" before each class: "We used to perform the military greeting every single time. In fact, sometimes he did not like the way we did it and made us do it again. I don't remember finding it strange. We just did it," explained Murat, also from Izmir. My recollections of our responses to this course and its teacher as students at Işık Lisesi are along the same lines. We never took it seriously and never bothered to question what we were doing there, or what the retired officer was doing in our school. Kader's analogy with the flag ceremony is a powerful one. As Kader said, "no student likes the flag ceremony and no student takes the military course seriously."

I show below that this has been changing recently with the increasing "politicization" of the course. The current students do take this course seriously and, in fact, many of them value the chance to learn about and discuss politics in the classroom. However, I suggest that the analytical and political significance of the course should not be analyzed based on the perceptions of the students only. To the contrary, their perception of this course as "insignificant" in the pre-1998 period should be posed as an important finding. I suggest that one of the main reasons why the *National Security Knowledge* course should be taken seriously, and viewed historically, is precisely because officers, as teachers-in-uniform, have "simply" been there asking all students to be good soldiers of the army of education since 1926. It is this acceptance that, I believe, is the greatest historical success of this course. Regardless of its content or effectiveness, it is very significant that a course on the military, designed and taught by the military, has been there in civilian education throughout Republican history. Military officers in their uniforms, sometimes with their guns, have frequented school halls and have been presented to students as "teachers" based on their military qualifications. The existence of this course in the high school curriculum has never been challenged publicly and students have learned to accept its reality as normal and routine, "just like the flag ceremony."

Strategic Thinking as a Way of Life: Students

The second reason why this course needs to be taken seriously has to do with recent developments. Many students, now, find this course important and educational because of its relevance to current debates. On the other hand, students who feel threatened by the military's vision of Turkey and by the pressure to express their (oppositional) political views in class have a very different relationship to the course. They take this course seriously not because they find it educational, but because it triggers their feelings of insecurity and "otherness."

As chapter five suggests, we are no longer dealing with a course on military organization, war, and military service, but with one on current politics. The students who have been attending this course since 1998 described it more as a course on politics than one on the military: "I learned a lot about the state"; "this course is about the state and about the military's role in government"; "we studied the national borders"; "it's a very useful course; we learn a lot about the country"; "we studied NATO and other international organizations and military's role in politics"; "we are taught useful information about our neighbors, our military and Atatürk"; "we learn all about Turkey's strategic position in the world and about the bad behavior of our neighbors"; "in every class, we discuss the issues that were raised on TV the night before; the topic of discussion recently has been Abdullah Öcalan" were some of the answers I received to my question about what was covered in this course.

Some went further to describe the course as a necessary part of their education. "I learn a lot in this course. The teacher knows that he is teaching us very important stuff," said Elif. She believed that she would need this "important stuff" when she had to interact with people in the future: "For instance, when you are in a situation where the military is being debated, you should not just remain silent or say something wrong. You should be able to say that our military is good, our military has good discipline, our military is orderly. For me, this is necessary knowledge." For Tamer, too, this course was preparing him to be a good citizen: "In the future, I will be representing my country. I want to be a useful citizen for my country. I don't want to do something wrong because of my ignorance.... This course teaches us why and how [political] things happen the way they do. For instance, the whole Apo[2] case."

The framework provided by this course (i.e., strategic analysis) came out prominently in all my group discussions, particularly with students in Istanbul. I sat there listening to long strategic analyses on Turkey with special emphasis on its relationship to neighboring countries. The students debated whether Greeks were indeed our enemies, where Russia's interests lay, why so many countries had come to the support of PKK, so on and so forth. The *National Security Knowledge* course meant current politics, which meant strategic analysis. Even when very critical statements were made by some of the students (criticizing the contents of the course and the teacher for being one-sided, even overly nationalistic), most students I interviewed in Istanbul agreed on two main assumptions: that Turkey was surrounded by enemies and that our military had to remain strong. Even oppositional statements had to take these "facts" into consideration.

Kemal and Mert had made critical remarks about the military course throughout our discussion. Kemal believed that what they were learning was "one-sided" and he was curious to learn about the arguments of "the other side." Mert was critical of the idea that everyone was our enemy: "Apo is our enemy. Greece is our enemy. If you listen to the *National Security* teacher, all European countries are our enemies. Even the United States is our enemy." He wondered if students in these countries saw the Turks as their enemies. Yet when I asked both of them what they thought about this course being taught by a military officer, they did not hesitate to suggest that he was "the most qualified instructor" to teach these issues. Kemal added that the biases of the officer-teachers should be considered normal: "We cannot prevent their nationalism. Of course they will be nationalist; they are soldiers."

Kemal, among others, believed that it was good that they had this course because "Turkey has an important strategic location." When I asked him for his views on the Kurdish issue, he immediately identified it with PKK and associated PKK with "our enemies": "PKK is controlled by other countries. They use PKK to weaken Turkey. We have spent billions of dollars on this issue and this has kept us weak." Another student added: "It would have been fine if they were indeed fighting for their rights, but the problem is all about the other countries trying to weaken Turkey." All the other students in the discussion group agreed. I asked them how the other countries were able to establish control over people who lived in remote villages and make them risk their lives by joining the war. Their answer was "brainwashing."

Alp was another student who was critical of the course. He found the textbook "funny": "It is not a necessary course. It creates animosity. For instance, with Greece." But then he added:

> Turkey is situated in a very important location strategically . . . between Europe and Asia. It is true that no country is good to us, none of our neighbors are . . . This course might seem funny to us but it might be good for people who know nothing about the world, for instance for students in the East. They might be learning what is what through this course. I mean, it can create some sort of unity in the East. Here, we are always engaged with things. We watch TV, read the news, we know who is doing what. But they don't . . .

According to Alp, there was no question that the death sentence of Abdullah Öcalan needed to be carried out. Sibel was also complaining about the way everyone was treated as an enemy in the military course, but there was no question in her mind either that all "our neighbors" were acting in animosity.

In all the interviews and discussion groups I conducted in Istanbul with students from a wide variety of backgrounds, there was one thing in common: As soon as I raised political issues in my questions, particularly the Kurdish issue, a long discussion on the strategic importance of Turkey and the animosity of Turkey's neighbors and other countries followed. All the students spoke as experts on, among others, France's, Britain's, Armenia's, Iran's, Syria's, Greece's and U.S. interests over Turkey. "The Games Played Over Turkey" was not only a chapter in their textbooks, but a significant aspect of their shared discourse on politics. Their political views differed widely, but not their emphasis on strategic analysis.

Şenay was the only exception to this rule. She was critical of everything about the *National Security Knowledge* course, starting with the title:

> First of all, there is the term 'national' in the title. That should not be there. When you have people go through x-rays, they all come out the same. We have the same bone structure, etc. Then there should not be any discrimination between people. Nationalism brings discrimination. Moreover, the textbook is horrible. There is a section in the textbook that is titled "The Games Played on Turkey." Can you believe that? How can they write such things? It is such a shame. I have no idea how they manage to see things this way . . .

According to Şenay, the course was about "how international organizations and agreements work against Turkey's interests and how all of our neighbors are our enemies." She saw this as a "peculiar" way of looking at the world but also realized that many of her friends went along with these ideas: "There is such strong racism everywhere, including my friends at school. Against the Kurds, against the Greeks . . ." For instance, she was alone in her class in arguing against the death penalty for Abdullah Öcalan and in sympathizing with Merve Kavakçı, the elected representative of the Virtue Party who could not become a member of the Grand National Assembly because she insisted on keeping her *türban* in the parliament.

After Merve Kavakçı was forced to leave the parliament due to the strong protest of other representatives, the prime minister had read a short speech where he had said that the parliament was "no place to oppose the state."[3] Şenay was confused by this speech and asked her officer-teacher in the following class: "I don't understand. Who is represented in the parliament? Is it the nation or the state? Is the Grand National Assembly an assembly of the representatives of the nation or of the state? Can you explain?" She said that she felt pity for the officer-teacher after she asked this question because he could not answer it: "He turned all red and looked so worried that I got scared something would happen to him." When I interviewed her, she was still curious about the answer to this question.

I asked Şenay if she thought that this course was being successful in making people see things in this "peculiar" way. She said: "I think it is successful. They want you to obey without thinking. And that's what people do. Those who refuse to stop thinking, leave the country." At her young age, she was pessimistic about the future of Turkey and tired of the racism she kept witnessing. She wanted to see "more curiosity and less judgment" around her, and longed for a "world without borders." Her family was Turkish, Muslim, and secular. It was her humanistic ideas and openness to differences that distinguished her from her own friends and from most of the other high school students that I interviewed in Istanbul.

For most students in Istanbul, learning about "national strategy" and "our enemies" was an asset, and an officer of the Turkish military was the most qualified person to teach these issues. One student who had earlier described the discourse of the textbook as "fascistic" said:

> There is no other course where we discuss political events. These are things we should know about. Particularly the games played on Turkey by its neighbors. We should be alert about these games. Plus, we are learning all these from the most qualified person, a military officer. I don't agree with him on many issues and the textbook is horrible, but his knowledge of these issues is superb. I am glad to be taking this course.

He expressed these views in a group of eight students. Everyone agreed with him. In another group of six students, Çigdem shared with us her feelings about her English teacher coming to class as a substitute for the *National Security Knowledge* teacher one day: "He was away in an operation and she came to class. It was so funny! It was funny to hear the English teacher talk about Atatürk's principles." All the students in the group laughed when she told us this story. For this group of students, it was normal for a military officer to be talking about Atatürk's principles, but not for a civilian language teacher.

Whose Security?

Compared with the students who had studied this course in the 1980s, the experience of current students is very different. *National Security Knowledge* is no longer a boring course where one only learns about military ranks; it is the main course where students discuss current politics, TV debates, and newspaper controversies. Yet an engagement with the course necessitates at least minimal identification with the "national self" whose security is being defined from a military perspective. Those who cannot identify with it have to deal with their locations of "otherness" and designated positions of "potential threat" on a daily basis.

I attended two *National Security Knowledge* classes in December 1999.[4] The officer, who was teaching the course in the only high school in the vicinity of his garrison, told me in advance that the two classes I would be participating in were very different from one another in terms of the make up of students. This was a small town in Western Turkey that had received some migration from the Eastern provinces in recent years and the tenth graders who were from the East had gathered in the same classroom. According to the officer-teacher, these students were not particularly "cultured" and they were shy. In other words, they had little to contribute to class discussions and, even if they had, they were too shy to participate. On the other hand, the other class was composed of mostly "local" students who were more outgoing and took active part in the course. The class dynamics were exactly as he described them: little discussion and a lot of lecture in the first class was followed by a lively, interactive classroom atmosphere in the second. Yet, my interpretation of this difference will depart significantly from the officer-teacher's.

There were ten students in the first class and all were male. There is a general belief that the military course is more important for male students because of compulsory male military service. This belief was expressed by most of the students I interviewed, although not all of them subscribed to it. They usually presented it as the general understanding that did not necessarily hold true for them. In this all-male class, it certainly would be an arguable statement to make. The students looked rather disinterested and bored as they listened to what was being said without making any comments or asking any questions. The officer-teacher tried to engage them in the topic of discussion by asking simple factual questions such as "What does EU stand for?" or "What is our type of government?" as well as by motivating them to articulate their ideas on current political events. For instance, he wondered if they approved of the call made by the European Union for the Turkish Chief of Staff to report to the Ministry of Defense, instead of the prime minister directly. He also wanted to know if they knew about the group of intellectuals called the "Second Republicanists" (İkinci Cumhuriyetçiler) and whether they embraced their views or not. None of the students articulated their views on these political questions. Each question was followed by an uncomfortable silence in the classroom. The students were not very keen on answering the factual questions, either. One or two of them volunteered the answer only after a silence and further probing. The majority remained silent for the whole class hour.

This stubborn silence in the classroom of the "students from the East" was broken only once by a critical question. Before the question was asked, the officer-teacher had declared the European Union's call for the Chief of Staff to be tied to the Ministry of Defense as inadmissible due to the special character of Turkey and had blamed the instability of the political system and the inadequacy of civilian politicians for this unique condition: "When there is no stability in the political system, you cannot have a civilian authority gain control over arms." The question, asked in a critical tone, was based on this claim: "But isn't the prime minister a civilian as well? What is the difference between a minister and a prime minister? They are both civilians." It was obvious that the officer-teacher did not like the question. His answer was not very satisfactory, either: "The difference is this: The prime minister rules over the Cabinet, but not over the individual ministers. The ministers are on their own; they are not tied to the Prime Ministry." The apparent concern was that there was no "chain of command" between a minister and a prime minister; but why would that make the prime minister a more trustworthy civilian (or less civilian?) than a minister of the same government? What the current organization meant for the hierarchical positioning of the Chief of Staff in relation to the ministers in the government and how it would change if the General Staff were to report to the Ministry of Defense was not discussed at all.

The topic of discussion that day was "national security." In both classes, the officer-teacher initiated the discussion by asking whether the students had watched the Hollywood movie *Braveheart*. Most of them had seen it. He seemed glad to get this answer because his reference to "old forms of warfare" was this movie:

Do you remember what war was like in *Braveheart*? The soldiers gather in a battlefield and they fight. The civilians have got nothing to do with these wars. Is this what wars are like today? No. Today the civilian population is also involved in wars. Let's give an example: The America–Iraq war [in 1991]. Or let's call it the war between Iraq and the multinational force composed of America, England, France, and Italy. When the strategic places in Iraq were bombed, of course the civilian population was hit as well.

In today's wars, civilians are also a part of the battle; they are also involved in war. This kind of war is called total warfare. This term was introduced for the first time by Mustafa Kemal Atatürk during the War of Independence.

Two other officers I interviewed had made the same claim: "Total warfare" was a military strategy introduced to the world by Atatürk. It was a sign of his genius. After explaining that the modern form of warfare was a contribution by Atatürk to military strategy, the officer-teacher explained "national security strategy" and the composition and workings of the National Security Council (by reading from the Constitution). He asked the students in the second class who was responsible for defining the "national security strategy" for the country. The first answer was: Turkish Armed Forces. The students were surprised to hear that this was wrong, and reformulated their answer: the General Staff. This, too, was wrong. Their third guess was the Grand National Assembly, which too was incorrect. The officer-teacher explained that the national security strategy was defined jointly by the National Security Council and the Cabinet.

The lecture continued with a discussion of what the European Union was about and the implications of Turkey's anticipated membership. The main topic of debate, in which both classes were encouraged to discuss, was whether the Chief of Staff be placed under the Ministry of Defense or not. No comments were made in the first class. According to the students in the second class, there was no need for this change. They were then asked about the group of intellectuals that have popularly been called *Second Republicanists*. The students had heard about it on TV but did not quite understand their views. Here is how the officer-teacher described their main arguments and his opposition to them:

> The *Second Republicanists* do not accept the Republic that was established by Atatürk and for which many martyrs were given. They suggest that Atatürk founded this Republic by force and that his principles should be rethought and, if necessary, abandoned. They desire a more libertarian Republic. For instance, they argue that university students should be free to wear everything they want, including the *türban*. They do not recognize Turks, either. They call all of us "people of Turkey" (*Türkiyeli*), not Turks.

This, I thought, was indeed a good summary of the key arguments made by *Second Republicanists*. He continued to explain how dangerous these views were and located the source of such thinking in a foreign power. According to this officer-teacher, the *Second Republicanists* were only puppets of an international conspiracy: "These are all games played over Turkey by other countries." His language was reflective of the course's textbook.

What was left with me at the end of these two hours was an admiration for this officer-teacher for being such a good lecturer and discussion leader (at least in the second class), and an alarmed sense of how far the securitization of politics had gone. He was very articulate, consistent in his views, and friendly in his approach to students. He obviously followed the latest political debates well and wanted his students to do the same as well. In the two hours I spent with them, a diversity of issues from the EU membership, political opposition (*Second Republicanists*), the *türban* issue at the universities, and the strong threat of Islamic fundamentalism and separatist movements in Turkey, to international politics, changing forms of warfare, and the role of the military in Turkish history (with references to Atatürk, the War of Independence, the 12 September 1980 coup d'etat, and the 1997 "28 February Decisions") were covered. Examples were given from Hollywood films, recent talk shows on television, newspapers, as well as from everyday life. He also had a copy of the 1982 Constitution in his hand and referred to it several times in describing the role of the National Security Council in Turkey. He even consulted the constitution when a student in the second class asked what the term *darbe* (coup d'etat) meant. To his dismay, there was no definition of "coup d'etat" in the constitution.

I attended these two classes after I had interviewed dozens of students in Istanbul and Diyarbakır. Their stories rang in my ears as I sat there listening to the well-organized lecture and observing the silence in the first class and the dynamic discussion on current political issues in the second class. I also remembered how boring this course was when I was a tenth grader in 1987. I would have much preferred to take this course from this particular officer-teacher and participate in the discussion of political events. Yet not all students who take this class today feel the same way about the openness of their officer-teachers in discussing taboo political issues in class. Some are glad to be learning about these issues and enjoy the class discussions; others are indifferent. Many others have expressed strong discomfort with having to take such a course, and not surprisingly, those who were critical were mostly "students from the East." Other critical views were expressed by members of ethno-religious minorities (Greek, Armenian, Jewish) and by devout Muslims who did not identify with the particular form of secularism in Turkey. The security of Turkey, as defined from a military perspective in their textbooks and in lectures, was based on their insecurity. They were identified as "threats" and their agency for dissent was taken away from them by the hegemonic conspiracy discourse. They were seen merely as puppets of Turkey's enemies.

Whose security did the concept of "national security" and its particular interpretations in the military course represent? Who was included in the national "self" and who was not? Who could express their views on current political issues freely and who could not? These questions were addressed by many students who felt "othered" in the hegemonic vision provided by the textbook and the officer-teacher in the course. Many talked about their silence in the classroom and complained about the pressure to articulate their views. Some had broken their silence and confronted the officer-teacher, sometimes with dire consequences.[5] Others, while remaining silent on critical issues during my interviews, simultaneously made sure to let me know *what* they were being silent about.

One difference that hardly came up in my interviews was gender. Only a few female students suggested that they felt alienated from the course "because it was mostly about issues that had nothing to do with me as a girl." Most other young women I interviewed seemed as engaged about the course as their male friends. To the contrary, some women seemed to think of this course as a way of asserting their "equality" with men. In their narratives, ethnic or religious identities appeared more central in determining the experience of this course, than gender. Some of them even felt offended that I was asking them to respond to a question as a "girl/woman"; for them, there was no "difference" between men and women. It is possible to interpret this approach to gender issues as a strategy for young women to be taken seriously (instead of being "reduced" to their gender identity) and to include themselves in the hegemonic military-nation. Yet, it also reveals the mechanisms through gender differences become invisible and silenced.

Loud Silences

The striking dichotomy that existed between the two classes I attended also marks my research experience in Western Turkey versus Diyarbakır. If most of my interviews with students in the West were characterized by loud articulations, almost all in Diyarbakır embodied loud silences. Piröz, a Kurdish woman in Diyarbakır, came to me after finishing the short, anonymous questionnaire I had asked them to fill out and said: "I did not want to declare the party I would like to vote for and you know why." She was referring the pro-Kurdish party HADEP, which, although legal and in office, was treated as a supporter of terrorism by the state. Helin, another Kurdish woman, talked extensively about the "ideological" one-sidedness of the *History and National Security Knowledge* textbooks and said that they were not learning the kind of history they were *really* interested in. When I asked what that was, she replied: "That's for us to know. I don't want to talk about it here." I received similar responses from at least a dozen students in Diyarbakır. Many of them complained about not being allowed to articulate certain views and not having access to certain books and newspapers. On rare occasions, they defined what these were in my interviews. When they did not, they made sure to point me in the right direction so that I knew what they were *not* voicing. Some of them, for instance, wrote in their questionnaires about the fact that they did not have access to the newspaper they would like to read on a daily basis, instead of writing its name.

During my interviews and group discussions in Diyarbakır in 1999, we often talked about issues that no one voiced but everyone assumed. As Ebru explained: "I am Kurdish and I am proud of it. But these days, you cannot even trust your best friend. You cannot talk to anyone." Ebru, along with all young people of her age in Diyarbakır, had grown up in the state of war. They did not even know what "normal" life was like. In Benjamin's terms, they represented the "tradition of the oppressed [which] teaches us that 'the state of emergency' in which we live is not the exception but the rule" (Walter Benjamin, quoted in Taussig 1992, 12). "State of emergency" was not a metaphor but an everyday reality for the young people of Diyarbakır: they had grown up in the *Olağanüstü Hal Bölgesi* (State of Emergency Zone). Their lives were lived under the shadow of heavy artillery and defined by various levels of silences and silencings. But many of them were "loud and clear" about the agency they had over these silences. Even when they did not feel secure enough to express their views, they did not want me (or anyone else) to assume that they did not have political preferences and ideas. They would not voice them, but they would make sure that I knew *what* they were not voicing. Their silences were well articulated and stubbornly claimed. In Taussig's (1992, 27) terms, the "unsaid" was present at all times.

I did not interview "the students from the East" in the small western town. Therefore, I cannot make a claim to provide a more informed or sound interpretation of their silence than the officer-teacher who had been teaching them for months. Yet my research interactions with a diverse base of students lead me to believe that experience of war weighs heavily on the silences of all "students from the East." Not only do their identity-claims as Kurds situate them as constituting a "threat" in the discourses of ethno-racial nationalism and of security which dominate the teaching of this course, but their past experiences in the East have mostly been defined by strong insecurity and fear of soldiers. Therefore, the silence I observed in the class of ten male students from the East can be read as a loud articulation of the insecurities produced by war and the discourses of security in Turkey in the past two decades. I read this silence as signifying fear and self-defense, rather than ignorance and shyness, and above all, as an expression of insecurity.

Almost all my Kurdish interviewees communicated fear of the uniform: "I developed a fear of soldiers after they burned my grandmother's house. I was only ten years old at that time. I still carry that fear with me," was Ahmet's remark. Another student said, "I have been afraid of soldiers all my life. I always live with the fear that they will stop me and take me away." For Nergis, who had grown up in Siirt, her fear and dislike of soldiers had to do with her gender: "In the East, all young girls hate soldiers because it is impossible to walk from place to place without being harassed by them. You have to pass the garrison on your way to school, there are soldiers on your way to the town center . . . there are soldiers everywhere! And they verbally harass you all the time!" In Nergis's eyes, the officer-teacher who taught the *National Security Knowledge* course at her school was not only a teacher, but also a male soldier, which made her feel doubly insecure.

According to Kartal, a student in Diyarbakır, this course was important and potentially useful, yet he also believed that "the fact that it is taught by a soldier in uniform has a negative impact on students. Why can't a civilian teacher teach the same course? When you see a soldier with his uniform and his gun come into the classroom, you can't get much out of it." I had heard stories of officers occasionally coming into the classroom with their guns in other cities as well, but it was a rare happening. In the Southeast, many officers—even retired officers—seemed to be doing it on a regular basis. The students believed that this was unique to their region: "Perhaps it is because we are in the *Olağanüstü Hal Bölgesi* (State of Emergency Zone). The officer who was teaching in my previous school would sometimes come right back from an operation with his gun and dirty clothes." Many others said that their officer-teacher carried a gun at all times. This was not to be taken lightly by the students who lived in constant fear.

Moreover, many students had family members or relatives fighting in the mountains against the soldiers. Aynur, a young woman who had graduated from a high school in a mixed town in the Southeast recalled: "Once, a Turkish student brought a human ear to the classroom. His relative who was in the Special Team had given it to him. He showed it to all the students. It is so strange to see something like that. It could be my sister's. Who knows?" Aynur's sister had joined the PKK when Aynur was a child and she had not seen her since. Aynur herself was strongly opposed to the PKK or to the use of violence in general, yet her sister had been fighting for the PKK for years, and the displayed body-part could well have been her sister's.

Aynur had developed good relations with the officer-teacher of the *National Security Knowledge* course throughout her tenth grade. Yet, despite her interest in the course, good relations with the teacher, and active participation in class discussions, she had flunk it together with all other students from her village:

> It was so clear. Half of the students in the class were Kurdish and most were from my village, and the other half were local, mostly Turkish. They all passed and we all failed. My failure came as a shock to everyone because the teacher had designated me the class president. He was very friendly throughout the year and we had a wonderful relationship. I was so naïve at that time. I actually believed that there could be good soldiers. He would ask me all sorts of questions about my village and I would explain things to him. Then I flunk! My exams were all good, but that did not matter. That was an eye-opener for me. Since then I have a negative image of soldiers and police. I can never forget that officer.

Aynur also believed that the officer-teacher had been friendly initially because he was trying to gather information about her "tribe." She felt deceived and betrayed.

Many other Kurdish students expressed strong opposition to being asked political questions in their military courses: "I am about to graduate from high school and I have not learned *any* politics. No one taught us. And now they ask us very political questions. Why?" Ebru said. She also remembered a disappointing event:

> One day they told us that we would be going on a picnic. We loved the idea and asked where we were going. They said it was a great place and they could not tell us because it was a surprise. We were all ready that day for a picnic and they took us to the garrison! A number of high level officers, colonels, and so on, met with us that day and asked us questions. They kept asking, "What do you think about Kurdistan?" We are only students! They have not taught us any politics until now. I think they should have, but they haven't. Now they ask us these questions. Our ideas are private. . . . On the way back, we asked our teachers, "why did we not go on a picnic? We were all hungry!" They said, "Isn't this better than a picnic?"

Abdullah was going to a private school in Diyarbakır where most of the students were the children of the police and of military officers. He was experiencing a different kind of pressure. Whenever the Kurdish issue was discussed, not only the teachers, but also the other students would look at him to see his reactions. Abdullah preferred to keep quiet, but he was tired of being treated as a potential terrorist and defined as "the enemy" by teachers and students alike.

All the students I interviewed who have gone to school in the Southeast were very critical of the effort by the officer-teachers to make them talk about political issues. They all believed that this was a unique characteristic of the schools in the State of Emergency Zone. Ebru exclaimed:

> I really want to participate in a *National Security* course in the West and see how it is done there. What do they teach the students there? They kept asking us what we thought about Apo and the PKK. I wonder if this is the real content of this course. They are not teaching us patriotism. They are teaching us separatism. They are the ones who are being separatist. Am I asking him why he is Turkish? Why are they asking us those questions?

Moreover, she was interested in military affairs: "These are mostly issues that concern men. But these days women join the military as well. I want to learn about things that have to do with the military organization, mobilization, and things like that. I don't want them to come and ask me my ideas on political subjects." She suggested that the course should remain in the curriculum but that it should be taught with the "real aim of teaching military issues." Piröz also complained about the contents of the course: "The course is all about political events. We keep talking about our neighbors. Iran, Iraq, Greece... Turkey's relations with other countries. I think this is wrong." Bawer did not want this course in the curriculum at all: "I don't think this course is of any use to us. Why? Let me not go into why this is the case." Here was another loud silence.

Among all my Kurdish interviewees, there was a strong sense that they were treated differently by the officer-teacher and that the course was undertaken in a unique manner in their region. Many were resisting the surveillance over their political views and activities by keeping silent. Yet Aynur, who was a university student in Istanbul when I interviewed her, had questions about how effective such resistance was. She believed that Kurdish students were internalizing a form of "self-hatred" and "self-denial" at schools and this course added to such feelings:

> They want us to hate ourselves. I look back now and realize how much they were successful. For instance, I was embarrassed to bring my mother to school because she did not speak Turkish. I realize some of these things now. Many people never realize it and carry this complex with them all their lives.... When I say "I am a Turk" I feel more secure. I feel like I can avoid certain dangers by doing that. The aim behind this is to distance you from your own nation, your own people. Why is this course not important in Kayseri yet very important in the Southeast? There is a reason.... The course is not about teaching military service. I think there are other issues behind it.

The experiences of religious minorities and devout Muslims in their *National Security Knowledge* classes were also based on similar insecurities. One officer-teacher told me proudly that he had had two students expelled from school because they did not believe in Atatürk's principles. They were religious students who were complaining about Atatürk's laicism as being anti-democratic and he got them expelled from the school because he concluded that it would be impossible to "convert" them into laicism: "I don't think those who don't believe in laicism should be going to secular schools." Another officer-teacher remembered a difficult situation in the classroom when an Armenian student spoke up to challenge his interpretation of the *tehcir* (deportation) of Armenians from Anatolia in 1915. Other students in the class rushed to make clear that he was an Armenian. The officer-teacher was proud of how he handled the situation: "I told the other students that there was nothing wrong with being an Armenian and explained the real story of 1915 to the student. I also gave him some material to read. I was able to change his views."

Saliba was an eleventh grader in Istanbul when I met her and was an active member of an Asyrrian (*Süryani*) youth organization. She seemed proud of her difference as a Christian in a predominantly Muslim society and was vocal about the discrimination she faced in society or at school. She had been particularly disturbed by the *National Security Knowledge* course and its officer-teacher at the beginning of the school year because he kept referring to non-Muslims as *gavur*, a slang term for "non-believer." Apparently he did not know that there were a couple of non-Muslims in the classroom. Saliba was one of them and she exploded one day: "I told him that he probably did not know the real meaning of *gavur*. It stands for people who don't believe in God. Christians and Jews believe in God. So they should not be called *gavur*. When I explained this, the teacher said that I had misunderstood him and that he did not mean it that way." She was very disturbed by the nationalist discourse of the course: "O.K., we are all nationalistic, but this is too much!" Saliba, like many of the other minority students I interviewed, was critical of the way the "national self" was interpreted in this course, but she was not opposed to a nationalist framework.

Niko remembered reading the deragatory terms used for Greeks in the *National Security Knowledge and History* textbooks while going to a private Greek high school in Istanbul:

> We used to talk about current politics in the *National Security* course. In the textbook, I was particularly disturbed by the sections on "internal enemies." Who are internal enemies? The minorities: Greeks, Armenians, and so on. But those sections were mostly skipped in class discussions. Sometimes we forced the teacher to comment on them. I was really obsessed by this business of "internal" and "external" enemies . . .

The depiction of Greeks and other minorities as potential enemies in history textbooks is not new (Copeaux 1998, Milas 2000). The historical narratives on the late Ottoman period and the War of Independence abound with such references, however, the incorporation of current politics with detailed strategic analysis of "internal and external threats" in the *National Security Knowledge* course is new. Especially when students are asked to participate in class discussions, these references gain new meaning. The feelings of insecurity experienced by students whose identities are depicted as potential threats to national security are intensified in such discussions. Many resist the call to articulate their political positions by remaining silent, others force the limits of the discussion by raising their own, usually critical, perspectives.

Conclusion

The 1980s have been characterized as a period of "depoliticization" in Turkey, particularly among the youth. The 1980s generation is often seen as a lost generation. Anthropologist Leyla Neyzi analyzes the construction of youth in public discourse during three periods in Turkish history. She argues that:

> in the first period (1923–1950), youth—and educated youth in particular—came to embody the new nation. In the second period (1950–1980), in which a student movement led to widespread violence between "leftists" and "rightists", youth were reconstructed in public discourse as rebels, and as a major threat to the nation. . . . The third, and current period (post-1980) . . . tends to represent contemporary youth as apolitical consumers. (Neyzi 2001, 412)

The intense political atmosphere of high schools and universities that had characterized the 1968 movement and its aftermath was ruptured by the 1980 coup d'etat and the subsequent military regime. The new laws, regulations, and their implementation prevented any discussion of politics in schools, particularly in the classroom. As Neyzi explains, the youth were seen as "potential rebels" who needed to be tamed. I remember my history teacher lecturing us, the eleventh graders, in the spring of 1989 about the "dangers of politics." She used to say:

> Now that you will be graduating from high school and going to university, you will start learning about different political groups. They will approach you at your universities and will try to divert you from your path. Don't listen to them! Some of them will be leftist, some of them rightist. You should always take the middle way and be a good Atatürkist.

She repeated this speech almost every week. Her repetitions have created the impact she must have intended: I can still remember them quite well. I can even remember the expression on her face and her tone of speech as she talked. It was as if she were revealing an important secret. The secret was the existence, and the dangers of, politics at the university! She and the other teachers had kept us "safe" so far, but now we would be on our own.

A strong dislike and fear of politics was present in the narratives of most of the students and young people I interviewed as well, especially the students in Istanbul. Quite frequently, they referred to "being politically organized" as a "crime." For instance, they were against Merve Kavakçı becoming a member of the Grand National Assembly with the *türban* because it was clear that she was "politically motivated." The phrase "politically organized" (*örgütlü*) came up again and again as an expression of outrage. Many of the students in Istanbul believed that the current regulation of not allowing female university students with the *türban* on campus was just and desirable because they were "being harmful by organizing and doing propaganda work." On the other hand, Nergis, a twenty-five-year-old university graduate who wears the *türban*, felt outraged at the overall negative connotation of politics: "When Merve Kavakçı entered the parliament, people opposed her and said that she was using the *türban* issue politically. *So what?* Isn't the parliament a place where people engage in politics? I don't like her as a person at all and I don't vote for her party. But she should at least be allowed to do politics in the parliament."

It can rightly be argued that the "fear of politics" that characterizes the 1980s and the 1990s generations in Turkey is not merely the result of active depoliticization that has marked the post-coup political culture, but is also a reflection of the post–Cold War world order and the rapidly "liberalizing" and "globalizing" world economy, which has turned populations into consumers. I suggest that this post-coup and post–Cold War political order is also a rapidly militarizing one in Turkey. The recent developments in the *National Security Course* point to a new phenomenon and a more militarist approach towards youth in Turkey. At least from the perspective of the military, high schools should no longer be the "depoliticized" spaces they were in the 1980s. Since 1998, students have been learning about and discussing political issues from their *National Security Knowledge* textbook and in the presence of a military officer. One of the officer-teachers I interviewed suggested that his main goal was to make students knowledgeable and aware enough that they can talk with (or against) their father as they watched the news every night. Several students in Istanbul used the exact same words to talk about their "gains" from this course. They felt good about being able to talk politics with their families as they watched TV or read newspapers. However, this politicization should be seen as a *controlled and militarized politicization.*

What counts as politics (security concerns) and who is qualified to "teach" politics (officers) has been put under the hegemony of the military perspective. I would argue that the approach to "organized politics" as a dangerous and undesirable activity among the students, which coexists with passionate political discussions framed through "strategic analysis," speaks to the success of the "controlled politicization" intended by the decision-makers. In military-strategic terms, politics has been "contained" in strategic analysis, which designates most political positions as dangerous in terms of national security. As the "situated knowledges" of the students suggest, not only is political discussion refigured here as strategic analysis, and thus militarized, but it also creates or reinforces strong insecurities in students whose identities (not belonging to the imagined Turkish, Sunni-Muslim, secular nation) or positionalities (being a youth in Diyarbakır) are associated with "threats."

Epilogue

One of my in-depth interviews was with Elif, a young woman who was both Kurdish and Alevi. It was a wonderful interview because she was very friendly, open, and willing to talk freely about all kinds of issues. She was in her early twenties; yet she looked and sounded much more mature. We had met at a crowded café in Istanbul but this was no obstacle to her talking about touchy political issues in a loud voice— so much so that I felt the need to look around a couple of times to see if anyone was listening. She was comfortably loud as she uttered taboo words and made critical statements. After the interview, as usual, I asked her to fill out my short questionnaire and went to the restroom to leave her alone with it. When I came back, she had finished it but had left two questions unanswered: the question about her mother tongue and the question about her religious beliefs. She asked me: "What should I write here?" I said that she could write whatever was her answer. She hesitated at first, and then wrote Kurdish and Alevi respectively. She then explained her hesitation to me: "I was not sure if it would be appropriate to write them in an official questionnaire. I did not want to put you in trouble."

As I think about this incident now, two things strike me and both make me feel uneasy. The first one makes me feel uneasy as a citizen of Turkey and the second one as a scholar. While Elif was quite articulate about her ethnic and religious allegiances during our long, taped conversation, it was difficult for her to put it down on paper. Although this was not a form of "self-hatred" in the way Aynur had described it, it was nevertheless a sign of the various levels of insecurity that was associated with these identities. The transition from speaking them out loud to putting them on paper was not a smooth one. People like Aynur and Elif had to constantly negotiate how they should define themselves in their everyday lives, and more importantly, in their relationship to the state. School was an official place for Aynur and she had not brought her mother there because her mother did not speak Turkish. For Elif, my questionnaire was an official document and she was not sure if she could write her mother tongue as Kurdish and her religious belief as Alevi.

Her perception of my academic research as being confined to "official" boundaries is what makes me feel uneasy as a scholar of Turkey. I cannot blame Elif. Academics have indeed done very little to challenge the official line in relation to the Kurdish issue, or other taboo problematics like militarism. For me, it was significant and disturbing that a twenty-three-year-old woman would hesitate to write her mother tongue and her religious belief on an anonymous questionnaire. It was not the first time, nor was it the last I had witnessed such hesitation and self-censorship. What was so striking in Elif's case was the discrepancy between her loud self-confidence during the interview and this hesitation when it came to filling out a questionnaire. Was she assuming that I would be censoring her statements during the interview as I concluded my "official" research? Why would she think that she would put *me* in trouble by writing "Kurdish" and "Alevi" in my questionnaire? Had the official discourse succeeded in making her believe that her identity claims constituted "threats" not only for "national security" but also for academic analysis? That was apparently the case.

This study has aimed to address the insecurities experienced by many young people like Elif in a highly militarized Turkey at the turn of the millennium. A militarized historiography, militarized gender relations, and militarized schools are only parts of the larger picture. Military's involvement in the economic realm through its own bank, factories, and companies, the disproportionate levels of military spending, the military's overwhelming physical presence throughout the country (particularly the Southeast), its role in daily politics, as well as in the shaping of culture in different realms of life are in need of further research and cultural criticism.[1]

Surprisingly, such critique has come recently from an officer of the Turkish military. In January 2001, a retired vice admiral, Atilla Kıyat, made revealing statements about the lack of civilian control over military decision-making:

> As soldiers, we define our own strategy, evaluate threats on our own, form the force structure that will fight against this threat again on our own, and then we ask for the money needed for it [from the Grand National Assembly]. We get the money and implement our plan. The civilians do not exercise an effective control in this process. They don't use the rights that the laws have given them.

Kıyat went further to discuss the monopoly exercised by the Armed Forces over the analysis of threats and definition of strategy in relation to key political issues:

> Terror began in the Southeast in early 1980s. Now we say that we have been very successful against terror.... It is true that under the designated strategy, we have been successful. We have stopped the bloodshed. But it lasted fifteen years and thousands of people died. In the future, we might face something like the Vietnam syndrome that America had to face. Large amounts of money were poured into this conflict at the expense of the country's development. Mistakes were made back in the 1970s. We built the problem on the assumption that Turkey could be divided. If we had built it on the assumption that Turkey is strong enough not to be divided ... perhaps there would have been no need for [an armed struggle]. We could have chosen to solve this problem by promoting freedom and not prohibitions, in which case our preventive measures would have been different. We could have succeeded with such measures in those days. We could perhaps have been a member of the European Union today. (Düzel 2001)

These views not only throw new light on the process that has led to fifteen years of war in Turkey, but they also stress the dangers of recent teaching in high schools where the military's assessments of "threat" and "strategy" are turning into political science "knowledge" in the classroom. Students are presented these assessments as the "truth" of Turkey's geo-strategic problems, legitimizing military buildup, and normalizing the use of military force in solving these problems. As I argued in the last two chapters, this development gains an added significance in a school system where an open discussion of politics is strongly discouraged. Politics is now defined as strategic analysis, with the military officer being the most qualified person to teach it. On the other hand, this perspective, which rests on a notion of constant threat from Turkey's "internal enemies," further marginalizes the non-Turkish and non-Muslim (or non-Sunni) students in schools, making them feel more and more insecure. Yet all of these insecurities, as well as the discourses that create them have their history. Far from being recent inventions, they rest on the "founding" discourses of "the state" and "the military" in Turkey.

Turkey's recent history has been characterized as a "revolution from above" (Trimberger 1978) with the military at center stage. This view rests on the assumption that states in the West have been formed through revolutions from *below*. Modernization, in many such accounts, is treated as an authentic feature of First World development, whereas the Third World has had to "imitate" the Western structures and culture of modernity. Recent theorizing on nationalism and state-formation has challenged this view. Historian Eugen Weber showed in the early 1970s that the revolution from below par excellence, that is the French revolution, in its larger sense rested on a number of state practices and discourses that turned peasants into Frenchmen [*sic*]. As Arif Dirlik (2002, 256) suggests, "the paradigm of colonialism may have much to tell us about state-building projects, especially with the emergence of the nation-state: in the state monopolization of the instruments of violence, in the use for the control of the population of new techniques of surveillance and inventory, and in the efforts to create homogeneous national cultures that erased local differences, to cite some of the most important." This was neither an inevitable nor an easy process. Nationhood was not an a priori condition, but a political and social project. As anthropologist Ernest Gellner succinctly put it: "Nationalism is not the awakening of nations to self-consciousness: it *invents* nations where they do not exist" (Gellner 1964, quoted in Anderson 1991, 6).

The Turkish nation has been invented as a "military-nation." Compulsory conscription and compulsory militarized education have helped this invention and its reinforcement. Yet it is not a seamless discourse. In fact, its current interpretations rest on contradictory assumptions that have to do with the tension between the understanding of nationalism as a force "from below" and modernization as one "from above." On the one hand, Turks are commended for having been a military-nation throughout history, with the national War of Independence being one of the most recent and best manifestations of this characteristic. On the other hand, it is suggested that it was the "Turkish military" that fought the war and established the state. The first assumption is based on a notion of "revolution from below" and on a narrative of national awakening, while the second one downplays "national" participation and singles out an institution ("the military") represented by its decision-makers (i.e., the officer cadre) for having carried out the revolution from above, both during and after the War of Independence. How do these two seemingly contradictory views coexist?[2]

The call made to high school students in the 1960s National Security Knowledge textbook to realize and recognize their responsibility to their military-nation embodies this contradiction:

> You, the heroic young SOLDIERS of our sacred homeland, which the Turkish Armed
> Forces have defended and will continue to defend with success, make-up a real ARMY

OF EDUCATION. The responsibility of the future has been placed on your shoulders, minds, and wrists. (*National Security Knowledge II* 1965, 3, original emphasis)

It is the students who are the "heroic young soldiers" of the homeland, yet the "Turkish Armed Forces" are identified as a separate body that has defended and will continue to defend the homeland. Despite the fact that the students are asked to join the Armed Forces, it is also made clear that the Armed Forces exist independently of these student-soldiers. If Turks as a military-nation are behind the victory of the War of Independence, why is it seen as a war that has been fought and won by the "Turkish Armed Forces"?

These are only some of the internal contradictions of the discourse. There are many more created in people's lived experiences. Journalist Nadire Mater's (1999) daring study of the experiences of young men fighting in the Southeast against the PKK as part of their "sacred duty to the nation" has offered challenging openings in this regard. Her ethnographic perspective has indeed overcome "the dissimulating political discourse of the modern state" and shown "the ways in which individual and collective modern bodies constitute themselves through war" (Shapiro 1996, 472). Mater's research with soldiers points to the contradictions and the overall costs of militarization since the 1980s from the perspectives of the very soldiers who make up the military. For instance, a taxi driver from Istanbul says, "I had wanted to go to Şırnak and I did...there was the nationalism thing: 'We love our country. We are Turks (*Türk evladıyız*).' But everything changes once you are inside the barracks," (1999, 63) and continues:

> These people have accepted to be citizens of the Turkish state. They don't want a separate state for Kurds. It is not possible anyway. The guy says "I want this", that is normal. Some look at them as terrorists. If I live in this country and pay my taxes, there are certain things that I want. You cannot look at the Kurds as terrorists.... In this country, there are Kurds, Armenians, Alevis, Sunnites....We have to live together. The people who live there are not guilty, you need to educate them. My ideas were different before I went there. (67)

Expressions of such transformations are not limited to those who used to be Turkish nationalists before military service. An Armenian, leftist ex-soldier reveals a similar account of transformation: "It is interesting, during military service I was close friends with an ultra-Turkish-nationalist (*ülkücü*)" (198). He mentions that when he came back, he was criticized by some for having "moved to the right" (199). His response was quite straightforward:

> I don't want death to be sanctified! If you think so, then die! I mean, when a bullet goes through, there is no more socialism, no more Kürdistan, no more ultra-nationalism ... The first thing on your mind is how to stop the bleeding, you know what I mean? The ones who sanctify death are performing the worst crime of history. Noone from the Turkish army or from among the politicians can provide an explanation for Ahmet's death. Neither side can explain to me why he was sent to his mother's lap in three pieces. I am angry with the leftists ... Perhaps an ultra-nationalist can easily send someone to die; an Islamist can send people for *jihad*. The left should be more careful about sending people to die. We should be the ones to sanctify life! (200)

Mehmedin Kitabı embodies a set of significant challenges to discourses of war and nationalism, both official and dissident, and implies a sound alternative to official and strategic accounts of war. First, it blurs the relationship between the opposing sides of this conflict (i.e., making it difficult to "take sides") both by its methodology and through the accounts that it presents. Second, it draws our attention to the human face and costs of war (see Scarry 1985) through the vivid and difficult accounts of pain and suffering by the ordinary soldiers who were the main actors in this conflict. Barnes suggests, "it is often forgotten that [wars] depend on ordinary soldiers, who make personal sacrifices to achieve advances and victories, and who suffer the consequences of retreats and defeats physically" (1995, 118). Nadire Mater and the accounts of the ex-soldiers in *Mehmedin Kitabı* make us remember this basic fact and force us to consider both its implications and consequences in relation to the Kurdish conflict.

My interviews with young people who have grown up in the war zone in the 1990s reveal the other side of the suffering. Almost all students have expressed strong fear of the uniform; their self-narratives were shaped by loud silences; and their lives by strong insecurities. Some of these insecurities had to do with everyday forms of terror in a war zone. Others were much deeper. Elif's hesitation to put down Kurdish and Alevi on an anonymous questionnaire in Istanbul, after giving an open and confident interview, points to some of those depths.

The contradictions and silences in both the seemingly intact discourse of militarized nationhood *and* individuals' experiences promise new openings in overcoming the dissimulating state discourse. The first step is to take them seriously. I believe that scholars of Turkey are faced with the task of analyzing the mechanisms that have created and sustained the myth of the military-nation, as well as of interrogating the many contradictions that lie beneath and within the masks of "the military" and "the state." Only then will we be able to hear some of the loud silences that have shaped Turkish culture and social sciences alike.

NOTES

Introduction

1. The full title was: *2000'li Yıllara Girerken Türk Ordusu* (Turkish Military Into the 2000s). It was prepared by Mehmet Özel, the Director for Fine Arts in the Ministry of Culture, and published by the Ankara Chamber of Commerce. A note on the first page reads: "This book has been reviewed by the General Staff."
2. Unless otherwise noted, all translations from the Turkish texts are mine.
3. For instance, in a speech in 1996, the Minister of Culture and Spokesperson for the government, Agah Oktay Güner, had also defined the Turkish nation as a military-nation (*Yeni Yüzyıl*, 29 March 1996).
4. A growing number of intellectuals and academics have started writing on various aspects of militarism in recent years (see Insel and Bayramoğlu 2004; Cizre 2003; Şen 1996). Tanel Demirel (2002) points to the need to examine the processes of internalization of the importance of the Turkish Armed Forces (TSK) among social actors, instead of explaining the existing social legitimacy of TSK with reference to "coercion." Journalist and writer Çetin Altan is also a rare exception. He has been writing about militarism periodically in his columns for many years.
5. 12 March 1971 and 28 February 1997 did not result in military regimes. The first is the date of an ultimatum given to the government, the second is the day of a meeting of the National Security Council at which decisions were made about the specific kinds of legislation that the government needed to pass in order to "protect the regime." The tension between the military high command and the government resulted in the resignation of Prime Minister Necmettin Erbakan (of the religious-oriented Refah/Welfare Party) and a change of government.
6. See Fidel 1975; Heper and Evin 1988; Özdemir 1989; Hale 1994; and Heper and Güney 2000; Cizre-Sakallıoğlu 1993; Cizre 2003. For recent critiques of the costs of such intervention in Turkey's relations with the European Union, see Rouleau 2000 and Frantz 2001.
7. Such an analysis would require a different kind of research, one that looked into the multifaceted "military system," which is composed of conscripted soldiers as well as professional officers; the barracks as well as the General Staff headquarters; differentiated interests of the officer corps as well as the mechanisms of their common seclusion from the society at large; military academies as well as field training sites; the families of the officers as well as the workers of ammunition factories. The relations between the "military system" and the "political system" would be central to such research.
8. "The state" was discussed in relation to "political organization" in early social-anthropological works, e.g., Fortes and Evans-Pritchard 1940. Pioneering studies on the anthropology of the state were conducted by Pierre Clastres in the 1970s. More recent works include Abélès 1990; Coronil 1997; Gupta 1995; Herzfeld 1996; Navaro-Yashin 1998 and 2002; Ong 1999; Taussig 1992 and 1997; Verdery 1991; and Williams 1991.

9. Anthropologist Laura Nader has been urging anthropologists to "study up" since the late 1960s (see Nader 1969; Starn 1999).
10. Cynthia Enloe (1989, 1993, 1995, 2000) has transformed the ways in which national and international politics are analyzed through her work on militarization and gender. Betty Reardon (1985) has drawn attention to the intricate links between sexism and "the war system" since the 1980s. Anthropologist Catherine Lutz (2001) has done an outstanding ethnography of Fayetteville, a military town in North Carolina, pointing to the prevalence of war and war preparation in shaping our "homes," self-understandings, and everyday practices. Recent ethnographic work on military service in a variety of contexts, from Bolivia (Gill 1997), to Israel (Helman 1997); South Africa (Cock 1991); South Korea (Kwon 2001); and the United States (Feinman 2000) has shown the centrality of this practice in defining gender relations and the state alike. Carol Cohn (1993) has examined the discourse of defense intellectuals and pointed to the gendered discourse(s) that shape the way we view militaries, wars, and defense. There are many others who have problematized wars and their impact on women, as well as their relationship to men and masculinity. Several dense and insightful collections on the relationship between women and war have come out in the past decade: Elshtain and Tobias 1990; Cooke and Woollacott 1993; Lorentzen and Turpin 1998 and Giles et al. 2003.
11. I borrow this term from Cynthia Enloe's (2000) compelling and insightful book *Maneuvers.*

Chapter One   The Myth of the Military-Nation

1. There is no difference between these two formulations in terms of meaning, although *ordu-millet* is the more popular one. *Ordu* means "military." *Asker* is literally "soldier," but is also used to mean "military." The term *ulus* is the Turkish equivalent of the Arabic *millet*, and means "nation." Both terms are in use in today's Turkey. Certain people prefer *ulus* because the term *millet* had a specific connotation in the Ottoman state system: it referred to the religious groups in the Empire (Muslim millet, Jewish millet, etc.).
2. The term used for "combatant" in this translation is "*mücahid*," which has Arabic and Islamic origins and means "the one who is engaged in *jihad* (holy war)." With the secularization of the polity and the language during the Republican years, words of Turkish origin were preferred to refer to the same phenomenon. For instance, for "combatant," the term "*savaşçı*" was used.
3. During this time there was a great deal of military cooperation between Prussia and the Ottoman Empire. A number of German commanders were invited by the Ottoman Sultan to train soldiers, set up the curriculum in military schools, and teach, as well as lead armies. Baron de Tott, Helmuth von Moltke, Liman von Sanders, and Colmar von der Goltz (or Goltz Pasha, as he is known in Turkey) were among these commanders. Goltz was killed in Baghdad in 1916 and buried in Istanbul (see Kayalı 1985 and Karabekir 2001).
4. Throughout the book, the names written in parenthesis refer to the surnames that the mentioned individuals adopted after 1934 when everyone became obliged to choose a surname. Before 1934, many people used their first name and middle name (and occasionally their father's first name in addition to their own). For instance, Afet Inan's early publications were signed "Afet" and Atatürk was known as Mustafa Kemal.
5. Hasan Ünder (1999a) underlines the traces of social Darwinism in Atatürk's ideas beyond his thinking about the military and suggests that this influence might have originated from his military education, which was based on curricula designed by German officer-teachers.
6. See Lewis (1961, 208) and Berkes (1978, 419–425). Sociologist Şerif Mardin (1997, 68) suggests that "nineteenth-century Ottoman officials, regardless of their generation or specific worldview, seem to have had the salvation of *devlet* [the state] as a uniform goal

and bent their minds to this ideal." Anthropologist Yael Navaro-Yashin (1998) has shown how this preoccupation of the elite with "saving the state" has remained a crucial aspect of the political culture of Turkey to this day.

7. On the modernization of the education system between 1839 and 1908, see Somel 2001.

8. For a more detailed analysis of the different strands of thought on issues related to identity and the state, see Mardin 1985.

9. Historian Halil Berktay suggests that between Yusuf Akçura and Ziya Gökalp, it was Akçura who contributed to the scientific study of Turkish history and to the development of history as a discipline in Turkey. Berktay claims that some of Ziya Gökalp's historical arguments were unfounded (see Berktay 1985). My aim here is not to judge the historicity of the various claims made about the "Turkish nation." My discussion in this chapter is limited to the development of the discourse on Turkish nationhood and, more specifically, to the tension between the concepts of "race" and "culture" in the various formulations of Turkish nationalism.

10. See also Murat Belge's (2001) discussion of Gökalp's status as the ideologue of Kemalist nationalism.

11. The Turkish interpretation of the relationship between state and religion is based primarily on the French concept of "laicism," which involves state-control over religion, rather than an absolute separation of state and the religious realm. This "control" has been institutionalized in Turkey in the *Diyanet İşleri Başkanlığı* (Directorate for Religious Affairs), a centralized body that administers all mosques, imams, and a variety of religious practices and organizations. For a discussion of the relationship between the Turkish and French interpretations of laicism in relation to the constraints put on the freedom of religious practices in the two countries, see Ewing (2000). According to Andrew Davison (1998, 133), Gökalp advocated the "complete disestablishment" between the realms of politics and religion. "He demanded the complete autonomy of political and religious spheres for the sake of both."

12. The Erzurum Congress, which was organized by *Şarki Anadolu Müdafaa-i Hukuk Cemiyeti* (Society for the Defence of the Rights of Eastern Anatolia), met on 23 July 1919. The Sivas Congress, which was organized by the *Anadolu Rumeli Müdafaa-i Hukuk-u Milliye Cemiyeti* (Society for the Defence of the National Rights of Anatolia and Thrace), met from 4–11 September 1919. Mustafa Kemal was elected president of the representative committees formed after both of these congresses (see Zürcher 1994, 156–157).

13. The original text is as follows: "Efendiler, bu hudut sırf askeri mülahazat ile çizilmiş bir hudut değildir, hududu millidir. Hududu milli olmak üzere tesbit edilmiştir. Fakat bu hudut dahilinde tasavvur edilmesin ki anasırı islamiyeden bir cins millet vardır. Bu hudut dahilinde Türk vardır, Çerkes vardır ve anasırı saire-i islamiye vardır. İşte bu hudut memzuç bir halde yaşıyan, bütün maksatlarını bütün manasiyle tevhidetmiş olan kardeş milletlerin hududu millisidir (hepsi islamdır, kardeştir sesleri). Bu hudut meselesini tesbit eden maddenin içerisinde büyük bir esas vardır. Fazla olarak o da bu vatan hududu dahilinde yaşıyan anasır-ı islamiyenin her birinin kendine mahsus olan muhitine, adatına, ırkına mahsus olan imtiyazatı bütün samimiyetle ve mukabilen kabul ve tasdik edilmiştir" (*Atatürk'ün Söylev ve Demeçleri I* [1997], 30). This text is only partly intelligible with today's Turkish, which has gone through seven decades of change including an extensive "clean-up" of all Arabic and Persian words which were a part of the Ottoman language. On the web site of the Turkish Grand National Assembly (http://www.tbmm.gov.tr/tarihce/ldlyyl.htm), this speech is presented with today's Turkish. It is interesting to note that, in the translation from Ottoman Turkish to contemporary Turkish, the term "*kardeş milletler*" (sibling nations) has been changed to "*kardeş unsurlar*" (sibling elements) while the term millet has remained the same in the remainder of the text.

14. "Efendiler . . . Burada maksut olan ve Meclisi âlinizi teşkil eden zevat yalnız Türk değildir, yalnız Çerkes değildir, yalnız Kürt değildir, yalnız Lâz değildir. Fakat hepsinden mürekkep anasır-ı islâmiyedir, sâmimî bir mecmuadır . . . Binaenaleyh muhafaza ve müdafaasiyle iştigal ettiğimiz millet bittabi bir unsurdan ibaret değildir. Muhtelif anasır-ı İslâmiyeden mürekkeptir. Bu mecmuayı teşkil eden her bir unsur islâm, bizim kardeşimiz ve menfaii tamamiyle müşterek olan vatandaşımızdır ve yine kabul ettiğimiz esasatın ilk satırlarında bu muhtelif anasır-ı islâmiye ki: Vatandaştır, yekdiğerine karşı hürmet-i mütekabile ile riayetkârdırlar ve yekdiğerinin her türlü hukukuna, ırkî, içtimaî, coğrafi hukukuna daima riayetkâr olduğunu tekrar ve teyidettik ve cümlemiz bugün samimiyetle kabul ettik. Binaenaleyh menafiimiz müşterektir. Tahsiline azmettiğimiz vahdet, yalnız Türk, yalnız Çerkes değil hepsinden memzuç bir unsur-u islâmdır" (*Atatürk'ün Söylev ve Demeçleri-I* [1997], 74–75).
15. As Kemal Kirişçi (2000) shows in relation to the immigration law and related citizenship practices, Turkish citizenship was not only ethnicist in theory, but also in practice. He concludes that Turkish citizenship is in need of "disaggregation." Ayhan Aktar (2000) provides a detailed analysis of the various state practices (such as employment practices, tax laws, and forced migration) that have discriminated against non-Muslim citizens.
16. The "caliph" was the name given to the supreme leader of the Muslim community after the death of the Prophet Muhammed. This title was claimed by the Ottoman sultans starting in the sixteenth Century when the possessions of the Prophet were appropriated in the conquest of Egypt. The Ottoman Sultans carried this title until the caliphate was abolished by the Grand National Assembly in 1924.
17. *Nakşibendi* is a major Sunni orthodox sect that still has a substantial number of followers in Turkey.
18. This was a nationalist organization established in 1912, during the Balkan Wars. In the transition from empire to nation-state, it became an important cultural and political site for the development of Turkish nationalism. In 1931, as Turkish nationalism turned into state ideology, the organization was closed down, only to be reestablished in 1949. As Füsun Üstel (2002a) notes, after 1949, the Turkish Hearths distanced themselves from official/bureaucratic nationalism and began identifying with a more conservative (and after 1980s, more Islam-defined) version of oppositional nationalism. For a more detailed study, see Üstel 1997.
19. The debate between Afet (Inan) and historian Fuad (Köprülü) during the First History Congress was emblematic of how this process was taking shape. Fuad (Köprülü)'s questioning of the methods used in the advancement of the Turkish History Thesis and his concern about the lack of primary sources available to discuss the accomplishment of the Turks in prehistoric Central Asia met with fierce criticism on the part of Afet (Inan). By the end of the Congress, Fuad (Köprülü) had assumed a defensive position; he made sure that he was not in opposition to any of the arguments proposed by this thesis and took back some of his criticisms (see Ersanlı-Behar 1992).
20. Her dissertation was first published in Geneva (Inan 1941) and, six years later, in Ankara by the Turkish Historical Society (Inan 1947).
21. Afet Inan's choice to work with Eugène Pittard in Geneva was not coincidental. Pittard's race-based anthropological work had provided one of the main references of the Turkish History Thesis. He was also the guest of honor at the Second Turkish History Congress in 1937.
22. To give a few examples: Şevket Aziz Kansu, the first scholar to hold an anthropology chair in Turkey, was one of the contributors to the race theories that provided the backbone of the Turkish History Thesis. In 1936, he wrote: "Anthropological study, instruction, and dissemination in our country means the analysis of our [bodily] constitution through bio-sociological anatomy and morphology" (Kansu 1936, 40). In 1937, he elaborated on the centrality of eugenics: "When we assert that the Turkish population issue is a

bio-sociological issue, we are trying to explain how we embrace all of its cultural, hygienic, eugenic, economic, and social aspects. The conquest of the Turkish land by the enlightened and technically minded children of the homeland; the colonization of the country for the country! This grand and lively issue is closely tied to the issue of bio-sociological culture . . . It should not be forgotten that nations progress with their higher children. The decadence of nations begins when birth rates in select families fall below the average" (Kansu 1937a, 410). For other writings on race, culture, anthropology, and eugenics, see Kansu 1934a; Kansu 1934b; Kerim 1934; Toksöz and Köyden 1936; Kansu 1937b; Kansu 1939; and Şenyürek 1940. Nazan Maksudyan's (2003) insightful M.A. thesis *Gauging Turkishness: Anthropology as Scientific-Fiction in Legitimizing Racist Nationalism (1925–1939)* demonstrates the extent to which anthropology was used as an instrument for translating "ideological myths into scientific truths."

23. Yusuf Akçura continued to play an active role in the development of Turkish nationalism until his death in 1935. As the President of the Turkish Historical Society, he chaired the First History Congress in 1932.

24. It was suggested that Armenians had never established their own state. In the current textbook used in the high school National Security Knowledge course, it is suggested that "Armenians are after the 'Big Armenian State' which they believe existed in history, but which in reality never did" (*Milli Güvenlik Bilgisi* 1998, 94).

25. The number of Turkish states established in history is officially regarded as 16, although in unofficial histories this number has steadily increased over time. In 1994, Ibrahim Kafesoğlu, a prominent nationalist historian, suggested that Turks have established close to 100 states throughout history (Kafesoğlu 1994, 450).

26. Historian Andreas Kazamias, among others, finds it paradoxical that "non-Moslems were being recruited and trained to become the guardians and rulers of a Moslem Empire" (Kazamias 1966, 28). In Turkish nationalist sources, the size and significance of the Janissaries is often downplayed, with the emphasis being placed on the fief-holding "Turkish" soldiers (see Ilhan 1989).

27. See Gülsoy 2000 for a detailed analysis of the conscription of non-Muslims in the nineteenth century Ottoman Empire.

28. This increase is also a reflection of the increasing anxiety in the wake of the Second World War and the need to keep more citizens in arms.

29. Certain parts of the country, particularly the Kurdish provinces in the East, were more resistant to sending young men to the military. As discussed in chapter two, one of the reasons cited by the government for the Dersim Operation in 1937 was their refusal to comply with the compulsory military service law. Kurds had not been a part of the regular army during Ottoman times either. They had mainly contributed to the war effort as "irregular cavalry units" (Zürcher 1996, 232).

30. One of the most tragic events that marked this era was the deportation (*tehcir*) and massacre of a large part of the Armenian population in Anatolia. Estimates of the number of people killed during the deportation of Armenians from their homes in various parts of Anatolia to Zor (a location in the desert in today's Syria) range from 300,000 to 1.5 million. The debate over whether these killings constitute a "genocide" (planned by the Ottoman state against all Armenians) or a "necessary war measure" based on the atrocities caused by Armenian nationalists and their collaboration with Russia against the Ottoman state continues to be a source of major conflict amongst scholars and between Turkish and Armenian diaspora communities in the U.S.A. and Europe, and strains the diplomatic relations between the Turkish and Armenian Republics as well (see Akçam 2000).

31. The same year (1931), Atatürk expressed this belief in a talk: "The Turkish nation loves its army and considers it the guardian of its ideals" (quoted in Parla 1991b, 169–170). In 1938, a publication of the Ministry of Culture used a more threatening version of this statement: "The Turkishness of anyone who does not love our soldiers and military service should be suspect" (Yalman 1938, 38).

Chapter Two   Women and the Myth: The World's First Woman Combat Pilot

1. Sabiha Gökçen died on 22 March 2001.
2. The quotation is from the Airport's English website. The Turkish website has the same introduction (http://www.sgairport.com/havaalani/eng/start.asp).
3. "Kissing someone's hand" is a way of paying respect and stands for kissing the outside of the hand and then touching it to the forehead. It is usually young people who (are expected to) kiss the hands of the elderly in this fashion.
4. In her 1956 interview, Gökçen gives a slightly different story of her first encounter with Atatürk. In this version, she shouts from among the crowd that she wants to see Atatürk and is able to attract Atatürk's attention. The rest of her encounter story is the same in the two versions.
5. Atatürk had five adopted daughters, including Sabiha Gökçen and Afet Inan.
6. Unless stated otherwise, all quotations from Halit Kıvanç's 1956 interview with Gökçen are Fred Stark's translations in the 1998 book.
7. Although this was the "predominant" picture (and certainly how Dersim was perceived by outsiders), the Dersim population was quite diverse in itself. There were Kurmanji speaking Kurds and Zaza speaking Kurds, each group belonging to a variety of Muslim sects, including Alevi, Sunni, and Şafi.
8. Alevis are a minority denomination among Muslims in Turkey. Their eclectic and heterodox creed and practices have often led the majority Sunni to view them as quasi heretics.
9. *Kızılbaş* literally means "redhead." It is a derogatory term used for Alevis.
10. To give a counterexample: In an encyclopedia entry he composed on the history of the Air Force (*Cumhuriyet Dönemi Türkiye Ansiklopedisi*), retired Colonel Enver Günsel (1985, 2630) notes the international recognition of "our woman pilot Sabiha Gökçen," without mentioning the Dersim Operation. Despite the significance of this operation as the first bombings undertaken by the young Turkish air force, it is written out of this detailed encyclopedic entry.
11. Arif Dirlik draws attention to the historical relationship between colonialism and nationalism: "There were . . . close parallels between colonization at home and abroad. The paradigm of colonialism may have much to tell us about state building projects, especially with the emergence of the nation-state: in the state monopolization of the instruments of violence, in the use for the control of the population of new techniques of surveillance and inventory, and in the efforts to create homogeneous national cultures that erased local differences, to cite some of the most important" (Dirlik 2002, 256).
12. Even after 1991, state policies on the use of the Kurdish language in public media have been contradictory. RTÜK (Radyo Televizyon Üst Kurulu—The Higher Board of Radios and Televisions) has penalized radio stations and TV channels for broadcasting in Kurdish or for playing Kurdish songs. One of the central debates in relation to Turkey's accession into the European Union has been the question of whether broadcasting in all languages, including Kurdish, would result in an increased threat of disintegration for Turkey. Many people have expressed the view that it would damage Turkey's "unitary structure of government." In 2003, the ruling AKP (Justice and Development Party) passed legislation legalizing the instruction of "all mother tongues" (including Kurdish) in private courses and allowing limited radio and TV broadcasting (See *2003 Regular Report on Turkey's Progress Towards Accession*, European Commission 2003).
13. In June 1998, I coordinated a four-day program hosted by three women's organizations based in Istanbul, *Cin.net Collective, Anakültür,* and *Women for Women's Human Rights,* and sponsored by the Heinrich Böll Foundation-Istanbul Office. Twelve women who worked in local community centers for women in different part of the Southeast were invited for visits to feminist organizations, the Women's Library and Information Center,

and NGOs specializing on women's issues, as well as a meeting with feminist magazines and a full-day workshop with NGO representatives. The community centers, called ÇATOMs (*Çok Amaçlı Toplum Merkezleri*-Multi-Purpose Community Centers), were established in 1995 by a governmental organization, Southeastern Anatolia Project Regional Development Administration, in collaboration with a non-governmental organization, TKV (*Türkiye Kalkınma Vakfı*-Development Foundation of Turkey). The exchange mentioned above took place during one of our meetings with women lawyers.

14. In the *Year-In-Review 2001* of the Committee on Women in NATO Forces, it is said that, in Turkey, "Starting in 1992, together with recruitment from other sources, women cadets were allowed to enter military academies" (77). The 2001 figures for the total number of woman officers in the Turkish Armed Forces is given as 918, out of a total force of more than 800 thousand (92). Turkey has the second largest military in NATO (after the United States), and one of the lowest ratios of women personnel (together with Italy and Poland). One can speculate that the recruitment of women into the military academies after the 1990s could have been a result of pressuring on the part of NATO, particularly the Committee on Women. The *Year-in-Review 2001* can be accessed at http://www.nato.int/ims/2001/win/win-2001.pdf.

15. For an insightful reading of Edib's autobiography in relation to Atatürk's *Nutuk* (The Speech), see Adak 2003.

16. We first explored Edib's treatment of Fatma Çavuş in *The Turkish Ordeal* and the relationship between women and war in the transition from the Ottoman Empire to the Turkish Republic in a graduate paper with Nilgün Uygun (see Uygun and Altınay 1996).

17. See, for instance, *Yeni Yüzyıl*, 9 January 1999, and *Anadolu Ajansı*, 11 September 1998.

18. On the development of second wave feminism in Turkey, see Ş. Tekeli 1986 and 1998, Sirman 1989. Şirin Tekeli notes that one reason behind the time lag between the first wave and the second was, much like in the West, the "illusion that the goals of the movement, such as suffrage, had been achieved" (Ş. Tekeli 1998, 338). Added to this "illusion" was the authoritarian Republican regime which promoted the single idea that gender equality was achieved thanks to Mustafa Kemal Atatürk (338). This was done at the same time as women's independent organizations were closed down by Atatürk and his government. The result was new generations of women who felt "indebted" to Atatürk for their rights and would do anything to protect "his" Republic. It was only in the early 1980s with the emergence of second wave feminism that this framework began to be challenged by women.

19. For an insightful review of the development of women's studies from Kemalism in the 1930s to feminism in the 1980s, see Y. Arat 1993.

20. For an insightful analysis of "silences" in the construction of gender ideologies in Turkey, see Sirman 2002.

21. Alakom's projection has recently been proven right. In 2003, historian Yavuz Selim Karakışla published a detailed analysis of the Kurdish Women's Organization, in which he reminds us that in the same year, 1919, another ethnic women's organization was founded by the Circassians, but that the two organizations were quite different in nature (Karakışla 2003).

22. In this context, looking at the relations between different groups of women is particularly important. Have women found ways to work against the ethnic divides, act in solidarity, and empower one another? (cf. Cockburn 1998 and 2004) Or have they been active agents of the processes of "othering"? In this case, we most likely would find examples of both. To my knowledge, no study has yet been done on this particular issue.

Chapter Three   Becoming a Man, Becoming a Citizen

1. In the last six years, I have had conversations, short and long, with more than 100 men and women of all ages (from early twenties to late seventies) about their experiences of and

ideas regarding military service. The analysis in this chapter is informed by these conversations and the sixteen in-depth interviews I did between 1997 and 1999.

2. All the names used in this chapter are pseudonyms. Some of my interviewees chose their own pseudonyms, otherwise, I assigned them myself.

3. The first conscription law in Britain was passed in 1916.

4. In the next section and in later chapters, I will talk about the relationship between military service and education, two major institutions of nationalized discipline.

5. According to Foucault, corporal punishment as public spectacle was a characteristic of pre-modern penal forms that started dying out by the end of the eighteenth and beginning of the nineteenth centuries. It was then that punishment became "the most hidden part of the penal process" (1979, 9).

6. One exception to this rule seems to be the experience of the soldiers who do the shorter term of one month by paying a compensation. These soldiers not only serve shorter terms, but are treated very differently by the military as well.

7. Let me remind the reader that the first use of this term in the English language that I have been able to identify was in an 1803 British publication about the French conscripted army, *The French Considered as a Military Nation Since the Commencement of Their Revolution.*

8. Sara Helman talks about a similar understanding of military service in Israel: "The construction and perception of military service as a community that overlaps society—rather than the state—has blurred the boundaries between state and society. Moreover, it has blurred the difference between membership in the state and membership in the associations of civil society. It has turned opposition to the state's war practices into opposition to the life-world itself" (Helman 1997, 326).

9. Mehmet Ali Birand suggested in 1991 that the number of soldiers in literacy training programs in the military was ten thousand.

10. One stark consequence of this attitude in relation to military service was the special treatment of non-Muslim men during World War II. Those who were in the military in 1939 were not given weapons, and in 1941, all non-Muslim men between the ages of 25 and 45 were recruited to the military to be kept in overcrowded camps. They were released a year later. This practice (called *yirmi kura askerlik*) not only disrupted the lives of thousands of non-Muslim men (Muslim men were not recruited), but also created fear and anxiety, particularly among the Jewish population, that they would be sent to concentration camps (Bali 1999).

11. Abdullah Öcalan is the leader of the PKK (Kurdish Workers' Party) that has been fighting against the Turkish government since 1984. He was captured in Kenya in February 1999 and sentenced to death after a one-month trial. During the EU-accession reforms of 2002, the Turkish parliament lifted the death sentence from the constitution. Öcalan now serves a life term in a special prison on the island of Imralı. In 1999, when this incident took place, there were intense debates about whether Öcalan should be hung or not.

12. Men become eligible for service at age 20. There is usually an age difference between regular conscripts and university graduates. When they enlist, all men are made to take a test and fill out forms that detail their characteristics and choices. University students are asked to choose between these two categories of service. The ultimate decision, however, is made by the military itself, depending on its needs which means that university students are not always assigned their choice of term.

13. The 1999 earthquakes in Izmit and Adapazarı had put serious burdens on the state and the economy.

14. Regular term for military service dropped to fifteen months (from eighteen months) in July 2003. For those with university degrees, regular term is twelve months and the short term is six months.

15. See the policy changes proposed by women's groups and feminist lawyers regarding the ammendment of the Turkish Penal Code so that "honor" can no longer be used to discriminate against women in the laws: *Kadın Bakış Açısıyla Türk Ceza Kanunu: TCK Tasarısı Değişiklik Talepleri* [2003].

16. The full declaration was published in *Kaos GL*, January 2003, 8.

17. "Eşcinseller Neden Savaşa Karşı?" (Why are Homosexuals Opposed to the War?), 20 December 2002, published on *www.savaskarsitlari.org*, 2 January 2003.

18. In Turkish, "*adam olmak*" or "*erkek olmak.*"

19. Turkey's troops were part of the UN forces in Korea from 1950 to 1953.

20. As pointed out in the previous chapter, there are only about 1,000 women officers in the military, many of them stationed in the headquarters, military schools, and hospitals. Very few of my interviewees mentioned having had contact with women officers.

21. One notable exception is the publication of the book *Mehmedin Kitabı* (Mater 1999), which publicized the critical responses of those who had fought in the Southeast to the war and military service. Although the book became a bestseller, the public debates around it remained limited. Serdar Şen's (1994) insightful book on the connections between military service, nationalism, and modernization was another important effort in problematizing the nature of military service.

22. One can argue that Kurdish nationalists were also against military service to the Turkish state during this time. Their resistance, however, was unidirectional: joining the PKK was not problematized.

Chapter Four   The Road Less Traveled:
Challenging Military Service

1. Originally published in *Sokak*, 11 February 1990. Reprinted with the title "Vicdani Ret Açıklaması-Vedat Zencir" in www.savaskarsitlari.org, 1 January 1998.

2. Osman Murat Ülke has been using the name Ossi both in his personal and public life for many years now. The other activists, too, prefer using their first names in their interactions with people. I follow the same convention in this chapter.

3. Details of the meeting, as well as summaries of some of the presentations, can be found in the publication *ICOM 93—Documentation: International Conscientious Objectors Meeting 1993, n.d.*

4. The report blames the government for "heavy-handed response to an escalation of the conflict in southeastern Turkey," while also blaming the PKK for human rights violations. See http://www.hrw.org/reports/1995/WR95/HELSINKI-16.htm#P655_198257 for details of this report.

5. See *Bakaya*, October 1993, the irregular periodical of the War Resisters' Association.

6. Aytek Özel and Menderes Meletli were interviewed by Ali Tevfik Berber in a program produced by Erhan Akyıldız.

7. This was changed only in 2003. The seventh reform package included amendments ruling that military courts would no longer be able to try civilians (see *2003 Regular Report on Turkey's Progress Towards Accession* [2003], 20).

8. See brochure titled *İzmir Savaş Karşıtları Derneği*, n.d.

9. See brochure titled *Vicdani Ret Kavramına İlişkin Belirlenimler*, published by ISKD, n.d.

10. See brochure titled *İzmir Savaş Karşıtları Derneği*, n.d.

11. See *Turkey: Osman Murat Ülke—Conscientious Objector Imprisoned for Life* [1998].

12. A marginal, reactionary Muslim sect.

13. It is illegal to employ anyone without registering them with SSK (*Sosyal Sigorta Kurumu*—Social Security Institution) and paying the applicable taxes. Because SSK has an updated list of all conscription evaders, they cannot be employed legally.

14. This is a shortened version of his declaration. The declaration as a whole can be read electronically at *www.savaskarsitlari.org*, "Mehmet Bal ile Dayanışma Komitesi'nin Basın Açıklaması," 31 October 2002.

15. A War Resisters' International report defines "total objectors and total objection" as follows: "These terms are used for COs who refuse to perform either military service or any form of substitute service. In countries where substitute service has not been instituted, certain COs may consider themselves total objectors, as they would refuse to perform any substitute service required of them" (Horeman and Stolwijk 1998, 16).

16. See *T.C. Genelkurmay Başkanlığı Askeri Savcılığı, Ankara*, 2002. A scanned version of the document can be accessed electronically at *www.savaskarsitlari.org/images/karar1.jpg*, *www.savaskarsitlari.org/images/karar2.jpg*, *www.savaskarsitlari.org/images/karar3.jpg*, and *www.savaskarsitlari.org/images/karar4.jpg*.

17. Murat Çelikkan is a columnist in the prestigious national daily *Radikal*. He mentioned Mehmet Bal's case in his column on 14 November (see Çelikkan 2002a).

18. The independent online news service, *www.bianet.org*, gave regular updates on Mehmet Bal's case. National dailies *Cumhuriyet* and *Radikal* ran short news stories, as well as long opinion pieces. Kurdish newspaper *Yeniden Özgür Gündem*, radio station *Özgür Radyo*, and the news agency *Dicle Haber Ajansı* also followed Bal's case closely. *Radikal* reported that a Socialist Member of Parliament in the Netherlands had asked the Dutch Foreign Ministry to inquire about Mehmet Bal's case and ask Turkey whether they planned to institute any legal measures to bring their military service law in line with the Copenhagen Criteria (*Radikal*, 28 November 2002).

19. Their names were Mustafa Şeyhoğlu, Erkan Ersöz, Sertaç Girgin, and Emir Üner.

20. Their statement, titled "Hiç Kimsenin Askeri Olmayacağız!" (We Will Not be Anybody's Soldiers), had a joint signature and was distributed to those attending the meeting.

21. The declarations were distributed to the audience as hand-outs. My translations here are from those handouts. They can also be viewed electronically at the War Resisters' website: www.savaskarsitlari.org.

22. The first was soon after his release in October at a meeting in Istanbul. He looked weak after more than a month of hunger strike, but also very content and calm.

23. The 2001 documentary *Ret 1111* (Objection 1111, referring to the Law no. 1111, which defines military service) by Cüneyt Şekerci and Hasan Çimen ends with this statement by Uğur, "Istemiyorsanız, gitmeyin!" (If you don't want it, don't do it!).

24. He was interviewed by reporter Hamza Aktan soon after his declaration of objection. See Hamza Aktan, "Sinek Kadar da Olsak Mide Bulandırıyoruz," *www.bianet.org*, 1 February 2003.

25. Mehmet Bal, interviewed by Hamza Aktan (see Aktan 2002).

Chapter Five   "The Army is a School, the School is an Army"
The Nation's Two Fronts

1. A significant exception to this rule is the administration of the military schools, which is under the jurisdiction of the Ministry of National Defense. Hasan Ünder has drawn attention to the tense discussions that took place in the Grand National Assembly and among educators in the early 1920s around the issue of whether the military schools should be tied to the Ministry of Education or to the Ministry of Defense. For the first year after the Law of Unification of Instruction had been passed, military schools were tied directly to the Ministry of Education; however, on 22 April 1925 another law (no. 637) was passed that transferred their administration and control to the Ministry of Defense. As such, the military schools have remained the only exception to the "unity of instruction" in Turkey (see Ünder 1999 for an excellent discussion of this process).

2. See *The Law of Higher Education*, Law Number: 2547, Date of Enactment: 4 November 1981, Published in the *Resmi Gazete* (Official Gazette) No: 17506; Date: 6 November 1981. (http://www.yok.gov.tr/webeng/law/content.html).

3. See Ismail Kaplan's (1998) detailed analysis of education policies throughout Republican history.

4. After the "Surname Law" was passed, the surname "Atatürk" was given to Mustafa Kemal by the Grand National Assembly on 24 November 1934.

5. The second part of this list has changed slightly over the years. The current law (passed in December 1979, published in the *Resmi Gazete* (Official Gazette) in February 1980 and modified in 1998) states that after staff officers (of ranks Colonel, Major, and Captain), priority should be given to officers (in the same ranks) who have graduated from the combatant classes of the Military College. Third on the list are graduates of other classes, and fourth are all other officers. See *Milli Güvenlik Bilgisi Öğretimi Yönetmeliği* (Regulations Regarding the Instruction of the National Security Knowledge Course) in *Resmi Gazete*, 2 February 1980, R. Gazete No. 16888, Karar No. 8/37 and modifications of the article in question in *Resmi Gazete*, 4 November 1998, R. Gazete No. 23513, Karar No. 98/11868.

6. Article 7 of the current regulations is as follows: "As a rule, National Security Knowledge courses are taught by regular officers who are graduates of Military Colleges. In the absence of such officers, or in cases where their numbers are not sufficient, other regular soldiers, retired soldiers, or soldiers who have resigned from their posts can be commissioned. If none of these soldiers are sufficient in number, then secondary school teachers who have performed their military service as reserve officers can be commissioned" *Resmi Gazete* (Official Gazette), 2 February 1980, R. Gazete No. 16888, Karar No. 8/37.

7. In my research, I have not been able to find an example of this practice. In fact, the notion that a civilian teacher could teach this course was foreign to both the teachers and the students I interviewed. Even in Turkey's Southeast where officers were engaged in active warfare between 1984 and 1999, they seem to have found the time to perform their teaching functions in high schools instead of relegating this role to civilian teachers (see chapter six).

8. It is strictly forbidden for them to teach in civilian clothes unless they are retired.

9. See http://www.meb.gov.tr for annual statistics.

10. Nationalism is one of the founding "Principles of Atatürk," others being Republicanism, Populism, Etatism, Laicism, and Reformism. These principles, known as the "Six Arrows" (*Altı Ok*), were first formulated in the 1927 and 1931 programs of the Republican People's Party (of which Atatürk was the "eternal leader") and were put into the constitution in 1937. The 1937 amendment was the addition of the statement "The Turkish Republic is Republicanist, Nationalist, Populist, Etatist, Laicist, and Reformist" in Article Two of the constitution, which remained in effect until 1961. These principles continued to inform the 1961 and 1982 constitutions, although they were given different interpretations and were not always referred to explicitly (see Parla 1992 and 1991c).

11. "Race" has been a much-debated category in the past century. It is now agreed upon by scholars that "racial difference" understood as "natural" "biological" difference is a cultural and political construction. As explained in the "American Anthropological Association Statement on 'Race,'" race is "an ideology about human differences" and that "evidence from the analysis of genetics (e.g., DNA) indicates that most physical variation, about 94%, lies *within* so-called racial groups" (http://www.aaanet.org/stmts/racepp.htm, Saturday, 10 February 2001). Nevertheless, "race" as an "ideology of human difference" and as a social marker of inequality exists in many societies. In Turkey, although it has been central in the construction of national identity, the term "race" does not have a popular usage. In other words, physical differences between

people are not necessarily associated with the idea of "race" or even "ethnicity." One possible exception to this rule is the general understanding that the "Kurds" have a darker complexion and only black hair. Although this understanding simplifies a complicated reality (e.g., there are many blond people among the Kurds and many people with darker complexion among people of other ethnicities), even in its extreme form, it signifies a relative difference and not an absolute one, as in "black" and "white." Another exception is the "racist" ideology promoted by certain ultranationalists; in the case of this ideology, the Turkish History Thesis has been taken to its logical conclusion to assume that Turks represent a homogeneous race. One alarming episode during the 17 August 1999 earthquake, where more than 30,000 people died, was the unwillingness of the Minister of Health, Osman Durmuş, to accept donated blood from Greece. His approach met with immense criticism and he had to back down and accept "Greek blood" (see Atay 1999 for a critical discussion).

12. This construction also silences the existence of a small community of Turkish Orthodox Christians, i.e., Christians who identify themselves as "Turks."

13. My usage of the term "strategic" throughout this text should be taken to imply military strategy.

14. For a discussion of the development of the national security state in the American context, see Hogan (1998).

15. *Türban* is the name that has been given to a special form of headscarf that is large and is worn in such a way that it completely conceals the hair and neck of the woman. This form of covering has become popular with the rise of the Islamist movement in Turkey, although not all women who wear the *türban* have been associated with Islamist groups or parties. The *türban* controversy has marked the politics of the 1980s and the 1990s, particularly in the universities of big cities. Several amendments in higher education laws have been made either allowing woman students to wear the *türban* or prohibiting them from doing so. The current law prohibits the covering of the hair and face in any form (see Göle 1991; Çakır 2000; Arat 2001).

16. For an insightful discussion of the xenophobic aspects of Turkish nationalism, see Belge (2002).

17. The report was written by the officials of the Ministry of National Defense, Ministry of National Education, Ministry of Interior, Ministry of Publications, the General Staff, and two officer-teachers. Six out of the eleven members of this committee were active or retired military officers (see *Millî Eğitim ile Ilgili Millî Savunma Komitesi Çalışmaları ve Raporu* [1961]).

18. In 2003, the History Foundation (*Türkiye Ekonomik ve Toplumsal Tarih Vakfı*), the Turkish Academy of Sciences (*Türkiye Bilimler Akademisi*), and the Human Rights Foundation of Turkey (*Türkiye Insan Hakları Vakfı*) coordinated a project whereby they examined a wide range of textbooks based on human rights criteria. In a report that I authored, the *National Security Knowledge* textbook was also examined and problematized as part of this project (Altinay 2003).

19. Anthropologist Sam Kaplan (1996) has shown that since the 1980 coup, the military has made a special effort to control the institutions of education, sometimes going as far as using slightly modified military laws and regulations for schools, teachers, and students.

20. The Higher Education Council is a national body that governs all higher education in Turkey. See *The Law of Higher Education*, Law Number: 2547, Date of Enactment: 4 November 1981, Published in the *Resmi Gazete* (Official Gazette) No: 17506; Date: 6 November 1981. According to Article 6, the Higher Education Council consists of twenty-two members, seven of whom are appointed by the President of Turkey, seven by the Council of Ministers, seven by the Inter-University Board, and one member by the Chief of the General Staff. Article 8 determines the number of appointees to the Higher Education Supervisory Board as ten, one of whom is appointed by the Chief of the General Staff.

Chapter Six   Silencing the Present:
Student-Soldiers and Officer-Teachers
Meet in the Classroom

1. I participated in two *National Security Knowledge* classes during my research and listened to the stories of about 75 young people from 40 different high schools in 12 cities and several small towns. The cities were: Ağrı, Ankara, Balıkesir, Cizre, Diyarbakır, Istanbul, Izmir, Kahramanmaraş, Kayseri, Kütahya, Mersin, and Siirt. All interviews took place in Diyarbakır, Istanbul, and Izmir. My research was mainly comprised of in-depth interviews with individual students and focus group discussions with groups of two to ten. About one-third of the students were from private high schools and two-thirds from public high schools. One-third had gone to high school in Diyarbakır, one-third in Istanbul, and the rest in other cities or small towns. The students were distributed evenly among lower-, middle-, and upper-class socioeconomic backgrounds (based on their own declarations of family income). About 40% were female and 60% male. During my interviews, I asked students to choose a pseudonym for themselves. About half of the names that appear in this chapter are self-designated names. I have assigned pseudonyms to the other half. No real names have been used. The age range of my interviewees was 16–35. All have gone to high school in the 1980s and the 1990s.
2. "Apo" is the short form of Abdullah, used here to refer to Abdullah Öcalan.
3. See Özyürek 2000 for a detailed and insightful discussion of the events surrounding the Merve Kavakçı incident.
4. It was thanks to a coincidence and to the openness of one of the officer-teachers I interviewed that I was able to participate in these classes. He was teaching on the day of our interview and asked me if I wanted to come to his classes. I was introduced to the students as a researcher who was interested in the *National Security Knowledge* course as part of her Ph.D. work in the United States.
5. Several students talked to me about having faced disciplinary measures for articulating controversial views.

Epilogue

1. See Parla 1998 for a discussion of what he calls "mercantile militarism." Anthropologist Sam Kaplan has explored the military's role in shaping education policies in his doctoral thesis (S. Kaplan 1996). Political scientist Ismail Kaplan has also done a comprehensive study of education policies in Turkey, pointing to its militarizing aspects (I. Kaplan 1998). Researcher Serdar Şen has written on the role of the military in shaping society. Şen conceptualizes the Armed Forces as an "ideological apparatus" and points to conscription as an important component of this apparatus (see Şen 1996). Ümit Cizre has been problematizing the role of the military in politics in novel ways (see Cizre-Sakallıoğlu 1993; Cizre 2003). A recent collection by Ahmet Insel and Ali Bayramoğlu (2004) provides an insightful set of articles on the role of the military in shaping political discourse, the economy, and other aspects of life.
2. Political scientist Nur Vergin addresses this second assumption in a 1997 op-ed: "The Turkish Republic has been founded by the military. This is correct. So what? I think and think, and force my memory, but I cannot find a single state (including the United States of America) that was not founded by the military. I cannot find it, because it does not exist. All states, always, are founded by people who possess arms; not by artisans, traders, or magicians" (Vergin 1997).

BIBLIOGRAPHY

2000'li Yıllara Girerken Türk Ordusu. [1999]. Ankara: Ankara Ticaret Odası ve T.C. Kültür Bakanlığı.

2003 Regular Report on Turkey's Progress Towards Accession. (2003). Brussels: European Commission.

Abélès, Marc. 1990. *Anthropologie de l'État.* Armand Colin.

Abu-Lughod, Lila. 1991. Writing Against Culture. In *Recapturing Anthropology: Working in the Present,* ed. Richard Fox, 137–162. Santa Fe, New Mexico: School of American Research Press.

Abrams, Philip. 1988. Notes on the Difficulty of Studying the State (1977). *Journal of Historical Sociology* 1(1): 58–89.

Adak, Hülya. 2003. National Myths and Self-Na(rra)tions: Mustafa Kemal's Nutuk and Halide Edib's Memoirs and The Turkish Ordeal. *South Atlantic Quarterly,* Special Issue: Relocating the Fault Lines: Turkey Beyond the East-West Divide, ed. Sibel Irzık and Güven Güzeldere. 102(2/3): 509–529.

Afet (Inan). 1939. Atatürk ve Tarih Tezi. *Belleten* 3: 243–246.

Afet (Inan). 1930. *Askerlik Vazifesi.* Istanbul: Devlet Matbaası.

Ahıska, Meltem. 2000. Gender and National Fantasy: Early Turkish Radio Drama. *New Perspectives on Turkey* 22(Spring): 25–60.

Ahmad, Feroz. 1993. *The Making of Modern Turkey.* London and New York: Routledge.

Aka, Kemal ve Mustafa Çiçekoğlu. 1950a. *Millî Savunma Bilgileri I.* Istanbul: Güven Basımevi.

Aka, Kemal ve Mustafa Çiçekoğlu.1950b. *Millî Savunma Bilgileri II.* Istanbul: Güven Basımevi.

Aka, Kemal ve Mustafa Çiçekoğlu.1950c. *Millî Savunma Bilgileri III.* Istanbul: Güven Basımevi.

Akçam, Taner. 2000. *Ermeni Tabusu Aralanırken: Diyalogdan Başka Çözüm Var Mı?* Istanbul: Su Yayınları.

Akçura, Yusuf. 1976 [1904]. *Üç Tarz-ı Siyaset.* Ankara: Türk Tarih Kurumu.

Aktan, Hamza. 2003. Sinek Kadar da Olsak Mide Bulandırıyoruz. *www.bianet.org,* 1 February.

Aktan, Hamza. 2002. Mehmet Bal Mehmetçik Olmayacak. *www.bianet.org,* 28 November.

Aktar, Ayhan. 2000. *Varlık Vergisi ve 'Türkleştirme' Politikaları.* Istanbul: İletişim Yayınları.

Akyüz, Yahya. 1983. Atatürk ve 1921 Eğitim Kongresi. In *Cumhuriyet Döneminde Eğitim.* Istanbul: Milli Eğitim Bakanlığı.

Alakom, Rohat. 1998. Araştırmalarda Fazla Adı Geçmeyen Bir Kuruluş: Kürt Kadınları Teali Cemaati. *Tarih ve Toplum* 171(March): 36–40.

Allison, Anne. 1994. *Nightwork: Sexuality, Pleasure, and Corporate Masculinity in a Tokyo Hostess Club.* Chicago: University of Chicago Press.

Alonso, Ana Maria. 1994. The Politics of Space, Time and Substance: State Formation, Nationalism, and Ethnicity. *Annual Review of Anthropology* 23: 379–405.

Altınay, Ayşe Gül. 2003. Militarizm ve İnsan Hakları Ekseninde Milli Güvenlik Dersi. In *Ders Kitaplarında İnsan Hakları: Tarama Sonuçları*, ed. Betül Çotuksöken, Ayşe Erzan, and Orhan Silier, 138–157. Istanbul: Türkiye Ekonomik ve Toplumsal Tarih Vakfı.

Altınay, Ayşe Gül. 2000a. *Vatan, Millet, Kadınlar*. Istanbul: İletişim Yayınları.

Altınay, Ayşe Gül. 2000b. Talking and Writing Our Sexuality: Feminist Activism on Virginity and Virginity Tests in Turkey. In *Women and Sexuality in Muslim Societies*, ed. Pınar İlkkaracan. Istanbul: Women for Women's Human Rights-New Ways.

Altınay, Ayşe Gül. 1999a. Askerlik ve Eğitim. *Birikim* 125/126(September/October): 200–208.

Altınay, Ayşe Gül. 1999b. Mehmetler, Askerlik ve Savaş. *Birikim* 127(November): 89–100.

Altınay, Ayşe Gül. 1999c. Mehmedin Kitabı: Challenging Narratives of War and Nationalism. *New Perspectives on Turkey* 21(Fall): 125–145.

Altınay, Ayşe Gül and Tanıl Bora. 2002. Ordu, Militarizm ve Milliyetçilik. *Milliyetçilik: Modern Türkiye'de Siyasi Düşünce Cilt 4*, ed. Tanıl Bora, 140–154. Istanbul: İletişim Yayınları.

Alvarez, Sonia E. 1997. Reweaving the Fabric of Collective Action: Social Movements and Challenges to "Actually Existing Democracy" in Brazil. In *Between Resistance and Revolution: Cultural Politics and Social Protest*, ed. Richard G. Fox and Orin Starn, 83–117. New Brunswick, New Jersey: Rutgers University Press.

Anderson, Benedict. 1991. *Imagined Communities: Reflections on the Origins and Spread of Nationalism*. Rev. ed. London: Verso.

Anderson, Martin, ed. 1982. *The Military Draft: Selected Readings on Conscription*. Stanford: Hoover Institution Press.

Arat, Yeşim. 2001. Group-Differentiated Rights and the Liberal Democratic State: Rethinking the Headscarf Controversy in Turkey. *New Perspectives on Turkey*, 25(Fall): 31–46.

Arat, Yeşim. 1997. The Project of Modernity and Women in Turkey. In *Rethinking Modernity and National İdentity in Turkey*, ed. Sibel Bozdoğan and Reşat Kasaba, 98–110. Seattle: University of Washington Press.

Arat, Yeşim. 1993. Women's Studies in Turkey: From Kemalism to Feminism. *New Perspectives in Turkey*, 9(Fall): 119–135.

Arat, Zehra. 1998. Educating the Daughters of the Republic. In *Deconstructing Images of "the Turkish Woman"*, ed. Zehra Arat, 157–180. New York: St. Martin's Press.

Asad, Talal, ed. 1973. *Anthropology and the Colonial Encounter*. New York: Humanities Press.

Atatürk'ün Askerliğe Dair Eserleri. [1959]. Ankara: İş Bankası.

Atatürk'ün Söylev ve Demeçleri I-III. [1997]. Türk Tarih Kurumu Basımevi.

Atay, Tayfun. 1999. Deprem, Kan ve Bakan. *Birikim* 125/126(September/October): 95–97.

Ayaz, Nevzat. 1994. Sunuş. In *Talim ve Terbiye Kurulu Başkanlığı (1983–1993)*, ed. Yusuf Ekinci, Mustafa Çandır, Turhan Soylu, and Onur Bağlum Keleş. Istanbul: Milli Eğitim Basımevi.

Aygen, Nermin. 1941. *Türk Beyinleri Üzerine İlk Antropolojik Araştırma*. Antropoloji ve Etnoloji Serisi, No.22. Ankara: Dil ve Tarih-Coğrafya Fakültesi Yayınları.

Bakhtin, M. M. 1994. *The Dialogic Imagination*. Ed. M. Holquist. Trans. C. Emerson and M. Holquist. Austin: University of Texas Press.

Balakrishnan, Gopal, ed. 1996. *Mapping the Nation*. London and New York: Verso.

Bali, Rıfat N. 1999. *Cumhuriyet Yıllarında Türkiye Yahudileri: Bir Türkleştirme Serüveni [1923–1945]*. Istanbul: İletişim Yayınları.

Barkey, Henri J. and Graham E. Fuller. 1998. *Turkey's Kurdish Question*. Lanham, Maryland: Rowman and Littlefield and the Carnegie Corporation of New York.

Barnes, Teresa A. The Heroes' Struggle: Life After the Liberation War for Four Ex-Combatants in Zimbabwe. In *Soldiers in Zimbabwe's Liberation War*, ed. N. Bhebe and T. Ranger. Harare: University of Zimbabwe Publications.

Barthes, Roland. 1972. *Mythologies*. Trans. Annette Lavers. New York: Noonday Press.

Belge, Murat. 2002. Türkiye'de Zenofobi ve Milliyetçilik. In *Milliyetçilik: Modern Türkiye'de Siyasi Düşünce Cilt 4*, ed. Tanıl Bora, 179–192. Istanbul: İletişim Yayınları.

Belge, Murat. 2001. Mustafa Kemal ve Kemalizm. In *Kemalizm: Modern Türkiye'de Siyasi Düşünce Cilt 2*, ed. Ahmet Insel, 29–43. Istanbul: İletişim Yayınları.

Ben-Ari, Eyal. 1998. *Mastering Soldiers: Conflict, Emotions, and the Enemy in an Israeli Military Unit.* New York and Oxford: Berghahn Books.

Ben-Eliezer, Uri. 1995. A Nation-in-Arms: State, Nation, and Militarism in Israel's First Years. *Comparative Study of Society and History* 18: 264–285.

Berghahn, V. R. 1982. *Militarism: The History of an International Debate, 1861–1979.* New York: St. Martin's Press.

Berkes, Niyazi. 1978. *Türkiye'de Çağdaşlaşma.* Istanbul: Doğu-Batı Yayınları.

Berktay, Fatmagül. 2002. Doğu ile Batı'nın Birleştiği Yer: Kadın İmgesinin Kurgulanışı. In *Modernleşme ve Batıcılık: Modern Türkiye'de Siyasi Düşünce Cilt 3*, ed. Uygur Kocabaşoğlu, 275–285. Istanbul: İletişim Yayınları.

Berktay, Fatmagül. 2001. Osmanlı'dan Cumhuriyet'e Feminizm. In *Tanzimat ve Meşrutiyetin Birikimi: Modern Türkiye'de Siyasi Düşünce Cilt 1*, ed. Mehmet Ö. Alkan, 348–360. Istanbul: İletişim Yayınları.

Berktay, Fatmagül. 1998. Cumhuriyetin 75 Yıllık Serüvenine Kadınlar Açısından Bakmak. In *75 Yılda Kadınlar ve Erkekler/Bilanço 98*, 1–11. Istanbul: Iş Bankası and Tarih Vakfı.

Berktay, Halil. 1990. Iktisat Tarihi: Osmanlı Devletinin Yükselişine Kadar Türklerin Iktisadî ve Toplumsal Tarihi. In *Türkiye Tarihi I*, ed. Sina Akşin et al., 25–137. Istanbul: Cem Yayınevi.

Berktay, Halil. 1985. Tarih Çalışmaları. *Tanzimat'tan Cumhuriyet'e Türkiye Ansiklopedisi* 9: 2456–2474.

Beşikçi, Ismail. 1992. *Tunceli Kanunu (1935) ve Dersim Jenosidi.* Ankara: Yurt Kitap-Yayın.

Bilal, Melissa, Lerna Ekmekçioğlu, and Belinda Mumcu. 2001. Hayganuş Mark'ın (1885–1966) Hayatı, Düşünceleri ve Etkinlikleri: "Feminizm: Bir Adalet Fermanı." *Toplumsal Tarih* 15(87): 48–56.

Bora Aksu and Asena Günal, eds. 2002. *90'larda Türkiye'de Feminizm.* Istanbul: İletişim Yayınları.

Bora, Tanıl. 2003. Ders Kitaplarında Milliyetçilik. In *Ders Kitaplarında Insan Hakları: Tarama Sonuçları*, ed. Betül Çotuksöken, Ayşe Erzan, and Orhan Silier, 65–89. Istanbul: Türkiye Ekonomik ve Toplumsal Tarih Vakfı.

Bora, Tanıl. 1999. "Millet-i Müselleha," *Radikal Iki*, 5 September.

Bourdieu, Pierre. 1999. Rethinking the State: Genesis and Structure of the Bureaucratic Field. In *State/Culture: State Formation After the Cultural Turn*, ed. George Steinmetz, 53–75. Ithaca and London: Cornell University Press.

Bozdemir, Mevlut. 1985. Ordu-Siyaset Ilişkileri. *Cumhuriyet Dönemi Türkiye Ansiklopedisi* 10: 2648–2660.

Buzan, Barry, Ole Wæver, and Jaap de Wilde. 1998. *Security: A New Framework for Analysis.* Boulder: Lynne Rienner.

Buzan, Barry. 1991. *People, States, Fear: An Agenda for International Security Studies in the Post-Cold War Era.* Boulder: Lynne Rienner.

Campbell, David. 1992. *Writing Security: United States Foreign Policy and the Politics of Identity.* Minneapolis: University of Minnesota Press.

Chatterjee, Partha. 1993. *The Nation and Its Fragments: Colonial and Postcolonial Histories.* New Jersey: Princeton University Press.

Chenoy, Anuradha M. 1998. Militarization, Conflict, and Women in South Asia. In *The Women and War Reader*, ed. Lorentzen, Lois Ann and Jennifer Turpin, 101–110. New York: New York University Press.

Cizre, Ümit. 2003. Demythologizing the National Security Concept: The Case of Turkey. *Middle East Journal* 57(2): 213–229.

Cizre-Sakallıoğlu, Ümit. 1993. *AP-Ordu İlişkileri: Bir İkilemin Anatomisi*. Istanbul: İletişim Yayınları.

Clastres, Pierre. 1987 [1974]. *Society Against the State: Essays in Political Anthropology*. Translated by Robert Hurley in collaboration with Abe Stein. New York: Zone Books.

Clifford, James and George E. Marcus, ed. 1986. *Writing Culture: The Poetics and Politics of Ethnography*. Berkeley: University of California Press.

Clifford, James. 1986. Introduction: Partial Truths. In *Writing Culture: The Poetics and Politics of Ethnography*, ed. James Clifford and George E. Marcus, 1–26. Berkeley: University of California Press.

Cock, Jacklyn. 1991. *Colonels and Cadres: War and Gender in South Africa*. Cape Town: Oxford University Press.

Cockburn, Cynthia. 2004. *The Line: Women, Partition and the Gender Order in Cyprus*. London and New York: Zed Books.

Cockburn, Cynthia. 1998. *The Space Between Us: Negotiating Gender and National Identities in Conflict*. London and New York: Zed Books.

Cohn, Bernard S. and Nicholas Dirks. 1988. Beyond the Fringe: The Nation State, Colonialism, and The Technologies of Power. *Journal of Historical Sociology* 1(2): 224–229.

Cohn, Carol. 1993. Wars, Wimps, and Women: Talking Gender and Thinking War. In *Gendering War Talk*, ed. Miriam Cooke and Angela Woollacott, 227–246. New Jersey: Princeton University Press.

Connell, R. W. 1995. *Masculinities*. Berkeley and Los Angeles: University of California Press.

Connell, R. W. 1987. *Gender and Power: Society, the Person and Sexual Politics*. Cambridge: Polity Press.

Cooke, Miriam and Angela Woollacott, ed. 1993. *Gendering War Talk*. New Jersey: Princeton University Press.

Copeaux, Etienne. 1998. *Tarih Ders Kitaplarında (1931–1993): Türk Tarih Tezinden Türk-Islam Sentezine*. Istanbul: Tarih Vakfı Yurt Yayınları.

Cornwall Andrea and Nancy Lindisfarne. 1994. *Dislocating Masculinity: Comparative Ethnographies*. London and New York: Routledge.

Coronil, Fernando. 1997. *The Magical State: Nature, Money, and Modernity in Venezuela*. Chicago: University of Chicago Press.

Corrigan Philip and Derek Sayer. 1985. *The Great Arch: English State Formation as Cultural Revolution*. Oxford and New York: Basil Blackwell.

Cumhuriyet. 2002. Vicdani Retçi Bal'a Destek. 25 November.

Cumhuriyet 2002. Vicdani Retçi Rapor Bekliyor. 18 November.

Çaha, Ömer. 1996. *Sivil Kadın: Türkiye'de Sivil Toplum ve Kadın*. Trans. Ertan Özensel. Konya: Vadi Yayınları.

Çakır, Ruşen. 2000. *Direniş ve İtaat: İki İktidar Arasında İslamcı Kadın*. Siyah-Beyaz Dizisi. Istanbul: Metis Yayınları.

Çakır, Serpil. 1994. *Osmanlı Kadın Hareketi*, Istanbul: Metis Yayınları.

Çelikkan, Murat. 2002a. 16 Gün Kaldı. *Radikal*, 14 November.

Çelikkan, Murat. 2002b. Eşcinsellik ve Askerlik. *Radikal*, 6 November.

Çoker, Fahri. 1985. Tanzimat ve Ordudaki Yenilikler. *Tanzimat'tan Cumhuriyet'e Türkiye Ansiklopedisi* 5: 1260–1266.

Davison, Andrew. 1998. *Secularism and Revivalism in Turkey: A Hermeneutic Reconsideration*. New Haven and London: Yale University Press.

Delaney, Carol. 1991. *The Seed and the Soil: Gender and Cosmology in Turkish Village Society*. Berkeley: University of California Press.

Demirdirek, Aynur. 1993. *Osmanlı Kadınlarının Hayat Hakkı Arayışlarının Bir Hikayesi*. Ankara: İmge Yayınları.

Demirel, Tanel. 2002. Türk Silahlı Kuvvetlerinin Toplumsal Meşruiyeti Üzerine. *Toplum ve Bilim* 93(Summer): 29–54.

Dewey, John. 1990. On Military Training in Schools. In *John Dewey: The Later Works, 1925–1953*, ed. Jo Ann Boydston, 124. Carbondale: Southern Illinois University Press.

Dirlik, Arif. 2002. History Without A Center? Reflections on Eurocentrism. In *Historiographical Traditions and Cultural Identities in the Nineteenth and Twentieth Centuries*, ed. Eckhardt Fuchs and Benedikt Stucktey, 247–284. Lanham, Md.: Rowman and Littlefield.

Dirlik, Arif. 1975. The Ideological Foundations of the New Life Movement: A Study in Counterrevolution. *Journal of Asian Studies* 34(4): 945–980.

Durakbaşa, Ayşe. 2000. *Halide Edip, Türk Modernleşmesi ve Feminizm*. Istanbul: İletişim Yayınları.

Durakbaşa, Ayşe. 1993. *Reappraisal of Halide Edib For A Critique of Turkish Modernization*. Ph.D. Dissertation. University of Essex.

Durakbaşa, Ayşe. 1988. Cumhuriyet Döneminde Kemalist Kadın Kimliğinin Oluşumu. *Tarih ve Toplum* 9(51): 167–171.

Düzel, Neşe. 2001. Ordu Siyasetin Dışında Olmalı. *Radikal*, 13 January.

Earle, Edward Mead. 1966. Adam Smith, Alexander Hamilton, Friedrich List: The Economic Foundations of Military Power. in *Makers of Modern Strategy: Military Thought from Machiavelli to Hitler*, ed. Edward Mead Earle, 117–154. New York: Atheneum.

Eckhardt Fuchs and Benedikt Stuchtey, ed. *Across Cultural Borders: Historiography in Global Perspective*. Lanham, Md.: Rowman and Littlefield. 2002

Edib, Halide (Adıvar). 1930. *Turkey Faces West: A Turkish View of Recent Changes and Their Origin*. London: Oxford University Press.

Edib, Halide (Adıvar). 1928. *The Turkish Ordeal*. New York and London: The Century Co.

Eley, Geoff and Ronald Grigor Suny. 1996. Introduction: From the Moment of Social History to the Work of Cultural Representation. In *Becoming National: A Reader*, ed. G. Eley and R. G. Suny. New York and Oxford: Oxford University Press.

Elshtain, Jean Bethke and Sheila Tobias, ed. 1990. *Women, Militarism, and War*. Savage, Maryland: Rowman and Littlefield Publishers.

Enloe, Cynthia. 2000. *Maneuvers: The International Politics of Militarizing Women's Lives*. University of California Press.

Enloe, Cynthia. 1995. Feminism, Nationalism and Militarism: Wariness Without Paralysis? In *Feminism, Nationalism and Militarism*, ed. Constance R. Sutton, 13–32. Association for Feminist Anthropology/American Anthropological Association.

Enloe, Cynthia. 1993. *The Morning After: Sexual Politics at the End of the Cold War*. Berkeley: University of California Press.

Enloe, Cynthia. 1989. *Bananas, Beaches and Bases: Making Feminist Sense of International Politics*. Berkeley: University of California Press.

Ersanlı-Behar, Büşra. 1992. *İktidar ve Tarih: Türkiye'de "Resmi Tarih" Tezinin Oluşumu (1929–1937)*. Istanbul: Afa Yayınları.

Escobar, Arturo. 1995. *Encountering Development: The Making and Unmaking of the Third World*. New Jersey: Princeton University Press.

Ewing, Katherine. 2000. Legislating Religious Freedom: Muslim Challenges to the Relationship between "Church" and "State" in Germany and France. *Daedalus* 129(4): 31–54.

Ewing, Katherine Pratt. 1997. *Arguing Sainthood: Modernity, Psychoanalysis, and Islam*. Durham: Duke University Press.

Fahmy, Khalid. 1999. The Nation and Its Deserters: Conscription in Mehmed Ali's Egypt. In *Arming the State: Military Conscription in the Middle East and Central Asia 1775–1925*, ed. Erik Jan Zürcher, 59–77. London and New York: I.B. Tauris.

Fahmy Khalid. 1997. *All the Pasha's Men: Mehmed Ali, His Army and the Making of Modern Egypt*. Cambridge: Cambridge University Press.

Feinman, Ilene Rose. 2000. *Citizenship Rites: Feminist Soldiers and Feminist Antimilitarists*. New York and London: New York University Press.

Fidel, Kenneth. 1975. Military Organization and Conspiracy in Turkey. In *Militarism in Developing Countries*, ed. Kenneth Fidel, 169–218. New Jersey: Transaction Books.

Forrest, Alan. 1993. Citizenship and Military Service. In *The French Revolution and the Meaning of Citizenship*, ed. Renée Waldinger, Philip Dawson, and Isser Woloch, 153–165. Westport, Connecticut and London: Greenwood Press.

Foucault, Michel. 1991. Politics and the Study of Discourse. In *The Foucault Effect: Studies in Governmentality*, ed. G. Burchell, C. Gordon, and P. Miller, 53–72. University of Chicago Press.

Foucault, Michel. 1990 [1978]. *The History of Sexuality: An Introduction*. Vol. 1. New York: Vintage Books.

Foucault, Michel. 1979. *Discipline and Punish: The Birth of the Prison*. New York: Vintage Books.

Fox, Richard G. and Orin Starn. 1997. Introduction. In *Between Resistance and Revolution: Cultural Politics and Social Protest*, ed. Richard G. Fox and Orin Starn, 1–16. New Brunswick, New Jersey: Rutgers University Press.

Frantz, Douglas. 2001. Military Bestrides Turkey's Path to the European Union. *The New York Times*, 14 January.

Galip, Reşit. 1933. Türk Tarih Inkılâbı ve Yabancı Tezler. *Ülkü* 2(9): 164–177.

Georgeon, François. 1996. *Türk Milliyetçiliğinin Kökenleri: Yusuf Akçura (1876–1935)*. 2nd ed. Istanbul: Tarih Vakfı Yurt Yayınları.

Giles, Wenona, Malathi de Alwis, Edith Klein, and Neluka Silva, ed. 2003. *Feminists Under Fire: Exchanges Across War Zones*. With Maja Korač, Djurdja Kneževič, Žarana Papič as Advisory Editors. Toronto: Between the Lines.

Gill, Lesley. 1997. Creating Citizens, Making Men: The Military and Masculinity in Bolivia. *Cultural Anthropology* 12(4): 527–550.

Goltz, Colmar, Freiherr von der. 1887. *The Nation in Arms*. Trans. Philip A. Ashworth. London: W.H. Allen and Co.

Goltz, Colmar, Freiherr von der. 1884. *Millet-i Müsellaha: Asrımızın Usul ve Ahval-i Askeriyesi*. Trans. Mehmet Tahir. Istanbul: Matbaa-i Ebuzziya (2nd ed., 1888).

Gökalp, Ziya. 1977. *Yeni Türkiye'nin Hedefleri*. Istanbul: Istanbul Matbaası.

Gökalp, Ziya. 1959. *Turkish Nationalism and Western Civilization: Selected Essays of Ziya Gökalp*. Trans. and ed. with an introduction by Niyazi Berkes. New York: Columbia University Press.

Gökçen, Sabiha. 1996. *Atatürk'le Bir Ömür*. 2nd ed. Prepared by Oktay Verel. Istanbul: Altın Kitaplar.

Gökçen, Sabiha. 1982. *Atatürk'ün İzinde Bir Ömür Böyle Geçti*. Prepared by Oktay Verel. Türk Hava Kurumu Yayınları.

Göktaş, Hıdır. 1987. Interview with Sabiha Gökçen (partly published in *Nokta*, 28 June 1987).

Göle, Nilüfer. 1996. *The Forbidden Modern: Civilization and Veiling*. Ann Arbor: The University of Michigan Press.

Göle, Nilüfer. 1991. *Modern Mahrem: Medeniyet ve Örtünme*. Istanbul: Metis Yayınları.

Gupta, Akhil. 1995. Blurred Boundaries: The Discourse of Corruption, the Culture of Politics, and the Imagined State. *American Ethnologist* 22(2): 375–402.

Gülsoy, Ufuk. 2000. *Osmanlı Gayrimüslimlerinin Askerlik Serüveni*. Istanbul: Simurg Yayınları.

Günaltay, Şemsettin and H. Reşit Tankut. 1938. *Dil ve Tarih Tezlerimiz Üzerine Gerekli Bazı Izahlar*. Istanbul: Devlet Basımevi.

Günaltay, Şemsettin. 1938. Türk Tarih Tezi Hakkındaki İntikatların Mahiyeti ve Tezin Kat'î Zaferi. *Belleten* 2: 337–365.

Günsel, Enver. 1985. Hava Kuvvetleri. *Cumhuriyet Dönemi Türkiye Ansiklopedisi* 10: 2626–2634.

Hale, William M. 1994. *Turkish Politics and the Military*. London and New York: Routledge.

Hamilton, General Sir Ian. 1910. *Compulsory Service: A Study of the Question in the Light of Experience*. London: John Murray.

Hanioğlu, Şükrü. 1985a. Osmanlıcılık. *Tanzimat'tan Cumhuriyet'e Türkiye Ansiklopedisi* 5: 1389–1393.

Hanioğlu, Şükrü. 1985b. Türkçülük. *Tanzimat'tan Cumhuriyet'e Türkiye Ansiklopedisi* 5: 1394–1399.

Haraway, Donna. 1991. *Simians, Cyborgs, and Women: The Reinvention of Nature*. New York: Routledge.

Havacılık ve Spor, 15 June 1937, no.193.

Hein, Laura and Mark Selden. 1998. Learning Citizenship from the Past: Textbook Nationalism, Global Context, and Social Change. *Bulletin of Concerned Asian Scholars* 30(2): 3–15.

Helman, Sara. 1997. Militarism and the Construction of Community. *Journal of Political and Military Sociology* 25(Winter): 305–332.

Heper, Metin and Aylin Güney. 2000. The Military and the Consolidation of Democracy: The Recent Turkish Experience. *Armed Forces and Society* 26(4): 635–657.

Heper, Metin and Ahmet Evin, ed. 1988. *State, Democracy, and the Military: Turkey in the 1980s*. Berlin and New York: W. de Gruyter.

Herzfeld, Michael. 1996. *Cultural Intimacy: Social Poetics in the Nation-State*. New York and London: Routledge.

Hobsbawm, E. J. 1990. *Nations and Nationalism Since 1870: Programme, Myth, Reality*. Cambridge University Press.

Hocaoğlu, Murat. 2002. *Eşcinsel Erkekler: Yirmi Beş Tanıklık*. Istanbul: Metis Yayınları.

Hogan, Michael J. 1998. *A Cross of Iron: Harry S. Truman and the Origins of the National Security State, 1945–1954*. New York: Cambridge University Press.

Horeman, Bart and Marc Stolwijk. 1998. *Refusing to Bear Arms: A World Survey of Conscription and Conscientious Objection to Military Service*. London: War Resisters' International.

Howard, Michael. 1978. *War and the Nation State*. Oxford: Clarendon Press.

Iba, Şaban. 1999. *Milli Güvenlik Devleti: Dünyada ve Türkiye'de Belgeleriyle Milli Güvenlik Ideolojisi ve Kurumlaşma*. Istanbul: Çivi Yazıları.

Ilhan, Suat. 1989. Askerliğin Kültürümüzdeki Yeri. *Erdem* 5(14): 349–363.

Ilkkaracan, Pinar, ed. 2000. *Women and Sexuality in Muslim Societies*. Istanbul: Women for Women's Human Rights-New Ways.

Ilkkaracan, Pinar. 1998. Exploring the Context of Women's Sexuality in Eastern Turkey. *Reproductive Health Matters* 6(12): 66–75.

İlyasoğlu, Aynur ve Necla Akgökçe, ed. 2001. *yerli bir feminizme doğru*. Istanbul: Sel Yayıncılık.

Inalcık, Halil. 1994. Osmanlı Devrinde Türk Ordusu. *Türk Kültürü* 375(July): 385–394.

Inalcık, Halil. 1964. Osmanlı Devrinde Türk Ordusu. *Türk Kültürü* 22(August): 49–56.

Inan, Afet. 1939. Atatürk ve Tarih Tezi. *Belleten* 3: 243–246.

Inan, Afet 1988 [1969]. *Medeni Bilgiler ve M. Kemal Atatürk'ün El Yazıları*. 2nd ed. Ankara: Türk Tarih Kurumu Basımevi.

Inan, Afet. 1947. *Türkiye Halkının Antropolojik Karakterleri ve Türkiye Tarihi: Türk Irkının Vatanı Anadolu*. Ankara: Türk Tarih Kurumu Basımevi.

Inan, Afet. 1941. *L'Anatolie, le pay de la "race" turque. Recherches sur les caractères anthropologiques des populations de la Turquie*. Introduction by Eugène Pittard. Geneve: Georg & Cie.

Insel, Ahmet and Ali Bayramoğlu. 2004. *Bir Zümre, Bir Parti: Türkiye'de Ordu*. Istanbul: İletişim Yayınları.

Jayawardena, Kumari. 1986. *Feminism and Nationalism in the Third World*. London: Zed Books.

Kadın Bakış Açısıyla Türk Ceza Kanunu: TCK Tasarısı Değişiklik Talepleri. 2003. TCK Kadın Çalışma Grubu.

Kadıoğlu, Ayşe. 1998. Cinselliğin İnkarı: Büyük Toplumsal Projelerin Nesnesi Olarak Türk Kadınları. In *75 Yılda Kadınlar ve Erkekler/Bilanço 98.* Istanbul: İşbankası ve Tarih Vakfı Yayınları.

Kafesoğlu, Ibrahim. 1994. Türk Ordusu. *Türk Kültürü* 32(376): 449–452.

Kafesoğlu, Ibrahim. 1976. Ordu-Millet. *Türk Kültürü* 14(167): 648–650.

Kalman, M. 1995. *Belge ve Tanıklarıyla Dersim Direnişleri.* Istanbul: Nujen Yayınları.

Kandiyoti, Deniz. 1994. The Paradoxes of Masculinity: Some Thoughts on Segregated Societies. In *Dislocating Masculinity: Comparative Ethnographies,* 197–213. London: Routledge.

Kandiyoti, Deniz. 1989. Women and the Turkish State: Political Actors or Symbolic Pawns. In *Women-Nation-State,* ed. Nira Yuval-Davis and Floya Anthias, 126–149. London: Macmillan Press.

Kansu, Şevket Aziz. 1939. Kültür Teorileri Hakkında. *Ülkü* 12(71): 398–408.

Kansu, Şevket Aziz. 1937a. İstikbal Sevgisi ve Bio-Sosyal Kültürümüz. *Ülkü* 8(48): 409–410.

Kansu, Şevket Aziz. 1937b. Hâmidin Antropolojik Tetkiki. *Ülkü* 9(51): 183–185.

Kansu, Şevket Aziz. 1936. Antropoloji'nin Tarifi ve Programı Hakkında (I). *Ülkü* 7(37): 34–40.

Kansu, Şevket Aziz. 1934a. Biyososyoloji. *Ülkü* 3(16): 253–262.

Kansu, Şevket Aziz. 1934b. Türk Topraklarının Adamı. *Ülkü* 4(20): 81–82.

Kaplan, Ismail. 1999. *Türkiye'de Milli Eğitim İdeolojisi ve Siyasal Toplumsallaşma Üzerindeki Etkisi.* Istanbul: İletişim Yayınları.

Kaplan, Ismail. 1998. *The Ideology of National Education in Turkey and Its Implications for Political Socialization.* Ph.D. Dissertation. Istanbul: Boğaziçi University.

Kaplan. Sam. 2003. Nuriye's Dilemma: Turkish Lessons of Democracy and the Gendered State. *American Ethnologist* 30(3): 401–417.

Kaplan, Sam. 1996. *Education and the Politics of National Culture in a Turkish Community, Circa 1990.* Ph.D. Dissertation. University of Chicago.

Karabekir, Kazım. 2001. *Türkiye'de ve Türk Ordusunda Almanlar.* Prepared by Orhan Hülagü ve Ömer Hakan Özalp. Istanbul: Emre Yayınları.

Karakışla, Yavuz Selim. 2003. Kürd Kadınları Teâli Cemiyeti (1919). *Toplumsal Tarih* 19(111): 14–24.

Karakışla, Yavuz Selim. 1999. Enver Paşa'nın Kurdurduğu Kadın Birinci Taburu: Osmanlı Ordusunda Kadın Askerler. *Tarih ve Toplum* 11(66): 15–24.

Kaya, Ali. 1999. *Başlangıcından Günümüze Dersim Tarihi.* Istanbul: Can Yayınları.

Kayalı, Kurtuluş. 1985. Osmanlı Devleti'nde Yenileşme Hareketleri ve Ordu. *Tanzimat'tan Cumhuriyet'e Türkiye Ansiklopedisi* 5: 1250–1258.

Kazamias, Andreas M. 1966. *Education and the Quest for Modernity in Turkey.* London: George Allen and Unwin.

Kerber, Linda. 1990. May All Our Citizens Be Soldiers and All Our Soldiers Citizens: The Ambiguities of Female Citizenship in the New Nation. In *Women, Militarism, and War,* ed. J. B.Elshtain and S. Tobias, 89–103. Savage, Maryland: Rowman and Littlefield Publishers.

Kerim, Fahrettin. 1934. Milli Nüfus Siyasetinde (Eugenique) Meselesinin Mahiyeti. *Ülkü* 3(15): 206–212.

Kıvanç Halit. 1998. *Bulutlarla Yarışan Kadın: Halit Kıvanç, Sabiha Gökçen'le Söyleşiyor/She Raced With the Clouds: Halit Kıvanç Interviews Sabiha Gökçen.* Trans. Fred Stark. Istanbul: Yapı Kredi.

Kiernan, V. G. 1973. Conscription and Society in Europe Before the War of 1914–18. In *War and Society: Historical Essays in Honour and Memory of J. R. Western 1928–1971,* ed. J. R. Western and M. R. D. Foot, 141–158. London: Paul Elek.

Kirişci, Kemal. 2000. Disaggregating Turkish Citizenship and Immigration Practices. *Middle Eastern Studies* 36(3): 1–22.

Kirişci, Kemal and Gareth M. Winrow. 1997. *The Kurdish Question and Turkey: An Example of a Trans-state Ethnic Conflict.* London: Frank Cass.

Koçoğlu, Yahya. 2001. *Azınlık Gençleri Anlatıyor.* Istanbul: Metis Yayınları.

Koloğlu, Orhan. 1999. Osmanlı Devleti'nde "Asker Millet" Anlayışının Oluşması, *Tarih ve Toplum* 32(192): 344–345.

Koonz, Claudia. 1987. *Mothers in the Fatherland: Women, the Family and Nazi Politics.* New York: St. Martin's Press.

Kurnaz, Şefika. 1993. *Balkan Harbinde Kadınlarımızın Konuşmaları.* Istanbul: Milli Eğitim Bakanlığı Yayınları.

Kurtcephe, İsrafil ve Mustafa Balcıoğlu. 1991. *Kara Harp Okulu Tarihi.* Ankara: Kara Harp Okulu Matbaası.

Kutay, Cemal. 1937. Kadınlarımız Asker Olacaklardır. *Yedigün* 240: 7–9.

Kwon, Insook. 2001. A Feminist Exploration of Military Conscription: The Gendering of the Connections Between Nationalism, Militarism and Citizenship in South Korea. *International Feminist Journal of Politics* 3(1): 26–54.

Langdon-Davies, John. 1919. *Militarism in Education: A Contribution to Educational Reconstruction.* London: The Swarthmore Press.

Leloğlu, Duygu. 2002. Şehir Efsanesi Değil Gerçek. *Radikal* 13 May.

Lerner, Daniel and Richard D. Robinson. 1960. Swords and Ploughshares: The Turkish Army as a Modernizing Force. *World Politics* 13(1): 19–44.

Lewis, Bernard. 1961. *The Emergence of Modern Turkey.* London and New York: Oxford University Press.

Lewis, Bernard. 1953. History-Writing and National Revival in Turkey. *Middle Eastern Affairs* June–July: 218–227.

Liebknecht, Karl. 1917. *Militarism.* New York: B. W. Huebsch

Lise Müfredat Programı. 1956. Ankara: Maarif Basımevi. T. C. Maarif Vekaleti.

Lorentzen, Lois Ann and Jennifer Turpin. 1998. *The Women and War Reader.* New York: New York University Press.

Lucassen, Jan and Erik Jan Zürcher. 1999. Introduction: Conscription and Resistance. The Historical Context. In *Arming the State: Military Conscription in the Middle East and Central Asia 1775–1925*, ed. Erik Jan Zürcher, 1–20. London and New York: I.B. Tauris.

Lutz, Catherine. 2002. Making War At Home in the United States: Militarization and the Current Crisis. *American Anthropologist* 104(3): 723–735.

Lutz, Catherine. 2001. *Homefront: A Military City and the American 20th Century.* Boston: Beacon Press.

Lutz, Catherine. 1999. Ethnography at the War Century's End. *Journal of Contemporary Ethnography* 28(6): 610–619

Lutz, Catherine. 1995. The Gender of Theory. In *Women Writing Culture*, ed. Ruth Behar and Deborah A. Gordon, 249–266. Berkeley: University of California Press.

Lutz, Catherine and Donald Nonini. 1999. The Economies of Violence and the Violence of Economies. In *Anthropological Theory Today*, ed. Henrietta L. Moore, 73–113. Polity Press.

Lutz, Catherine and Lesley Bartlett. 1995. JROTC: Making Soldiers in Public Schools. *The Education Digest* 61(3): 9–14.

Lutz, Catherine A. and Jane L. Collins. 1993. *Reading National Geographic.* Chicago and London: University of Chicago Press.

Maarif Sergisi Rehberi. 1933. Istanbul: Devlet Matbaası.

Maksudyan, Nazan. 2003. *Gauging Turkishness: Anthropology as Science-Fiction in Legitimizing Racist Nationalism (1925–1939).* M.A. Thesis. Boğaziçi University.

Malkki, Liisa H. 1995. Refugees and Exile: From "Refugee Studies" to the National Order of Things. *Annual Review of Anthropology* 24: 495–523.

Mançer, Selin. 2002. Anlat, Anlat: Askerlik Anıları. *Max*, 11: 100–103.

Marcus, George E. 1995. Ethnography in/of the World System: The Emergence of Multi-Sited Ethnography. *Annual Review of Anthropology* 24: 95–117.

Mardin, Şerif. 1997. Projects as Methodology: Some Thoughts on Modern Turkish Social Science. In *Rethinking Modernity and National Identity in Turkey*, ed. Sibel Bozdoğan and Reşat Kasaba, 64–80. Seattle: University of Washington Press.

Mardin, Şerif. 1989 [1964]. *Jön Türklerin Siyasi Fikirleri: 1895–1908*. Istanbul: İletişim Yayınları.

Mardin, Şerif. 1985. 19. yy'da Düşünce Akımları ve Osmanlı Devleti. *Tanzimat'tan Cumhuriyet'e Türkiye Ansiklopedisi* 2: 342–351.

Mater, Nadire. 1999. *Mehmedin Kitabı: Güneydoğu'da Savaşmış Askerler Anlatıyor*. İstanbul: Metis Yayınları.

McClintock, Anne. 1997. "No Longer in a Future Heaven": Gender, Race and Nationalism. *Dangerous Liaisons: Gender, Nation, and Postcolonial Perspectives*, ed. Anne McClintock, Aamir Mufti, and Ella Shohat, 89–112. Minneapolis: University of Minnesota Press.

Meyer, John W. 1999. The Changing Cultural Content of the Nation-State: A World Society Perspective. In *State/Culture: State Formation After the Cultural Turn*, ed. George Steinmetz, 123–143. Ithaca and London: Cornell University Press.

Milas, Herkül. 2000. *Türk Romanı ve "Öteki": Ulusal Kimlikte Yunan İmajı*. Istanbul: Sabancı University Press.

Millî Eğitim ile Ilgili Millî Savunma Komitesi Çalışmaları ve Raporu [1961] Ankara: Millî Eğitim Basımevi.

Milli Güvenlik Bilgisi Öğretimi Yönetmeliği, 28.12.1979, Karar No: 8/37, *Resmi Gazete*, February 2, 1980, R. Gazete No: 16888. (with modifications in 1983, 1987, 1993, 1996, and 1998).

Millî Güvenlik Bilgileri I [1965] Istanbul: Okat Yayınevi.

Millî Güvenlik Bilgileri III [1965] Istanbul: Okat Yayınevi.

Millî Güvenlik Bilgisi [1998] Istanbul: Milli Eğitim Basımevi.

Millî Güvenlik Bilgisi [1987] İstanbul: Milli Eğitim Basımevi.

Millî Güvenlik Bilgisi I-II-III [1973] Istanbul: Milli Eğitim Basımevi.

Millî Savunma I [1952] Istanbul: Milli Eğitim Basımevi.

Mintz, Sidney [1960] *Worker in the Cane: A Puerto Rican Life History*. New Haven: Yale University Press.

Mitchell, Timothy. 1999. Society, Economy, and the State Effect. In *State/Culture: State Formation After the Cultural Turn*, ed. George Steinmetz, 76–97. Ithaca and London: Cornell University Press.

Mosse, George L. 1993. *Confronting the Nation: Jewish and Western Nationalism*. Hanover and London: Brandeis University Press.

Nader, Laura. 1969. "Up the Anthropologist"—Perspectives Gained From Studying Up. In *Reinventing Anthropology*, ed. D. Hymes, 284–311. New York: Random House.

Nagel, Joanne. 1998. Masculinity and Nationalism: Gender and Sexuality in The Making of Nations. *Ethnic and Racial Studies* 21(2): 242–269.

Navaro-Yashin, Yael. 2003. "Life is Dead Here": Sensing the Political in "No Man's Land.". *Anthropological Theory* 3(1): 107–125.

Navaro-Yashin, Yael. 2002. *Faces of the State: Secularism and Public Life in Turkey*. Princeton and Oxford: Princeton University Press.

Navaro-Yashin, Yael. 1998. *Travesty and Truth: Politics of Culture and Fantasies of the State in Turkey*. Ph.D. Dissertation, Princeton University.

Neumann, Sigmund. 1966. Engels and Marx: Military Concepts of the Social Revolutionaries. In *Makers of Modern Strategy: Military Thought from Machiavelli to Hitler*, ed. Edward Mead Earle, 155–171. New York: Atheneum.

New York Times, The. 1951. Turkish Woman to Serve As Fighter Pilot in Korea. 29 January.

New York Times, The. 1937. The Flying Amazon of Turkey. 19 September.

New York Times, The. 1937. Turkish Paradox. 20 June.

New York Times, The. 1937. Turkey Combats Uprising of Kurds. 17 June.

New York Times, The. 1936. Women Fliers Prepare to Serve if War Comes. 30 March.

Neyzi, Leyla. 2001. Object or Subject? The Paradox of Youth in Turkey. *International Journal of Middle Eastern Studies* 33(3): 411–432.

Neyzi, Leyla. 2000. Remembering to Forget: Sabbateanism, National Identity and Subjectivity in Turkey. Paper presented at the conference *Intersecting Times: The Work of Memory in South Eastern Europe.* Center for the Study of Southeastern Europe, University of Wales. Clyne Castle, Swansea, 25–28 June.

Neyzi, Leyla. 1999a. Gülümser's Story: Life History Narratives, Memory and Belonging in Turkey. *New Perspectives on Turkey* 20(Spring): 1–26.

Neyzi, Leyla. 1999b. *İstanbul'da Hatırlamak ve Unutmak: Birey, Bellek ve Aidiyet.* İstanbul: Tarih Vakfı Yurt Yayınları.

Nokta. 1987. Hedef Doğrudan Dersim İdi. 28 June.

Ong, Aiwa. 1999. Clash of Civilizations or Asian Liberalism? An Anthropology of the State and Citizenship. In *Anthropological Theory Today,* ed. Henrietta L. Moore, 48–66. Cambridge: Polity Press.

Onur, Nureddin. 1937. *Kan Grupları Bakımından Türk Irkının Menşei Hakkında Bir Etüd.* İkinci Türk Tarih Kongresi. İstanbul: Devlet Basımevi.

Ortaylı, İlber. 1985. Tanzimat. *Tanzimat'tan Cumhuriyet'e Türkiye Ansiklopedisi* 6: 1545–1547.

Os, Nicole A. N. M. van. 2001. Osmanlı Müslümanlarında Feminizm. In *Tanzimat ve Meşrutiyetin Birikimi: Modern Türkiye'de Siyasi Düşünce Cilt 1,* ed. Tanıl Bora, 335–347. İstanbul: İletişim Yayınları.

Özdağ, Ümit. 1991. *Ordu-Siyaset İlişkisi: Atatürk ve İnönü Dönemleri.* Ankara: Gündoğan Yayınları.

Özdemir, Hikmet. 1995. Milli Güvenlik Kurulu. *Cumhuriyet Dönemi Türkiye Ansiklopedisi* 11: 54–58.

Özdemir, Hikmet. 1989. *Rejim ve Asker.* İstanbul: Afa Yayıncılık.

Özyürek, Esra. 2000. Mecliste Başörtüsü Düğümü. In *Vatan, Millet, Kadınlar,* ed. Ayşe Gül Altınay, 339–357. İstanbul: İletişim Yayınları.

Palmer, R. R. 1966. Frederick the Great, Guibert, Bülow: From Dynastic to National War. In *Makers of Modern Strategy: Military Thought from Machiavelli to Hitler,* ed. Edward Mead Earle, 49–74. New York: Atheneum.

Parla, Ayşe. 2001. The "Honor" of the State: Virginity Examinations in Turkey. *Feminist Studies* 27(1): 65–90.

Parla, Taha. 1998. Mercantile Militarism in Turkey, 1960–1998. *New Perspectives on Turkey* 19(Fall): 29–52.

Parla, Taha. 1992. *Kemalist Tek-Parti İdeolojisi ve CHP'nin Altı Ok'u.* Türkiye'de Siyasal Kültürün Resmî Kaynakları, Cilt 3. İstanbul: İletişim Yayınları.

Parla, Taha. 1991a. *Atatürk'ün Nutuk'u.* Türkiye'de Siyasal Kültürün Resmî Kaynakları, Cilt 1. İstanbul: İletişim Yayınları.

Parla, Taha. 1991b. *Atatürk'ün Söylev ve Demeçleri.* Türkiye'de Siyasal Kültürün Resmî Kaynakları, Cilt 2. İstanbul: İletişim Yayınları.

Parla, Taha. 1991c. *Türkiye'de Anayasalar.* Cep Üniversitesi. İstanbul: İletişim Yayınları.

Parla, Taha. 1985. *The Social and Political Thought of Ziya Gökalp, 1876–1924.* Leiden: E.J. Brill.

Radikal. 2002. Vicdani Retçi Bal'a Tahliye. 28 November.

Reardon, Betty. 1985. *Sexism and the War System.* New York: Columbia University, Teacher's College Press.

Rouleau, Eric. 2000. Turkey's Dream of Democracy. *Foreign Affairs* 79(6): 100–114.

Rosaldo, Renato. 1993 [1989]. *Culture and Truth: The Remaking of Social Analysis*. Boston: Beacon Press.

Reiter, Rayna R., ed. 1975. *Toward an Anthropology of Women*. New York: Monthly Review Press.

Rosaldo, Michelle and Louise Lamphere, ed. 1974. *Woman, Culture and Society*. Stanford: Stanford University Press.

Sakallıoğlu, Ümit. 1995. Ordu ve Siyaset. *Cumhuriyet Dönemi Türkiye Ansiklopedisi* 14: 1000–1004.

Sakaoğlu, Necdet. 1992. *Cumhuriyet Dönemi Eğitim Tarihi*. Cep Üniversitesi. Istanbul: İletişim Yayınları.

Sakaoğlu, Necdet. 1991. *Osmanlı Eğitim Tarihi*. Cep Üniversitesi. Istanbul: İletişim Yayınları.

Saktanber, Ayşe. 2001. Kemalist Kadın Hakları Söylemi. In *Kemalizm: Modern Türkiye'de Siyasi Düşünce Cilt 2*, ed. Ahmet Insel, 323–333. Istanbul: İletişim Yayınları.

Saktanber, Ayşe. 1995. Women in the Media in Turkey: The Free, Available Woman or the Good Wife and Selfless Mother. In *Women in Modern Turkish Society*, ed. ŞirinTekeli, 153–169. London and New Jersey: Zed Books.

Sancar, Serpil. 2001. Türkler/Kürtler, Anneler ve Siyaset: Savaşta Çocuklarını Kaybetmiş Türk ve Kürt Anneler Üzerine Bir Yorum. *Toplum ve Bilim* Fall: 22–40.

Sarıbaş, Şermin. 2002. Suç ve Ceza'da Kendimi Okudum. *Hürriyet Pazar*, 22 December.

Scarry, Elaine. 1985. *The Body in Pain: The Making and Unmaking of the World*. Oxford: Oxford University Press.

Schirmer, Jennifer. 1994. The Claiming of Space and the Body Politic within National-Security States: The Plaza de Mayo Madres and the Greenham Common Women. In *Remapping Memory: The Politics of TimeSpace*, ed. J. Boyarin, 185–220. Minneapolis and London: University of Minnesota Press.

Schöpflin, George. 1997. The Functions of Myth and a Taxonomy of Myths. In *Myths and Nationhood*, ed. G. Hosking and G. Schöpflin, 19–35. London and New York: Routledge.

Scott, James. 1985. *Weapons of the Weak: Everyday Forms of Peasant Resistance*. New Haven: Yale University Press.

Scott, Joan. 1986. Gender: A Useful Category of Historical Analysis. *The American Historical Review* 91(5): 1053–1075.

Shapiro, Michael J. 2000. National Times and Other Times: Re-thinking Citizenship. *Cultural Studies* 14(1): 79–98.

Shapiro Michael J. and Hayward R. Alker, ed. 1996. *Challenging Boundaries: Global Flows, Territorial Identities*. Minneapolis: University of Minnesota Press.

Sıtkı, Celal. 1933. Askerlikten Dönüş. *Ülkü* 1(3): 250–54.

Silva, Neluka. 2003. Introduction to Part I. In *Feminists Under Fire: Exchanges Across War Zones*, ed. Wenona Giles, Malathi de Alwis, Edith Klein, Neluka Silva (coeditors) with Maja Korač, Djurdja Kneževič, Žarana Papič (advisory editors), 37–40. Toronto: Between the Lines.

Sinclair-Webb, Emma. 2000. "Our Bülent is Now a Commando": Military Service and Manhood in Turkey. In *Imagined Masculinities: Male Identity and Culture in the Modern Middle East*, ed. Mai Ghoussoub and Emma Sinclair-Webb, 65–91. London: Saqi Books.

Sirman, Nükhet. 2002. Kadınların Milliyeti. In *Milliyetçilik: Modern Türkiye'de Siyasi Düşünce Cilt 4*, ed. Tanıl Bora, 226–244. Istanbul: İletişim Yayınları.

Sirman, Nükhet. 2000. Gender Construction and Nationalist Discourse: Dethroning the Father in the Early Turkish Novel. In *Gender and Identity Construction: Women of Central Asia, the Caucasus and Turkey*, ed. Feride Acar and Ayşe Güneş-Ayata, 162–176. Leiden: Brill.

Sirman, Nükhet. 1989. Feminism in Turkey: A Short History. *New Perspectives on Turkey* 3(1): 1–34.

Somel, Akşin. 2001. *The Modernization of Public Education in the Ottoman Empire, 1839–1908: Islamization, Autocracy, and Discipline.* Leiden and Boston: Brill.

Spencer, Jonathan. 1990. Writing Within: Anthropology, Nationalism, and Culture in Sri Lanka. *Current Anthropology* 31(3): 283–300.

Starn, Orin. 1999. *Nightwatch: The Politics of Protest in the Andes.* Durham and London: Duke University Press.

Starn, Orin. 1991. Missing the Revolution: Anthropologists and the War in Peru. *Cultural Anthropology* 6(3): 63–91.

Şen, Serdar. 1996. *Cumhuriyet Kültürünün Oluşum Sürecinde Bir Ideolojik Aygıt olarak Silahlı Kuvvetler ve Modernizm.* Istanbul: Sarmal Yayınevi.

Şenyürek, Muzaffer. 1940. Kan Grupları ve Irk. *Ülkü* 15(90): 500–502.

Tan. 1937. İlk Kadın Tayyarecimiz Sabiha Gökçenin Dersimde Kahramanca Hizmetleri. 15 June.

Tankut, Hasan Reşit. 1937. *Dil ve Irk Münasebetleri Hakkında.* Ikinci Türk Tarih Kongresi. Istanbul: Devlet Basımevi.

Tanör, Bülent. 1985. Anayasal Gelişmelere Toplu Bir Bakış. *Tanzimat'tan Cumhuriyet'e Türkiye Ansiklopedisi* 1: 10–26.

Tarih I. 1931. Istanbul: Devlet Matbaası.

Tarih II. 1931. Istanbul: Devlet Matbaası.

Tarih III. 1931. Istanbul: Devlet Matbaası.

Tarih IV. 1934. 2nd ed. Istanbul: Devlet Matbaası.

Taussig, Michael. 1997. *The Magic of the State.* New York and London: Routledge.

Taussig, Michael. 1992. *The Nervous System.* New York and London: Routledge.

TBMM Zabıt Ceridesi, 21 June 1927, Inikat: 79, C: 1 Devre: II, Cilt: 33.

T.C. Genelkurmay Başkanlığı Askeri Savcılığı, Ankara. 2002. Kovuşturmaya Yer Olmadığı Kararı. Evrak No. 2002/832, Esas No. 2002/713, Karar No. 2002/270, 26 November.

Tekeli, Ilhan. 1998. *Tarih Bilinci ve Gençlik: Karşılaştırmalı Avrupa ve Türkiye Araştırması.* Istanbul: Tarih Vakfı Yurt Yayınları.

Tekeli, Ilhan. 1985. Osmanlı Imparatorluğu'nden Günümüze Eğitim Kurumlarının Gelişimi. *Tanzimat'tan Cumhuriyet'e Türkiye Ansiklopedisi* 3: 650–673.

Tekeli, Şirin. 1998. Birinci ve Ikinci Dalga Feminist Hareketlerin Karşılaştırmalı Incelemesi Üzerine Bir Deneme. In *75 Yılda Kadınlar ve Erkekler/Bilanço 98,* 337–346. Istanbul: İşbankası & Tarih Vakfı Yayınları.

Tekeli, Şirin. 1986. Emergence of the New Feminist Movement in Turkey. In *The New Women's Movements,* ed. D. Dahlerup, 179–199. London: Sage.

The French Considered as a Military Nation Since the Commencement of Their Revolution. 1803. London: Egerton.

Thongchai Winichakul. 1994. *Siam Mapped: A History of the Geo-Body of a Nation.* Honolulu: University of Hawai'i Press.

Tilly, Charles. 1992. *Coercion, Capital, and European States, AD 990–1992.* Cambridge, Blackwell.

Tilly, Charles. 1985. War Making and State-making as Organized Crime. In *Bringing the State Back In,* ed. P. B. Evans, D. Rueschemeyer, and T. Skocpol, 169–191. Cambridge: Cambridge University Press.

Tipi, Tahir. 1941. *Askerliğe Hazırlık.* Lise Kitapları. Kızlar İçin. Ankara: Maarif Matbaası.

Tipi, Tahir. 1941. *Askerliğe Hazırlık II.* Ankara: Maarif Basımevi.

Toksöz Ahmet Ihsan and K. Köyden. 1936. Dr. Besim Ömer Akalın ve Nüfus İşimiz. *Ülkü* 7(39): 205–209.

Tolstoy, Leo. 1990 [1905]. Patriotism and Government. In *Classics of International Relations*, 2nd ed., ed. John A. Vasquez, 40–42. New Jersey: Prentice Hall.

Toprak, Zafer. 1988. Cumhuriyet Halk Fırkasından Önce Kurulan Parti: Kadınlar Halk Fırkası. *Tarih ve Toplum* 9(51): 30–31.

Toska, Zehra. 1998. Cumhuriyet'in Kadın İdeali: Eşiği Aşanlar ve Aşamayanlar. In *75 Yılda Kadınlar ve Erkekler/Bilanço 98*, 71–88. İstanbul: İşbankası & Tarih Vakfı Yayınları.

Trimberger, Ellen Kay. 1978. *Revolution From Above: Military Bureaucracts and Development in Japan, Turkey, Egypt, and Peru*. New Brunswick, New Jersey: Transaction Books.

Trouillot, Michel-Rolph. 1995. *Silencing the Past: Power and the Production of History*. Boston: Beacon Press.

Tunçay, Mete. 1989. Kadınlar Halk Fırkası. *Tarih ve Toplum* 11(62): 46.

Turkey: Osman Murat Ülke – Conscientious Objector Imprisoned for Life. 1998. Amnesty International Report. AI Index: EUR 44/22/98.

Türk Tarihi, Silahlı Kuvvetleri ve Atatürkçülük. [1973]. Genelkurmay Başkanlığı 50nci Yıl Yayını.

Türker, Yıldırım. 2002. Vicdanın Redde Bakan Fotoğrafı. *Radikal 2*, 4 November.

Türkiye Cumhuriyeti Maarifi 1923–1943. [1944]. Ankara: Maarif Matbaası.

Türkiye Cumhuriyetinde Ayaklanmalar, (1924–1938). [1972]. T. C. Genel Kurmay Harp Tarihi Başkanlığı Resmî Yayınları, Seri no: 8.

Ulubay, Necdet. 1961. *Millî Savunma I*. Istanbul: Hüsnütabiat Matbaası.

Ulubay, Necdet. 1962. *Milli Güvenlik Bilgileri-Lise 1*. Istanbul: Hüsnütabiat Matbaası.

Uygun, Nilgün and Ayşe Gül Altınay. 1996. From (Our) Homes To The Battlefront: Whose History? *Unpublished paper*.

Uzunçarşıoğlu, Ismail Hakkı. 1939. Türk Tarihi Yazılırken: Atatürk'ün Alâka ve Görüşlerine Dair Hatıralar. *Belleten* 3: 349–353.

Ünder, Hasan. 1999a. Milleti Müsellaha ve Medeni Bilgiler. *Tarih ve Toplum* 32(192): 48–56.

Ünder, Hasan. 1999b. Birinci Heyeti Ilmiye'de Tevhid-i Tedrisat Tartışması. *Tarih ve Toplum* 32(186): 349–354.

Üskül, Zafer. 1995. Olağanüstü Hal. *Cumhuriyet Dönemi Türkiye Ansiklopedisi* 14: 1170–1178.

Üstel, Füsun. 2002a. Türk Ocakları. In *Milliyetçilik: Modern Türkiye'de Siyasi Düşünce Cilt 4*, ed. Tanıl Bora, 263–268. Istanbul: İletişim Yayınları.

Üstel, Füsun. 2002b. Türkiye Cumhuriyeti'nde Resmi Yurttaş Profilinin Evrimi. In *Milliyetçilik: Modern Türkiye'de Siyasi Düşünce Cilt 4*, ed. Tanıl Bora, 275–283. Istanbul: İletişim Yayınları.

Üstel, Füsun. 1997. *Imparatorluktan Ulus-Devlete Türk Milliyetçiliği: Türk Ocakları (1912–1931)*. Istanbul: İletişim Yayınları.

Vagts, Alfred. 1959 [1937]. *A History of Militarism: Civilian and Military*. Meridian Books, Inc.

Van Tuyll, Hubert P. 1994. Militarism, The United States, and The Cold War. *Armed Forces and Society* 20(4): 519–529.

Veldet, Hıfzı. 1935. Türk Hukukunda Kadının Yeri. *Ülkü* 5(28): 268–276.

Verdery, Katherine. 1996. Whither "Nation" and "Nationalism"? In *Mapping the Nation*, ed. G. Balakrishnan, 226–234. London and New York: Verso.

Verdery, Katherine. 1991. *Nationalist Ideology under Socialism: Identity and Cultural Politics in Ceauşescu's Romania*. Berkeley: University of California Press.

Vergin, Nur. 1997. Ordunun Ne Olduğuna Dair Gündem Dışı Bir Pazar Sohbeti. *Yeni Yüzyıl*. 15 June, p. 19.

Visweswaran, Kamala. 1994. *Fictions of Feminist Ethnography*. Minneapolis: University of Minnesota Press.

Walby, Sylvia. 1996. Woman and Nation. In *Mapping the Nation*, ed. G. Balakrishnan, 235–254. London and New York: Verso.

Weber, Eugen. 1976. *Peasants Into Frenchmen: The Modernization Of Rural France, 1870–1914*. Stanford: Stanford University Press.

Weldes, Jutta, Mark Laffey, Hugh Gusterson, and Raymond Duvall. ed. 1999. *Cultures of Insecurity: States, Communities, and the Production of Danger.* Minneapolis and London: University of Minnesota Press.
Weldes, Jutta, Mark Laffey, Hugh Gusterson, and Raymond Duvall. 1999. Introduction: Constructing Insecurity. In *Cultures of Insecurity: States, Communities, and the Production of Danger*, ed. J. Weldes et al. Minneapolis and London: University of Minnesota Press.
Williams, Brackette F. 1991. *Stains on My Name, War in My Veins: Guyana and the Politics of Cultural Struggle.* Durham: Duke University Press.
Wolf, Eric. 1982. *Europe and the People Without History.* Berkeley and Los Angeles: University of California Press.
Woloch, Isser. 1994. *The New Regime: Transformations of the French Civic Order, 1789–1820s.* New York, W.W. Norton&Company.
Woolf, Virginia. 1966 [1938]. *Three Guineas.* San Diego and New York: Harcourt.
Yaman, Kadri. 1938. *Yurt Müdafaasında Türk Gençliği.* Istanbul: Devlet Basımevi.
Yalman, Ahmet Emin. 1937. Yüz Senelik Dersim İşi Şifa Yolunda. *Tan.* 15 June.
Yelda. 1998. *Çoğunluk Aydınlarında Irkçılık.* Istanbul: Belge Yayınları.
Yeğen, Mesut. 2002. Yurttaşlık ve Türklük. *Toplum ve Bilim*, 93(Summer): 200–217.
Yeğen, Mesut. 1999. *Devlet Söyleminde Kürt Sorunu.* Istanbul: İletişim.
Yıldız, Ahmet. 2001. *Ne Mutlu Türküm Diyebilene: Türk Ulusal Kimliğinin Etno-Seküler Sınırları (1919–1938).* Istanbul: İletişim Yayınları.
Yuval-Davis, Nira. 1997. *Gender and Nation.* London: Sage Publications.
Yücel, Hasan-Ali. 1998. *Pazartesi Konuşmaları.* Ankara: T. C. Kültür Bakanlığı Yayınları.
Zihnioğlu, Yaprak. 2003. *Kadınsız Inkılap: Nezihe Muhittin, Kadınlar Halk Fırkası, Kadın Birliği.* Istanbul: Metis Yayınları.
Zihnioğlu, Yaprak. 1999. Bir Osmanlı Türk Kadın Hakları Savunucusu: Nezihe Muhittin. *Tarih ve Toplum* 183: 132–139.
Zürcher, Erik Jan, ed. 1999. *Arming the State: Military Conscription in the Middle East and Central Asia 1775–1925.* London and New York: I.B.Tauris.
Zürcher, Eric Jan. 1996. Little Mehmet in the Desert: The Ottoman Soldier's Experience. *In Facing Armageddon: The First World War Experienced*, ed. Hugh Cecil with Peter Liddle, 230–241. London: Leo Cooper.
Zürcher, Eric Jan. 1994. *Turkey: A Modern History.* London and New York: I.B. Tauris.

INDEX